COMMUNICATING
· THE WORD OF GOD ·

JOHN N.M.WIJNGAARDS

MAYHEW-McCRIMMON
Great Wakering

First published in Great Britain in 1978 by
MAYHEW-McCRIMMON LTD
Great Wakering, Essex, England

© Copyright 1978 John N. M. Wijngaards

ISBN 0 85597 259 9

Cover design: Nick Snode
Published and printed by Mayhew-McCrimmon Ltd.

To my mother
who taught me to listen
and my father
who showed me how to communicate.

CONTENTS

CHAPTER ONE

INTRODUCTION

ON HOW TO USE THIS BOOK

This book offers a "do-it-yourself course on scriptural communication. It is addressed to preachers, teachers, parents and those with equivalent responsibilities. The purpose of this book is eminently practical. It doesn't seek to advance theological reflection or biblical research. Its overriding aim is to help all those who ask themselves: "How can I transmit the message of Scripture in an attractive manner and as effectively as possible?"

The nature of this book, its contribution as well as its limitations, will be better understood when one knows how and why it arose. The first section therefore of this chapter gives the reader some information about its origins.

The book has grown out of a course and is presented as a course. The practical implications of this for the reader will be spelled out in a second section.

The third and fourth sections of the chapter present the choice of techniques open to teachers and preachers respectively. They may stimulate the reader to examine his own degree of creativity and, perhaps, encourage him to widen his scope.

The final section of this chapter lists the objections which are sometimes raised against a more intensive pastoral use of Scripture. The answers to these objections are then worked out as positive principles in chapters two to five.

A WORD ABOUT ORIGINS

In 1962, while I was a student at the Biblical Institute in Rome, I attended a retreat given by the well-known Scripture scholar, Fr. Barnabas Aherne. In one of his conferences he told us the story of

David's sin. What struck me most was not the moral – I am sorry to say! – but the unusual technique. I was surprised at the force of the biblical story. His way of alternating narration and reflection opened my eyes to the potential of biblical narrative. It brought out into the open a defect in preachers I had always been vaguely aware of: all they normally talk about are themes illustrated by examples.

When I started teaching at the Major Seminary in Hyderabad in India, the matter came to my attention again through an analysis of the sermons preached by our deacons. It was found that they composed their sermons for the greater part from the instructions and sermons they had heard before entering the seminary. Six years of philosophy, theology, Bible studies and heaven-knows-what-else had apparently made little difference to their preaching. The reason proved simple enough. It is one thing to study a subject academically, quite another to know how to transform it into material for instruction. I decided to integrate into my lecture programme a special course on how to communicate Scripture.

About the same time I was approached for advice by the NBCLC at Bangalore, the pastoral centre that coordinates and promotes the biblical, catechetical and liturgical apostolate for the whole of India. I was asked to design and give advanced courses on Scripture for diocesan directors, college lecturers, novice mistresses and others who play a prominent part in the apostolate. I discovered with them the same need I had encountered in the seminary. I found that, on the whole, teachers and catechists receive far too little guidance on how to make use of the Bible for lessons and instructions.

These were the beginnings. I soon realised that hardly anything had been published about the practical questions that interest pastors most. I had to find my own way through trial and error. When I started fifteen years ago I recommended five techniques, with a good amount of hesitation. In the course of time I learned to discard and to add; I gained confidence as well as experience. The twenty-two techniques offered in this book are the result of this long and exciting search, and of the interest and imagination of the more than a thousand priests, nuns, teachers and seminarians who have attended my courses over the years.

Whenever I gave the course, I used to insist that the participants spend most of the available time in actual practice. I used to illustrate each technique with one or more examples that I had worked out myself. I then required that each technique be presented and evaluated in small groups. Finally, the technique was presented once more by one of the participants before the whole group, in a form that was meant to resemble the pastoral situation as closely as possible. This 'public practical', as we used to call it, led to further evaluations and discussions. The discerning reader will recognise in the second part of this book this same process of learning: the introductions leading up to the techniques, the explanations of the techniques themselves, the examples in which they are worked out and the (schoolmasterly) hints and suggestions that flow from the evaluations. I hope that the reader will look with tolerance on the frequent switches in topic and style that are unavoidable in such a direct presentation of a learning process.

A "DO-IT-YOURSELF" COURSE

It is my experience that in order to communicate Scripture well, one needs to acquire
> * some basic skills;
> * knowledge of various techniques; and
> * familiarity with Scripture.

The basic skills we need most are interpretation, narration, description and decoding.

We should know how to determine accurately the *meaning* of a text. We should be able to distinguish its 'fundamental assertion' from the details of the presentation.

We should master the art of story telling. From an analysis of a biblical narrative we should be able to build our own account that should preserve the force of the original story and at the same time produce a presentation that will be appreciated by our specific audience.

We should be able to express ourselves in visual language. Vivid descriptions, good characterizations and life-like portraits should belong to our stock-in-trade.

We should be able to read Scripture to others in such a way that the message is fully understood.

A "technique" means a particular method of presenting a Bible text. It involves a philosophy, an insight, a concept which is the rational basis of a particular approach. A technique also usually fits a particular pastoral situation. It finds its practical expression in a definite arrangement of the material. The technique "motif-inspired exposition of a text", for instance, demands a correct understanding of the "motif" and of what is essential and what may not be essential (the philosophy). The technique focusses attention on one sentence of the Gospel reading which contains the "motif", and then illustrates this theme from other scriptural texts (the arrangement). This technique is ideally suited for the ordinary Sunday sermon (the situation).

In the beginning all this may sound rather analytical and involved. One might get the impression that techniques consist of rigid schemes with complicated rules. Nothing is further removed from what I intend to promote. Freedom of expression, imagination and a very personal rendering are essential for any measure of success. The technique merely suggests an approach that will help a person to draw out new aspects of the biblical message and to increase the forms of presentation open to him. In soccer one has to learn such techniques as 'stopping' a ball that arrives from mid-air, 'dribbling', 'tackling' an opponent, and so on. Once a player masters these techniques he will put them to use in a very personal style almost without thinking. The same applies to our biblical techniques. 'Schemes' and 'rules' will figure most prominently only during 'training'.

We may need some real training, and by training I mean: acquiring facility by repeated practice. No one will become a good storyteller overnight nor can anyone hope to get fluency and complete control in any technique at the first attempt. Communication, like other complex actions, can only be learned by putting theory into practice: by effort, evaluation and correction.

If anyone were to ask me what I would suggest as a simple self-training programme for those who want to benefit from the experience contained in this book, I would recommend the following procedure.

First, I would suggest, one should read the whole book in one go from cover to cover to get a general and superficial knowledge of its contents.

Then one should select a particular chapter that offers skills and techniques that seem immediately relevant. This chapter should then be read more carefully.

If the technique is totally new to us, we may feel more confident about it if we begin by imitating an example that is worked out in the book. As soon as possible, however, we should try to apply the technique to texts selected by ourselves.

It is important to allow some time for a brief evaluation of our presentation after it is finished. We should take note of what we have actually said; of what seemed successful and what not; of what we should do differently next time. We check this against the suggestions made in the book.

We should practise a technique more than once in this manner before turning to something else. A few initial failures should not deceive us into thinking that a particular skill or technique is beyond us. One often needs time to "catch on".

A SPECIAL WORD TO TEACHERS

A difficulty which some persons experience is the inability to find appropriate Scripture texts. Teachers, especially, complain about this problem. The Old Testament seems strange and remote. They are not familiar enough with Scripture in general to know where to turn for good ideas. They often have to work under time pressure, so that they gratefully snatch up the first idea that comes to mind while on their way to the classroom. In the past such people have often begged me to supply them with lists of Bible texts that lend themselves to one or other of the techniques.

I have often tried to explain that providing such lists would not be a satisfactory way of helping a person in his or her task. Every christian preacher or teacher should learn to use the Bible itself as the source book. Dependence on derived or intermediate texts will be harmful if it means that the communicator is not familiar with the scriptural text itself (see more about this in Chapter Two). Short-term, immediate solutions will affect the quality of our communication task. They will frustrate its purpose and will eventually prove a greater loss of time.

The reader will forgive me for inserting a parable at this stage. In India I have often watched stone-cutters at work. From morning till night they handle hammer and chisel to hew building stones from rock. A major operation for them is the splitting of huge boulders into smaller parts. They do this by driving wedges into the rock along a line suggested by the natural grain. It may take three men two full days to split a big boulder into two halves. Recently some stone-cutters have discovered that they can obtain the same result in a shorter time by drilling a hole in a place along the dividing line of the grain, inserting a charge of dynamite and causing an explosion of just the right strength. Doing more work in less time they have substantially increased their profits. However, not every stone-cutter sees it this way. Many are too busy splitting their next boulder to take time off to learn a new skill. They can only think in terms of sharper chisels, better wedges and stronger hammers. They don't grasp that their problem could be solved better by a qualitative rather than a quantitative approach.

A teacher is helped most if he or she discovers that the Bible is not as unwieldy, formidable and unreadable a book as one might subconsciously assume. By being able to handle the Bible itself, one possesses a constant supply of lessons and instructions. In the beginning one can learn from other books where to look for inspiration. But one should always go back to the Bible itself and become familiar with the text as we find it there. A useful suggestion here is to follow the 'treasury approach'. This means that one considers the passages with which one is familiar as a kind of 'treasury' and then gradually adds to the treasury any new text one discovers. Having built up such a treasury of Bible texts the teacher will not find it tiresome or time-consuming to present a personal and inspiring programme of religious instruction. He or she will also convincingly instil a similar respect for, and love of, Scripture in the pupils.

Juniors in *primary school* (9-11 years old) learn most from narration and characterization. Religious instruction at this stage does not aim so much at clarifying concepts as at creating in the child an experience that will stay. Even when the froth of immediate interest wears off, the impression of a story or a portrait will remain.

The techniques that seem especially suited for children of this age group are:

(1) simple free narration (pp. 103-107);
(2) simple portrait (pp. 124-128);
(3) commentated reading (pp. 191-195);
(4) reading illustrated by acting (pp. 195-196);
(5) one-point example (pp. 137-138).

The lessons of an instruction programme can be held together by themes. To show how a programme can be built up I will give in an appendix (pp.249-254) a religious instruction syllabus for one term, in which topics and techniques for 40 twenty-minute instructions are spelled out. This sample programme for one term could be, for some teachers, a way of training themselves in the skills and techniques.

Teenagers in *secondary schools* require a more systematic

introduction to doctrine and Scripture. To keep their interest they need more variety in the way in which topics are presented. Whenever possible, they need to be more personally involved in the process of formulating questions and seeking answers. Especially recommended for them are:

(1) story-reflection-story (pp. 108-112);
(2) portrait-reflection (pp. 129-133);
(3) exposition of a motif (pp. 147-160);
(4) imaginative elaboration (pp. 168-172);
(5) witness (pp. 239-246);
(6) commentated reading (pp. 191-195).

Many other techniques, such as mystery ramble, simple guided reading, one-point example, etc., will also come in handy as elements of a varied presentation.

Teenagers respond well to forms of 'sharing' in which they can play a more direct role. As I have explained above, I will present the techniques of 'sharing' and of 'prayer' in a companion volume to this book under the title *Prayer with the Bible*.

ON SERMONS AND CONFERENCES

The time for the *ordinary Sunday sermon* is usually so short (8-12 minutes) that one needs to organise the material in compact form. Many preachers waste time by repeating the same message, by drawing a moral that is already obvious by long-winded introductions and perorations. A good sermon should contain both information and motivation: information on some point of doctrine, ethics, liturgy, etc., from which the faithful can learn something new: motivation by a direct confrontation with the Word of God. Excellent sermons can be constructed with these techniques:

(1) motif-inspired exposition of a text (pp. 147-149);
(2) mystery ramble (pp. 172-176);
(3) spotlight exegesis (pp. 206-213);
(4) witness (pp. 229-246);
(5) story-reflection-story (pp. 108-112);
(6) portrait-reflection (pp. 129-133);
(7) imaginative elaboration (pp. 168-172);
(8) simple free narration (pp. 103-107).

Often a preacher is called upon to give *a very short homily* (3-6 minutes). The occasion may be a weekday Mass in a convent or a prayer service in a school. One cannot do more than present one idea, one thought, one point of inspiration. Suitable techniques for this kind of miniature sermon are:

    (1) spotlight exegesis (pp. 206-213);
    (2) simple portrait (pp. 125-128);
    (3) one-point example (pp. 137-138);
    (4) exposition of a motif (pp. 147-160);
    (5) reflection on a proverb (pp. 220-221 & 225-227);
    (6) reflection on a law (pp. 220-225);
    (7) comparative Gospel study (pp. 213-220);
    (8) theological perspective (pp. 165-168).

Some of these techniques lend themselves to a series of short presentations (e.g. for six weekdays on the run). This also applies to exposition of a motif (see pp.151-160), to comparative Gospel studies (pp. 213-220); and to reflections on proverbs or laws (pp. 220-227).

Spiritual conferences given on recollection days or as part of a retreat leave the preacher more time and scope. They are also more demanding and require thorough preparation, both regarding content and presentation. Although a conference should contain more instruction, it should not on that account become a lecture. The audience should be given the opportunity of entering more deeply into the meaning of God's Word. Recommended techniques are:

    (1) story-reflection-story (pp. 108-112);
    (2) homily-type conference (p. 206);
    (3) portrait reflection (pp. 129-133);
    (4) exposition of a motif (pp. 147-160);
    (5) comparative Gospel study (pp. 213-220);
    (6) witness (pp. 229-246).

REFLECTIONS ON THE ROLE OF SCRIPTURE

The discussion of the skills and techniques is the main purpose of this book. It rightly takes up the lion's share of the available space (Part Two). Yet I thought the book would be incomplete without at least some discussion of the general principles on which my whole approach is based. Unless people agree with me that Scripture should be both message and medium, they will not see the need of attaching so much weight to 'scriptural' techniques of communication. (Part One).

Why is it necessary to give such a prominent place to the biblical text in preaching and instruction? Can't christians be good christians without being encumbered with knowledge of the Bible? Chapter Two on "Biblical Revival" explains that listening to God's Word in Scripture is a precious element in a christian's experience of God. The Bible should be made accessible to people so that they can nourish their spiritual life through direct contact with it.

But what about secularist trends in theology? Isn't Scripture part and parcel of an out-of-date, mythopoeic view of reality? What authority has Scripture today? Chapter Three offers some considerations that may help us find a personal solution. Even though modern theology has not yet formulated a new, convincing world view that would integrate our secularist thinking with the truths of faith, this should not diminish our confidence in God's Word. Faith precedes human thought. The same process that causes the confusion among theologians, has also set afoot a 'holy disquiet' that makes Scripture more relevant than ever.

Don't biblical instructions smack of a paternalism of a bygone age? Chapter Four on "Listening and Asking Questions" points out the unfortunate connotations 'preaching' has acquired in the minds of many. Following the example of Christ we should avoid one-way communication. We should always take our starting-point from the problems and aspirations of our audience.

In our sensation-ridden society topics must be new, interesting and unexpected, to captivate people's attention. Aren't many sermons stereotyped and boring? Has the biblical message not been heard so often that for many people it has become monotonous and flat?

Chapter Five tackles this problem head on. Boredom does not arise from quoting the Bible, but from generalizations, repetitions and lack of imagination. The Bible contains all the elements that can excite and hold people's attention: human-interest stories, poetry, the quaint and the unfamiliar, the unpredictable word. As communicators we should exploit such elements so that the message retains its interest value.

PART ONE

SCRIPTURE AS MESSAGE
AND MEDIUM

CHAPTER TWO

BIBLICAL REVIVAL

The decline in church attendance in many countries has not meant a decline of interest in the Bible. Radio broadcasts on biblical topics, Bible documentaries on TV and biblical films are still proving amazingly popular. There is a steady market for versions of Scripture, either complete or in selected parts. Books on the Old Testament, on Palestine, on Jesus Christ or any other related problem continue to sell remarkably well. The Bible remains 'in', even with many who don't reckon themselves as any longer belonging to organised christianity.

Within the Catholic Church biblical revival has given new life to small groups. Bible-sharing groups are mushrooming all over the world. We meet them in ever increasing numbers in countries as far apart as Brazil, the Philippines, Ghana, Mozambique, Indonesia, Guatemala, France and the United States, to mention just a few. They differ in orientation and method of work from one another, but basic to them all seems to be the realisation that Christ manifests himself most readily in a small community and that our whole life should be guided by the inspired Word of God.

Promotion of biblical revival is one of the avowed purposes of renewal in the Catholic Church. I still remember how on one occasion Pope John XXIII summoned all the priests and seminarians studying in Rome for a special conference. The meeting was arranged in the big church of San Ignazio. Thousands of students from all the seven universities of Rome gathered to listen to the Holy Father. It was an impressive scene. Pope John with his ever-ebullient eloquence spoke of the saintliness required in today's world. And one means to acquire this saintliness, he said, was familiarity with Sacred Scripture. He quoted the Apocalypse where an angel gives a scroll to John the Evangelist and says: 'Take it and eat; it will be bitter to your stomach, but sweet as honey to your mouth' (Rev 10, 9). John had to take the book and eat it, that he might preach the prophecies contained in it. Such, said the Pope, is once more the task of every priest, and in fact of every christian, in the changing world.

In its dogmatic Constitution on Divine Revelation, the Second Vatican Council voiced an intense longing, manifest throughout the Church, when it stated: "We hope for a new stimulus for the life of the Spirit from a growing reverence for the Word of God". Such a revival should begin with those who exercise leadership. "All the sacred ministers must hold fast to the Sacred Scriptures through diligent reading and careful study, especially the priests who represent Christ". Essentially it is a process that involves all the faithful. "The growth in insight into the realities and words that are being passed on . . . also comes about through the contemplation and study of believers who ponder these things in their hearts. It comes from the intimate sense of the spiritual realities which they experience." The Council urged all the christian faithful

> "to learn the surpassing knowledge of Jesus Christ (Phil 3, 8) by frequent reading of the divine Scriptures . . . Let them go gladly to the sacred text itself, whether in the sacred Liturgy, which is full of the divine Word, or in devout reading, or in such suitable exercises and various other helps which, with the approval and guidance of the pastors of the Church, are happily spreading everywhere in our day. Let them remember, however, that prayer should accompany the reading of Sacred Scripture, so that a dialogue takes place between God and man. For (as St. Ambrose says) 'We speak to him when we pray; we listen to him when we read the divine oracles'."

WHAT IS BIBLICAL REVIVAL?

The biblical revival in the Church means a rediscovery of the fact that the inspired Word of God should be the source of inspiration for every christian.

Sometimes one comes across the remark, "In the past centuries the Catholic Church did away with the Bible. Now it has been rediscovered". This is not correct. The biblical revival does not mean that the Bible needs an official recognition within the Church that it did not receive in the past. Vatican II declared: "The Church has always venerated the Divine Scriptures just as she venerates the Body of the Lord". There hasn't been anything wrong with the *theory* of the Bible's central place in the Church. Together with tradition, it has always been accepted as the supreme rule of faith. The proclamation of the Word of God in epistle and gospel always enjoyed a place of honour in the Eucharistic celebration. The liturgical prayers for each day, the breviary which the Church prescribed for her priests, were almost entirely taken from the Bible. Study of Scripture was always recognised as an indispensable element of theology, preaching and catechetical instruction. Whenever the priest spoke the words of institution during the Eucharist, when he anointed the sick, or absolved the sinner, he knew he was pronouncing scriptural words, the Words of God. The prominent role of the Bible in worship, doctrine and morality was officially recognised throughout the centuries.

What had gone wrong since the Middle Ages was not the Bible's role in the official Church, but its role in the life of every individual. By a number of almost imperceptible developments, the Bible, while maintained on its golden throne, was isolated from the day-to-day life of most of the faithful. In the beginning there was nothing intentional about this. The official translation of the Bible was in Latin and so the reading of the text naturally became the privilege of theologians and clerics. Theology itself was undergoing a process of synthesis, in which Aristotelian, neo-Platonic and Arab philosophies were integrated into a christian world view. In many a theological treatise, scriptural texts gradually assumed the subservient role of being 'inspired proofs' in support of doctrinal or moral structures built up by their authors. When the Reformation tried to remedy these errors, by bringing the Bible back to the ordinary people, the leadership in the Catholic Church reacted with a good amount of fear and panic. This was the time when the Latin Vulgate was made the normative text (to counteract spurious translations by imposing a norm that could be easily checked), when the reading of Scripture by individuals was restricted or even forbidden (lest by misinterpretation people be led into heresy) and when Protestant initiatives to make the Bible accessible were met with hostility and suspicion. The Bible was still revered and held in awe, seen from a distance on its golden throne, but within the Church it was as far removed from the life of the ordinary people as Queen Victoria or Louis XIV were from their lowly subjects.

The biblical movement in the Church is essentially an attempt to liberate the Bible from this splendid isolation. The lack of contact with the inspired Word itself had led to a great impoverishment of spiritual life and theological reflection. Just as Pius X's decree on frequent communion helped to restore the ordinary people's contact with Christ in the Blessed Sacrament, so the biblical revival seeks to make God speak directly to each of the faithful through a personal study of Scripture.

Speaking about study, it may be useful to discredit another false impression one sometimes encounters. There are people who confuse biblical revival with the progress in scriptural research. The rise of modern sciences, such as archaeology, linguistics, text criticism, etc. opened a new era for scriptural studies. Through our better knowledge of the ancient Middle East and the old Semitic languages, we have learnt much about the Bible that had remained obscure in previous centuries. Many new insights were obtained. Theology greatly benefited from the better understanding gained in this way. But all this new knowledge neither caused the biblical revival nor could it ever bring it about. The new scriptural studies are a help, a means of reading Scripture better. But the purpose of the biblical movement is essentially a different thing, namely, that Sacred Scripture should become the food by which one's life of faith and service is nourished day by day. Biblical research aims at improving the quality of our knowledge; the biblical revival aims at improving the quality of christian living.

Scriptural renewal in the Church is therefore a renewed attention, a renewed response to the actually inspired Word of God. I speak of the actually inspired Word, the very expression used by the Holy Spirit. When God, in his infinite mercy, wanted to redeem man, he wished to express himself to man in human language. God spoke through human instruments. He adapted himself to our way of thinking, our way of formulating realities in words; but yet, in and through the human words of the Bible, it is God himself who addresses us. The almighty, eternal, everlasting Majesty of God bows down to us, tiny creatures. He deigns to express his message of infinite love in a language that we can understand. To make every christian aware of this Word, to make him listen to the message God addresses to him in Scripture, this and nothing else is the purpose of biblical revival.

EXTRACTS OR SUMMARIES WON'T DO

Is there really any need for people to read the actual words of Scripture, to be familiar with the actual text? Sometimes one meets

Fig. 1. Mary reading the Scriptures
(Robert Campin; 1375-1444).

the opinion, even among priests, that immediate contact with Scripture is not a necessity. It helps; it edifies; but it is not *a necessity*. It is then argued: many of our good Catholics get by without knowledge of the inspired texts. Our catechisms, our prayer books, our sermons are all somehow or other derived from Scripture. Why then the need to go back to Scripture itself? Why go back to the lemon, when its juice has already, so to say, been squeezed out for us by able theologians?

It is difficult to meet this kind of objection. As the argument makes use of some half-truths as its stepping-stones, its fallacy is not so obvious. It is true that the Word of God can reach us through a sermon or an instruction even when Scripture is not explicitly quoted. A sermon *can* be 'scriptural' in a true sense even if the actual words of the text are not referred to. Also, the label 'a necessity' can be denied to many normal aspects of christian life. Is a mature and adult understanding of faith "a necessity"? Is christian witness in one's place of work or daily surroundings "a necessity"? Is experience of the Spirit "a necessity"? The question arises whether the objection itself does not stem from a tradition which stressed duties and devotions, but allowed the quality of christian experience to be impoverished.

Sacred Scripture is not a textbook containing truths that can be derived from it. The Bible is God speaking to me and speech cannot be treated in this manner. Suppose someone has a friend who comes to visit him. The two may be talking to one another for quite a long time. The actual news, the contents of what the friend says may be comparatively little, yet the other enjoys his conversation. He listens to his friend with patience. He laughs with him and jokes with him, and shares his worries. In other words, through their talk they grow in mutual friendship and understanding. They exchange far more than a few scraps of news. What would we think of a friend who said: "Don't waste my time! Why all this idle talk? Make a brief summary of what you have to say and send it to me through the mail"? The words of a friend can never be summarised, because what we want is to have contact with that friend himself. In the same way God's words in Scripture can never be summarised, can never be substituted by truths derived from them.

God does not so much reveal truths in Scripture; he reveals himself. When he speaks or writes to you, you have no choice but to pay attention. St. Gregory said: "What is Sacred Scripture but a letter

Fig. 2. St. Jerome. "Who does not know Scripture, does not know Christ".
(Lucas van Leyden; 1495-1533).

of Omnipotent God to his creature? And certainly if you received a letter from your earthly emperor, you would not allow anything to come in your way, you would not give sleep to your eyes until you had understood what this earthly emperor had written to you. The Emperor of heaven, the God and Lord of men and angels, has sent a letter of vital importance to you! And yet, my dear son, you neglect to read that letter with great interest. Be diligent, therefore, and meditate daily on the words of your Creator!" If we are far away from home and someone who is dear to us sends us a letter, we are anxious to read it because it reaffirms our relationship. The person concerned may not have much news to communicate, but we are glad to see his or her handwriting. We enjoy reading their words even if the ideas they communicate are familiar. As St. John Chrysostom says: "When we receive a letter from a friend, we pay attention not only to the content of it, but also to the affection of the writer expressed in it". And so it is with Sacred Scripture; we can derive certain doctrines from it but we can never substitute these doctrines for the living contact with God himself through the words that he inspired.

What theological statement on God's mercy can ever replace the parable of the Prodigal Son in Jesus' own words? What 'Life of Christ' can win our hearts better than the simple and yet profound narration of the gospels themselves? What pastoral counselling book can introduce us better into the spirit of the apostolate than the enthusiastic letters of that greatest of apostles, St. Paul? However great, however famous a theologian may be, could his words ever overshadow the incomparable pronouncements of our Lord Jesus himself? He who does not know Scripture, does not know Christ', said St. Jerome, and Pope Pius XII reiterates, 'It is in Scripture that all come to know Christ'. No substitution, no derivation will do here. If we want our people to know God, if we want them to grow in his love, we will have to teach them how to listen to his own words, the inspired words addressed to each of them.

HOW TO MAKE SCRIPTURE OUR DAILY FOOD

No one can subsist for the rest of his life on the intellectual treasures acquired in the family or at school. A person's spiritual life cannot keep floating forever on devotions begun as a child. Each one of us needs constant re-kindling of our ideals. Each one of us needs new impulses and fresh ideas. Without periodical sowing, ploughing and irrigation, our minds and hearts grow more barren than a parched piece of land. We need to grow by personal reading and reflection. And in this process of renewal and maturing, Sacred Scripture should have an important place. This applies to everyone, teachers, religious and priests included.

Throughout life, the Bible should be our chief meditation book. We should always have it ready at hand. We should turn to it in preference to others when making our meditation. When we read another book, we should watch out especially for references to Scripture and, on meeting one, we should put our book aside and read the passage from Scripture itself, paying attention to the new aspect we may have discovered in it. Different books of Scripture may appeal to us in different stages of our life. In our continuous discovery of new realities, in our effort to keep abreast with the thought of the Church, Sacred Scripture will prove to be the store from which the householder can produce 'things old and new' (Mt 14, 52).

I was once assisting an old lady on her deathbed. On my asking what more I could do for her, she said: "Read to me from the Bible". I took the copy lying near her pillow. She requested me to read from Chapter 15 in the first letter to the Corinthians, where St. Paul speaks about our resurrection with Christ. While I was reading, I could see that she was moved and greatly comforted. God's Word meant something to her. I found that various sentences had been underlined with pencil. During her life she must have often meditated on this text and now it gave her strength and comfort. That is what Scripture is supposed to do in our lives too. It should feed our conviction; it should re-kindle our love; it should become dear to us as God's own assurance to each person. A christian who has discovered this value of Scripture has found a great treasure.

A common difficulty experienced by people is the inability to pray. The dryness and aridity so normal in a spiritual life may have been aggravated by the many distractions of our daily routine. We may find, all of a sudden, that we hardly pray at all. We may notice with concern that it is only with the greatest effort that we manage to pay attention at Holy Mass and other Church functions. Our own personal prayer may have dwindled to intercession for a small list of private intentions, without being that true communion with God that we would like it to be. For this kind of experience, no ready-made medicine can be supplied. If even great saints like St. Teresa of Avila struggled with this problem, how much more can *we* expect to have it as one of our crosses? Yet there is one remedy that the Church has always recommended, namely, to have recourse to biblical prayer.

Our root problem may be that we have forgotten to listen to what God is trying to say to us. It may be a combination of filling our lives with too much noise and imagining that prayer means us speaking to God. The solution might lie in creating some space in our daily routine during which we place ourselves in God's presence in silence, and in which we devoutly read some part of Scripture with the desire to listen to what God is telling us. Adopting this practice may make us discover that prayer is, after all, a natural thing; that a response rises spontaneously from our heart whenever we are struck by something God is telling us through a sacred text.

I can think of no better text to express the right attitude towards Scripture than the *Imitation of Christ*, (Book III, Chapter 2). The text has taken the form of a prayer. The prayer lends itself well as an introduction: it puts us into the right frame of mind before we start reading the inspired words.

'Speak Lord, your servant is listening (1 Kings 3,10). I am your servant. Grant me insight that I may learn to understand your testimonies!' (Ps 118,125).
'Incline my heart to the words of your mouth. May your word descend as the dew in the morning'.

Many years ago, the people of Israel said to Moses: "If you speak to us, we shall listen. It is better that the Lord does not speak to us, otherwise we may die" (Ex 20,19). Not thus, O Lord, not thus I pray. But humbly and urgently I beg you in the words of the prophet Samuel: "Speak, Lord, your servant is listening" (1 Kings 3,10).

Let not Moses speak to me or one of the prophets. Rather it should be you yourself, Lord my God, you who inspire and enlighten all prophets, who should speak to me. You don't need them. By yourself you can give me perfect instruction. But they can do nothing without you.
They may make their words resound, but they cannot impart the Spirit.
They speak beautiful words but, if you keep silent, they can't kindle the heart.
They communicate the letter, but you explain its meaning.
They announce mysteries, but it is you who reveal the sense of what has been said.
They proclaim commandments, you help us to observe them.

Fig. 3. "Speak to me, Lord"
A. da Fonseca

They point out the way, but you give the strength to walk on it.
They reach us from outside, but you instruct and enlighten our hearts.
They irrigate the soil, but you give fertility.
They call out words, but it is you who help us to understand them while we listen.
Therefore let not Moses speak to me, but you, Lord my God, eternal Truth. Let it not happen to me that, admonished from without, but not kindled within, I die without fruit. May I not come to condemnation for having heard your word but failed to put it into practice; having known it but failed to love it; having believed it but failed to live it.
"Speak therefore, O Lord, your servant is listening" (1 Kings 3,10).
"For you have the words of eternal life" (Jn 6,69).
Speak to me that I may feel comfort in my soul and that I may improve my whole life, to your praise and glory and eternal honour!'

COMMUNICATING THE WORD

If Scripture means something to us in our own spiritual lives and if we have understood the importance of such personal contact with the inspired Word for every christian, we will draw some conclusions that may have a far-reaching influence on all the ways in which we communicate Scripture to others.

Children need the help of their parents and teachers to learn about God. Adult christians need the Word of God proclaimed to them in the liturgical readings and the prophetic word of the preacher. But such forms of instruction cannot replace the personal study and reflection that should be done by each individual. Neither can such an outside proclamation of Scripture be a substitute for the personal reading of the Bible and prayer in response to it.

Our instructions will have to be scriptural, not only in content, but also in the sense that they help people appreciate Scripture and meditate on it for themselves. Our public reading, our teaching and preaching should be such as to put people directly in touch with the inspired Word. Vatican II decreed: "Easy access to Sacred Scripture should be provided for all the christian faithful". The Council Fathers were mainly thinking of making readable and low-cost translations of Scripture available. However, the same principle could well be applied

Fig. 4. Portrait of a Girl by Jan Sluyters (1928).
Do we make God's Word accessible to children?

to all our oral communication about God. It should aim at making the Word of God easily accessible to the faithful.

Christ is the great Sacrament of the Church: he is present to us in many ways. He rules and guides us through the Holy Father and the bishops he gives us as our leaders. He meets us in every christian. He offers Mass through the hands of the priest. He absolves sins by the words of his minister. He comes to take possession of us in the wonderful mystery of Holy Communion. And in a special way Christ remains present with us through Sacred Scripture. The biblical revival aims at making this presence of Christ a reality in the life of every christian.

But don't we live in a different age? Can the intellectuals of our world let their lives be ruled by the Bible? Has Scripture still any authority today? Does it affect the *social* conditions of our world?

CHAPTER THREE

THE AUTHORITY OF SCRIPTURE TODAY

'Power' has been defined as the ability to make one's own values and aims accepted by others; the ability to influence others; the ability to limit another person's alternatives of behaviour. 'Authority' is commonly understood as the legitimate use of such power.

Considered in itself the authority of Scripture will not change or diminish in the course of time, as it proceeds from the power of the Almighty itself. However, as authority necessarily terminates in society, and thus in human persons belonging to a specific age and culture, the authority of the Scriptures will also depend on the changes affecting society in a particular age and culture. The question: 'What is the authority of Scripture today?' is therefore a very relevant one. We might paraphrase it as meaning: 'How can Scripture influence the people of our own age?' It is this aspect that I would like to discuss, restricting myself to a few salient points and observations.

I believe that the crisis of authority in modern society is an important factor that should not be overlooked. Added to this, we find that modern secularism seems to reject the very idea of a Revelation as such. In spite of these negative factors, or perhaps as a reaction to them, the Gospel seems to be stirring in many christians a new 'Holy Disquiet'. This holds the promise of great possibilities.

THE CRISIS OF AUTHORITY

Research on attitudes among youth has amply demonstrated that present day society is undergoing a crisis of authority. The reasons for this crisis have to be sought in the sociological changes taking place.

First of all, in our times, more than ever before, people are flooded by a multiplicity of contradictory statements and opinions.

Through the modern means of communication, people soon learn to see that the same event can be reported in different ways, can be variously interpreted and may lead to opposing views. Every opinion is to some extent relative. This basic possibility of contradiction is the first reason for the shaking of confidence in authority.

The second reason lies in the conflict between the avowed aims of society and the realities of life. Education, for instance, promises a preparation for life, but in actual fact most subjects taught in secondary education have no direct bearing on the real problems of life, on economics, politics and human relationships. A similar conflict is experienced between the licence promoted by modern society in films and novels on the one hand, and the public defence of morality on the other. To modern youth it often seems that society no longer knows any more what it wants, and that authority virtually stands for the maintenance of that society.

The third reason for a crisis in authority is a renewed appreciation of the individuality and liberty of every person. Freedom in every respect, with regard to the choice of one's life-partner, with regard to one's profession, or the exercise of one's religious convictions, are values accepted everywhere. On the other hand, conventions, traditions and the 'establishment' are being discredited. Authority, which is often experienced as a curtailing of freedom, finds it more difficult to justify itself.

Undoubtedly this attitude towards authority has also had an influence on the authority of the Bible. Paul Tillich draws attention to this in a sermon on Jesus' authority. Having introduced Jesus' discussions with the chief priests on his authority (Lk 20,1-28), he observes:

> Jesus, as well as his foes, acknowledges authority. They struggle about *valid* authority, not about authority as such. And this is what we find everywhere in the Bible and the life of the Church.
> Paul fights with the original disciples, including Peter, about the foundations of apostolic authority. The bishops fight with the enthusiasts about the leadership in the Church.
> The popes fight with the princes about the ultimate source of political authority.
> The reformers fight with the hierarchs about the interpretation of the Bible.
> The theologians fight with the scientists about the criteria of ultimate truth.
> None of the struggling groups denies authority, but each of them

"Hands up all those who are against voting by a show of hands."

Fig. 5. Typical modern mix-up.
From "Punch", 28 Sept. 1977.

denies the authority of the other group.

But if the authority is split in itself, which authority decides? Is not split authority the end of authority? Was not the split produced by the Reformation the end of the authority of the Church? Is not the split about interpretation of the Bible the end of the Biblical authority? Is not the split between theologians and scientists the end of intellectual authority? Is not the split between father and mother the end of parental authority? Was not the split between the gods of polytheism the end of their divine authority? Is not the split in one's conscience the end of the authority of one's conscience? If one has to choose between different authorities, not *they* but *oneself* is ultimate authority for oneself, and this means: there is no authority for him.

SECULARISM AND THE IDEA OF REVELATION

According to the traditional christian concepts, revelation means 'God speaking to men'. To describe this concept in crude terms: Almighty God, who lives in the heavens above the heavens, has spoken to man through his mediators, the prophets. In the course of time, God sent his only-begotten Son, who was born into the world as a child of Mary, and who thus, as the God-man, became the tangible self-manifestation of God: 'The Word became flesh'. The revelation given by God through his prophets and especially through his own Son, was expressed in writing in the Holy Scriptures. These Scriptures, however much written under the instrumentality of man, should be considered therefore the very word of God himself.

This traditional view of revelation and inspiration has been undermined by our modern scientific world outlook. To the men of old, the world in which we live was a strange mixture of the secular and the Divine. God's presence and direct intervention were seen in natural events, in supposed miracles and in the acquisition of new knowledge. To men of our age God speaking through human mediators, the incarnation and the inspiration of the holy writings seem to be part of that ancient mythopoeic thinking. This is all the more so because of our present-day knowledge of comparative religion. In practically all major religions we find the conviction that God has spoken through holy men, that God has manifested himself in various forms, and that God's word has found expression in sacred writings.

Many attempts on the part of christian belief and christian

theology have been made to answer this objection. However, in my opinion a comprehensive and convincing answer has not yet been found or at least has not yet been sufficiently accepted everywhere. As a result, there is real confusion among many christians and theologians. In spite of their continuing belief and readiness to respond to God's self-revelation, they are unable to outline the theoretical justification for revelation and inspiration in our secularised world. College students will tell us: "The Bible is out of date. Like all the other sacred books of the world, the Bible presents a view of the world that no longer fits our society. Religion with its stress on miracles, divine interventions, revelation and divinely dictated writings simply belongs to the past".

This secularist objection to the Bible is perhaps the greatest factor undermining the authority of Scripture today. I am convinced that the Bible will lose its hold on believers if we do not formulate a convincing answer to this objection. And it is a fact that in spite of all our goodwill and the intense efforts of so many scholars, we are still basically groping in the dark and looking for a renewed insight that will integrate our acceptance of a personal and self-revealing God, into our modern view of the world. Until this has been achieved, the authority of Scripture will necessarily be on the wane.

However, there is a consoling observation that we can make. Often in the history of christianity, living christian faith has preceded theological understanding. A new sense of mystery raises its head. This renewed response to the biblical message, then often points to better things to come in the theology of the future.

THE GOSPEL AND HOLY DISQUIET

The present crisis in christianity, caused as it has been by the changing sociological and ideological structures of mankind, has at the same time given rise to a renewed understanding of the Gospel as the norm of perpetual self-criticism and the cause of lasting holy unrest. The characteristic christian of today turns away from man-made beliefs, customs and practices, and tries to put himself once more under the immediate influence of Jesus' authoritative words.

A fore-runner of this new understanding of Scripture was Kierkegaard (1813-1855). He was one of the first to develop what we might call the theology of 'disquiet'.

"Just as a fisherman, after he has set out his nets, brings movement into the water to drive the fish towards the nets and thus to
catch more; just as the hunter employs a group of drivers to
encircle a part of the forest and to make them drive the wild
animals to the place where he is ready to shoot them, so God
himself tries to catch those who want to receive his love by
means of disquiet among men. Christianity is disquiet of the
strongest intensity and the greatest extent; one cannot imagine a
disquiet greater than this; it strives to bring man's existence to
disquiet until man's deepest kernel has been affected, until
everything is blown up and everything has faded. Wherever
someone becomes christian, there disquiet will be present and
wherever someone was christian in the past there disquiet can be
shown" (11,2:8,29).
"Spirit is disquiet; christianity is the deepest kind of disquiet
brought about in existing structures, as we find written in the
New Testament. However, many christians have made
christianity into a reason for complacency, 'so that we may
enjoy life fully' " (11,2a 317).

In his book on *The End of Conventional Christianity*, Dr. W. H.
van de Pol describes how the pillars of conventional christian belief
and practice have been shaken by theology over the past 50 years. He
shows that, apart from outside reasons leading to the re-appraisal of
true christian values, there has been in the movement itself a genuine
core of renewed understanding of Scripture. Also in its most radical
form, in the 'God-is-Dead Theology', there remains in reformed
christianity a final and irrevocable appeal to the authority of Jesus'
challenging words.

'Among many christians there is a strong conviction that the
decline of conventional christianity is just as unavoidable as the
death of God in our secular society. This conviction itself rests
on the belief that conventional christianity with its official
bourgeois morals has become in fact a radical negation of the
message of Jesus of Nazareth. Pierre Barton who wrote a book
The Comfortable Pew at the invitation of the Anglican Synod of
Canada, and who has already sold more than 10,000 copies of
it, was led by this conviction about conventional christianity to
break with any christian church. But he does not want to break
with the Jesus of Nazareth. Conventional christianity and the
preaching of Jesus are being contrasted with one another ever

more. This is expressed equally forcefully in the exceptionally rich and captivating book of Werner and Lotte Pelz *God is No More.'*

What is true of theology, also proves to be true of the life of many ordinary christians. In an analysis of the renewal of christian faith among intellectuals of Europe, Simon Jelsma contrasts the complacency and self-assurance of many conventional christians with the new attitudes of reformed christians. In his exposition he claims to be especially influenced by his experience with Roman Catholic college students. When describing these young intellectuals, whom he calls the 'rebel christians', he writes as follows:

The rebels discover a world full of questions, responsibilities, challenges, risks and expectations. They want to live and work in this dynamic world. They rise and make ready to leave the old, dilapidated building of the past. Tents and camping equipment are taken for the journey. Before them they see the endless desert. At the other side of the horizon they know there will be the promised land. God is a story. Every day they have to rise again and continue the journey. While walking on the track they sing and pray. At night they make camp as possibilities allow them. They dream of new perspectives, of liberation, of happiness, of the end of a reign of terror. From day to day they have to seek oases, new wells, food for one day. The weather and the colour of the sky change and keep changing. Life means for them living in open space and being always on the move. The security of enclosure no longer exists.

By becoming again 'the desert church' some christians of today make themselves once more totally dependent on the Word of God. The very crisis which, at first sight, seemed to undermine the authority of the Bible today, would also seem to have become a providential setting in which the true function of God's Word may be re-established for many.

I am far from suggesting that all is well in the State of Denmark. Our times are confusing and the confusion is one reason why people refer to the Bible less than they should. The points I want to make are:

    1. There is a good reason for the confusion, viz. the search of theology for an adequate contemporary expression of faith.

This search is important, it should continue and we should accept the unpleasant consequences of it.

2. The more radical christian groups do not reject the Bible. In fact, all of us can learn from their determination to be true to the Gospel.

SCRIPTURE IN THE PASTORAL MINISTRY

The whole situation reminds me somehow of the "temptations of St. James" – a popular theme in medieval stories and art. Twentieth-century snobs that we are, we smile at the naivety of ideas expressed in it. We feel ourselves much superior to the "unresolved conflict" they manifest. But are we really so superior? The exciting story of how Hermogenes the Magician (human wisdom!) sends a host of sinister allies to tempt St. James the Greater (faith), so masterfully depicted by Hieronymus Bosch (see Fig. 6), could well symbolize what is happening to many people today. The shapes and the forms are different today – Bosch understood that well! – but the reality of our faith being assaulted, and ourselves being "tempted" in many ways, can hardly be denied. Perhaps, the answer lies not so much in trying to meet Hermogenes on his own ground, as in putting oneself under the protection of the "angel of God", as Bosch suggests in his painting!

Today, more than ever, the minister of the Word will have to spend all his energies on conveying the central message of the Bible itself. Fidelity to God's word requires the ability to distinguish the ever-present and ever-relevant demand of God from what is passing and time-bound. The message of Scripture should be disentangled from religious concepts that are contrary to our modern scientific outlook or which have a theology of God and man that is unacceptable to contemporary society. This 'demythologization' will have to be done. We have to do it without doing an injustice to the revelation of God itself: this may prove a difficult task. While openly admitting the difficulty, let us not stop proclaiming the Word on account of that.

A NEW KIND OF AUTHORITY

Scripture has authority today, not only because it is the Word God spoke, but especially in the sense that it exercises an influence on people in their everyday lives. Theology's inability to give a com-

Fig. 6. Hermogenes directing the assaults on St. James.
By Hieronymus Bosch (1450-1516).

prehensive and adequate reply to the intellectual queries of our age, need not stand in the way of Scripture addressing people in a meaningful way. In fact, it seems quite certain that this is the kind of authority the Bible is supposed to have. An unusual kind of authority, no doubt, but of the same kind as the authority exercised by Jesus. Two oracles of Isaiah may help us to reflect on this authority. They describe the "Servant of Yahweh":

> "This person is my servant.
> I uphold him.
> He is the one I have elected.·
> I am pleased with him.
> I have put my Spirit upon him.
> It is his task to establish a just way of life for all
>   mankind.
> He does not cry out,
> nor shout aloud.
> He does not make his voice heard in the street.
> A damaged reed he does not break,
> nor quench a wavering flame.
> But he establishes a just way of life by truth.
> With unshakeable and unflinching determination
> he will eventually constitute a just way of life on
>   the earth.
> Eventually even the farthest lands will live by his
>   guidance."
>
> Is 42,1-4

> "The Lord Yahweh has given me
> a disciple's tongue.
> He provides me with speech
> so that I may know how to reply to the wearied.
> Each morning he wakes me to hear,
> to listen like a disciple.
> The Lord Yahweh has opened my ear."
>
> Is 50,4-5

Is 42, 1-4 is an oracle. Yahweh is speaking. He is introducing a person to us and asserting that this person fulfils an important mission. Commentators used to be divided in opposing camps on the question whether Yahweh's oracle refers to an individual person or to Israel as a nation. Now the opinions of commentators seem to converge towards an intermediate position. Yahweh introduces an ideal person who was originally understood more in terms of a future outstanding individual leader of supreme holiness (the messianic interpretation). For practical purposes we may call this new ideal person introduced by Yahweh "the new Israelite".

A study of Deutero-Isaiah (Is 44-45) reveals to what kind of society this "new Israelite" belonged. Small groups of faithful Jews had returned to Palestine from their lands of exile. Generally speaking they were poor, badly organized, disheartened and constantly harrassed by enemies. They had very little political security to depend on. Their temple lay in ruins and even after it had been restored lacked the lustre of Solomon's times. Material progress was hampered by frequent civil wars and heavy taxation on all income. From a religious point of view there was a good deal of uncertainty about the extent to which God's promises were still holding good. It is against this background that we understand "the new Israelite". *He is a man of humble status, fighting the odds of adverse circumstances, but determined to be faithful to Yahweh.*

There is little room for boasting or triumphalism in such a picture. There is little left of the glamour of a Moses, the victorious conquest of a Joshua or the majestic splendour of Solomon's court. But here Yahweh's oracle makes its first decisive pronouncement. Yahweh adopts this "new Israelite". *He is chosen by Yahweh to be his special instrument of salvation.* The title "Yahweh's servant" had always been reserved to great leaders as Moses (Dt 34,5; Jos 1,1-2; 1 Kgs 8,53.56; 2 Kgs 21,8); Joshua (Jos 24,29; Jdg 2,8), David (Ps 89, 3-20; 2 Sam 7,5; 1 Kgs 11,34) or the prophets in general (2 Kgs 17,13). Here Yahweh calls the new Israelite "my servant". By this the new Israelite is raised to the status of being a new Moses, a new Joshua and a new David. Also, the Jews were well aware that God made a free use of his power to *elect* the instruments of Salvation. In this way he had "elected" Jacob rather than Esau (Dt 4,37; Mal 1,2), "elected" the Levites from all tribes (Dt 18,5; 21,5), "elected" Jerusalem rather than any other city for his temple (1 Kgs 8,44. 48; etc.) and "elected" the king who was pleasing to him (Dt 17,15). The new Israelite receives a similar election. Yahweh had fastened his love on him. He gives him his Spirit as he had done to his chosen leaders of the past.

Is 50,4-5 adds another dimension to the picture. Yahweh's servant is also *a disciple.* He is a man under instruction, a man who lives from listening to God's Word. In the past God's Word had been spoken directly only to some privileged few, to mediators of the covenant and prophets. Now in this new era God addresses his new servant without such intermediaries. He speaks directly to him. He "has opened his ears". The new servant of Yahweh wakes up every day to listen to the Word God will speak to him within the situation of that day.

THE UNEXPECTED TASK

Early Israelite theology was heavily self-centered. The emphasis fell on Yahweh's election of the nation to the exclusion of other peoples (Ex 19, 5-6; Dt 7,6). Although Yahweh was considered in some way the God of all the nations, he was thought of as having singled out Israel for a specially close relationship (Dt. 32,8-9). Deutero-Isaiah revolutionizes this concept by asserting that God's salvific Will *embraces all the nations of the world*. "All the ends of the earth shall see the salvation of our God" (Is 52,10). "That my salvation may reach to the ends of the earth" (Is 49,6). "Turn to me and be saved, all the ends of the earth" (Is 45,22). "That men may know, from the rising of the sun unto the west, that there is none besides me. I am the Lord, and there is no other" (Is 45,6). The stress is on the universal extent of the new Israelite's mission. He has to work "for all mankind" (Is 42,1). His mission is not limited to Palestine, but extends to the whole world, even to the farthest lands (Is 42,4).

What message of salvation is it the new Israelite has to carry to the world? Other oracles of Deutero-Isaiah leave no doubt about *the religious content of the message*. The mission should lead all nations to acknowledge Yahweh as the only God. "To me every knee shall bow, every tongue shall swear" (Is 45,23). The mission will only be completed when the nations of the earth will have come to Israel with the humble admission: "God is with you only and there is no other, no God besides him" (Is 45,14). This no doubt is the ultimate aim, the fulness of salvation, which will result from ever more non-Jewish nations giving up their superstitious and idolatrous practices and submitting whole-heartedly to Yahweh's convenant.

In the particular oracles we are discussing now, stress is not laid directly on this religious function. Rather it is stated most forcibly that the new Israelite has to bring to mankind "a just way of life", much in the same way as kings and political rulers are supposed to establish a realm of justice (see Jos 24,25; Ps 72,1-4;101,1-8). Deutero-Isaiah himself interprets this future realm of justice to imply that the eyes that are blind will be opened, that prisoners will be brought out of jail: "from the prison those who sit in darkness" (Is 42,7). All through his prophecies we find the stress on this *social dimension of the new servant's mission*. God is deeply concerned about the sub-human conditions of the people. "When the poor and needy seek water, and there is none, and their tongue is parched with thirst, I the Lord will answer them" (Is 41,17). "This is a people robbed and plundered. They are all of them trapped in holes and hidden in prisons" (Is 42,22). With eyes of pity God looks down on the "have-nots" who suffer in jail, or hunger and thirst, or are smitten by the scorching wind and the sun (Is 49,7-10). It is the task of his servant to establish a human way of life for all mankind.

At this point the traditional Israelite would expect a command from God to initiate a new world-wide holy war. He would expect a "military conquest of the earth", much on the lines of the victorious occupation of Palestine in the past. The message of Deutero-Isaiah explicitly rejects such a concept.The new Israelite will have to achieve his mission, not by violence or domination, but *by persistent service and persuasion*. He is tender-hearted and meek. He does not crush, even if he could easily do so, but tries to win the hearts of men by truth (Is 42, 2-3). Although suffering is not mentioned directly in Is 42,1-4, it is clearly implied. The real victory of Yahweh's new servant will not lie in political power or military triumphs, but in delivering mankind through the vicarious sufferings and humiliations undertaken in his mission (Is 52,13–53,12). This is an entirely new and profound understanding of the way in which God will work salvation. To some extent Old Testament theology here reaches its climax. It prepares the way for the ever-surprising reality of Christ's victorious passion. It was an insight so precious that it could form the foundation for expressing Christ's own mission.

THE NEW AUTHORITY OF GOD'S WORD

Is 42,1-4 became a basic text for the New Testament understanding of redemption. In the oldest traditions *Jesus' baptism* and this oracle are inextricably interwoven. It is at his baptism that the Father presents Jesus as his new servant "in whom my soul delights" (Mt 3,16-17; Mk 1,10-11; Lk 3,21-22). It was the coming of the Spirit upon Jesus at his baptism that marked the beginning of his mission (see also Jn 1,32-33). Also in other Gospel texts, the evangelists frequently characterize Jesus' mission with a reference to our text. Because Jesus was the new servant of Yahweh, he established his just way of life by truth (Is 42,3; Jn 8,44-46). Matthew quotes Isaiah 42,1-4 in full (Mt 12,18-21) to explain why Jesus proclaimed his message in a humble and peaceful manner (Mt 12,15-17).

It is not difficult to see how *the image of this new servant of Yahweh* suited Jesus to perfection (Acts 3,13). Jesus had come to bring salvation for all mankind. His salvation embraced the whole man: it brought the good news of repentance and acceptance, but also liberation to prisoners, sight to the blind and help to the oppressed (Lk 4,18-19). Jesus' way of redemption also was one of persuasion in truth, of meekness and gentleness, of vicarious suffering. Jesus was, in fact, the perfect realization of what God had in mind when he inspired the Deutero-Isaian passages.

Jesus' meekness and humbleness do not result in weakness. *Jesus exercises authority by the results he obtains.* "He will lead the truth to victory: in his name the nations will put their hope" (Mt 12,20-21; cf. Is 42,4). "See, my servant will prosper, he shall be lifted up, exalted, rise to great heights" (Is 52,13: cf. Jn 17,1-4). "I will make you the light of the nations so that my salvation will reach till the ends of the earth" (Is 49,6; cf. Lk 2,32). There is mystery and paradox here: Jesus, who is the Word that is God and that became flesh, can be challenged: "they did not accept him" (Jn 1,11). Yet he will be victorious because he is the light that darkness cannot overpower (Jn 1,5).

Through these reflections we may have found a key to solve the present-day crisis of Scriptural authority. Rather than one-sidedly concentrating on theoretical problems and theological studies, we should measure the impact of our mission, the mission of the Church, on people's lives today. As Yahweh's servants we cannot doubt the universality of our mission. We are called to bring about the salvation of all mankind. But this salvation should include the whole man, and should perhaps especially in the situation of today, begin with a determined effort to bring about "a just way of life" for everyone. It should achieve its end not by triumphalism or domination, but by suffering and truth. The assurance of ultimate victory will then also have a special meaning for us today. However insignificant and small we may be as a Church of believers, we will "eventually establish a just way of life on the earth".

CHAPTER FOUR

ON LISTENING AND ASKING QUESTIONS

Scripture is God's Word to man. It has a definite message. It is proclaimed with divine sanction. It would hardly be correct to reduce it to a mere stepping stone in our own process of thinking. The Bible is much more than a collection of useful examples and stories. The biblical text is a sacrament that somehow conveys God's own Word to us, however much its literary origins are human. The inspired message of Scripture is not to be questioned by man, but to be received with faith and obedience.

All this is right in theory, but in practice much goes wrong. Quite often our proclamation of the scriptural message turns into a monologue that defeats its own purpose. To be humanly effective, human speech should include both statement and response, should be a cycle in which communication flows between speaker and listener. Monologues are ineffective because the listener tends to disregard their message.

An ordinary Sunday sermon may provide a classical example of one-way communication. The priest talks for ten minutes without questions, responses or interruptions. Our Catholic audiences have grown accustomed to sitting rigid through the performance. A cautious smile may be tolerated. Relaxed laughter or applause are definitely out. The preparation of the message and its delivery are one hundred per cent the work of the priest. The faithful share in the process only by listening, which they have to do in a posture of frozen immobility.

Such a situation is highly unsatisfactory, especially today. The monologue type sermon or lecture smacks of paternalism and the establishment. In the minds of people it is readily associated with the pre-democratic forms of communication prevalent in the past. It seems to perpetuate the unwanted distinction between an omniscient clergy and an ignorant and docile laity. For such reasons this very process of communication arouses resentment and resistance among thinking Catholics, particularly if they are young. It is not leadership or authority itself that is questioned here, but the un-democratic and condescending way in which it is exercised.

The problem mentioned here affects sermons and other forms of instruction, whatever their topic may be. But when the topic is taken from the Bible, the problem is often aggravated by the way scriptural authority is understood and presented. If all the stress is laid on obedience to God's Word and passive submission to whatever it decrees, resentment and irritation will be unavoidable. If such feelings of resistance are provoked, the real authority of Scripture, its effective influence on people, will be weakened. It is useful to reflect a little on the implications of all this.

If the Bible is a way in which God communicates with man, it is implied that the person who reads or hears Scripture proclaimed also has a part to play. Effective communication comes about only when both partners have an equal share. The question of the authority of one partner does not diminish the share to be given to the other partner. Even if the brigadier gives orders to a corporal, the corporal will have to contribute actively by asking for clarifications, by providing complementary information or making alternative suggestions when required. The final decision of what should be done may be the brigadier's; the process of communication between the two belongs to both.

Sacred Scripture and its pastoral use demand a very active involvement of the person who is to benefit from them. Proclaiming the Word of God does not necessarily mean therefore adopting an authoritarian model of preaching or instruction. The Word of God is like a grain of wheat gently thrown on a piece of soil in the hope that it may grow. It is like an invitation to share in a wedding feast. Although the Word of God is God's and has, therefore, a message of its own, it does not address man in a uniform and stereotyped way. It doesn't speak only to instruct or command; it also questions, suggests, prods and persuades.

THE PREACHER AS COMMUNICATOR

It is difficult to trace the exact origins of the classical form of the sermon, such as is still associated in the minds of many with the proclamation of Scripture. Probably it arose during the Middle Ages and was a combination of the art of homily popular with the early Fathers of the Church, and classical oratory as it had been taught by Greek and Roman masters.

It may not be altogether a waste of time to read a satirical description of the 'oratorical sermon' given by Erasmus in his book *Praise of Folly* (1508).

'Tell me, my friend, what comedian, what vendor in the market place would you not prefer to these gentlemen who in their sermons make such a farce of public speech, while to everyone's entertainment, they claim to follow the rules laid down by the ancient masters of oratory? Good Lord, see how wildly they gesticulate; how they vary the pitch of their voice according to circumstances; how melodiously they speak on other occasions; how they sway with their bodies; how they pull a variety of faces; how they fill the whole church with their cries! And this art of preaching is handed down from one monk to another as if it were a great secret!

Although I am not really supposed to know anything about it, I will tell you all about it, basing myself on guess-work of course. First, they invoke help from above, a habit they learnt from poets. Then, if they wish to speak about christian charity, they will refer in their opening words to the Egyptian river the Nile; or if they intend to expound the mystery of the Cross, they consider it a brainwave to take their opening from the Babylonian dragon Bel; or if they want to discuss fasting, they will start with the twelve signs of the Zodiac; or again, if they have chosen Faith as their topic, their introductory reflections will be about the squareness of a circle. I was myself once among the audience of a preacher who was utterly stupid – I am sorry, I meant to say who was very learned – who claimed before a huge number of people that he was going to explain the mysteries of the Blessed Trinity. To give evidence of his extraordinary learning and to please the theologians who were present, he adopted an entirely new approach. Namely, he began to discuss letters, syllables, and words; he then discussed how noun and verb should be in agreement, and that the same is true of noun and adjective. Many were puzzled at all this; some could be heard to mutter to themselves the ancient saying of Horace: "What is all this nonsense going to lead to!" Eventually the preacher reached the conclusion that the image of the Trinity could be traced in such striking similarities in the first principles of grammar that no mathematician could have drawn it more clearly on a blackboard. . . . .

Fig. 7. Demosthenes, the model of many preachers.
Greek statue (300 B.C.).

After this unusual introduction, everyone, including the theologians, was listening with open mouths, overcome by amazement . . . And their appreciation was justified. For had ever anyone, even the famous Demosthenes among the Greeks, or Cicero among the Romans, invented such a clever introduction? These ancient masters considered an introduction defective if it was not adequately connected with the main topic; they were of the opinion that also swine-herds begin in this fashion, whose only master is nature. But these learned scholars of our own time are of the opinion that their 'forerunner' — for this is what they call the introduction — only satisfies the demands of oratory if it has nothing in common with the rest of their sermon, so that their hearers may full of surprise, utter the well-known words: "What on earth is he driving at?"

In the third part of their speech — which is actually the sermon part itself — they explain a small passage from the Gospel, but they do this quickly and superficially, whereas in fact this should have been their main task.

Then, when the fourth part of the sermon comes round, the speaker assumes a new character and introduces a theological question, normally one which floats between heaven and earth, obviously convinced that tackling such a question is also part of preaching. This is the moment when real theological pride manifests itself. They throw about their splendid titles at this juncture, such as: sublime teachers, profound and super-profound teachers, indisputable teachers, etc. Then they bamboozle the simple people with syllogisms, majors, minors, conclusions, corollaries, suppositions and more such scholastic nonsense.

The only thing that still remains is the fifth part of the sermon; in which the preacher has to prove himself a perfect artist. Here they produce one or other daft and stupid fairy tale, derived, unless I am mistaken, from the 'Historical Mirror' or the 'Acts of the Romans'. Somehow they succeed in drawing an allegorical, moral and religious message from it. . . . They have also learnt that joking is one of the requisites of oratory and so they attempt to spice their words with a few witty statements here and there. But, dear Venus, their jokes are so witty and so to the point that one can characterise them best with the saying: "It's like an ass playing the lyre". . . . In this way they succeed in making their sermon a chimera, a monster such as even Horace could not have imagined when he described a painting in which a being appeared with a woman's head on the rump of a horse . . . Now you will understand, I believe, what an impression this sort of person makes on me, especially because by their ludicrous pomposity and loud-mouthed, ridiculous stupidities they impose a kind of tyranny on the world. And then they imagine themselves to be preachers like Paul and Anthony of Padua!'

Erasmus had a sharp tongue. His criticism is cutting. For all we know, his remarks may do an injustice to many sane and biblical preachers of his age. What strikes me most in his sketch of the preacher is how the classical art of oratory had begun to dominate the scene. Preachers would adopt the oratorical sequence of having an introduction, a 'corpus', additional reasons and a peroration. They tried to follow the rules laid down by Greek and Roman masters as closely as possible. Even Erasmus, in spite of his criticism, refers to these classical teachers when he seeks a norm of evaluation. From this we can see that gradually a certain 'model' of preaching was universally accepted which became the standard almost to our own days.

Of course, there were variations on the model. John Wesley, a great preacher in a later century, was much more biblical and had a style of his own. Yet, in one way he and other evangelical preachers like him confirmed the 'model' of the preacher who tells people what is wrong with their lives and who proclaims the truths of Scripture.

Wesley was extraordinarily successful. Preaching in halls and prisons, in open spaces and among the toiling, uneducated masses, he drew crowds of up to 80,000. It is said that, before he died in 1791, he had travelled 225,000 miles within Britain and preached 50,000 sermons. Preaching the Word of God to others with this charism of prophetic authority also extended itself outside the Sunday service in church. Teachers would 'preach' to their pupils; catechists would 'preach' to catechumens; even parents in their homes shared in this universal charism by 'preaching' to their children.

I hope the reader understands that I am not against preaching as such, which we will have to do from time to time, but against the stereotype 'model' that has somehow for many people become identical with 'communicating the Word of God'. In their mind's eye they see the preacher as a stern and sincere individual who feels called upon to impart to others truths and commandments revealed by God, which have to be accepted unconditionally. And for many, consciously or unconsciously, this image of the preacher is projected back on to Jesus. They imagine that Jesus was, to an extreme degree, such a 'preacher'. After all, Jesus knew what is right and wrong; he knew everything, didn't he? So in the Gospel we find that Jesus preaches all the time . . .

JESUS' MODELS OF PREACHING

If we study the gospels we find that Jesus did not have one single, uniform way of communicating the Word. On the contrary we find him adopting quite different styles according to the needs of his audience. (As I will draw my illustrations mainly from St Luke's Gospel, references after a text in brackets refer to this gospel, unless another evangelist is indicated).

Jesus spoke in the synagogues during the sabbath service (6,6; 14,10; etc.). On those occasions Jesus followed the procedure of rabbis in his day. As he did in Nazareth (4,16-30), he would first read out a Scripture passage and then give his commentary on it. People admired the easy and gracious manner in which Jesus spoke. His style was different from that of the scribes, because he taught with authority (4,31-32).

Another kind of situation described in the gospel is Jesus 'speaking to the crowds'. People flocked to him from all directions and wanted to hear his instruction. Jesus would then sit down in their

Fig. 8. Jesus the Teacher.
Quinten Matsÿs (1465-1530)

midst and address them. At times this was done outside in an open space (6,17-19); at other times in a house (5,17-26; 8,19-21); sometimes from a boat while people stood on the shore (5,1-3) or in the Temple (19,47; 21,38). Here also Jesus spoke as a prophet; he taught with authority (Mt 7,28-29). But all the same there were important differences in his approach. No longer is Jesus simply a 'preacher' who imposes ideas on others. No, he feels himself the responsible 'elder brother' who wants his 'family members' to discover for themselves what is the truth.

Hardly ever do we hear Jesus quote the Old Testament when addressing the ordinary people. Rather, he begins his instructions from observations that reflect their own culture and thinking. He speaks about their everyday experience, about the flowers in the field, about sowing and reaping, about a shepherd looking after his sheep, about the village girls going to a marriage, about fishermen hauling in their net, about the experiences of travellers on a lonely road. For Jesus such realities of daily life are not just the wrapping in which he presents divine teaching; no, he teaches the crowds how they can infer the nature of religious realities from their daily experiences. "If you then, bad as you are, know how to give your children what is good for them, how much more will the heavenly Father give the Holy Spirit to those who ask him!" (11,13).

Jesus begins the process of thought with the needs of the people. This is seen best in the way his miracles come about. Jesus' miracles never start with an idea launched by Jesus himself. They always respond to a need; to people being hungry, to a boat being threatened by a storm, to a mother who weeps over her son at his burial, to blind persons, lepers, paralysed or hunch-backed individuals who suffer and need his help. Much of Jesus' preaching is done by these acts of genuine concern. Again, we would be wrong to think of Jesus' miracles as diplomatic proofs invented to support his doctrine; rather, Jesus thinks with the people and knows that his actions are governed by their needs.

Jesus wanted the people to think for themselves, that is why he taught them in parables. The apostles were surprised at this. They would have expected plain language. Jesus realised that people would only accept his message if he could make them think for themselves. In order to understand, they should listen and listen again; in order to perceive, they should see and see again. Only then would they be converted and healed (Mt 13,10-15).

When Jesus speaks to the Twelve, whom he has chosen to be his close companions, he pours out his heart with extensive explanations (Mt 13,18-23; 36-43) and detailed instructions (Mt 10,1-42; 18, 1-35; etc.). Frequently these instructions are very similar to his personal talks with individuals, such as the rich young man (18,18-23), Nicodemus (Jn 3,1-16), the Samaritan woman (Jn 4,1-26), Mary and Martha (Lk 10,38-42). Here again we find that in every single case Jesus listens as much as he speaks. His words are provoked by the needs of the person in question, not prompted by a preconceived ideal that he wants to impose.

Jesus adopts a totally different style when he is confronted with the scribes and pharisees. Let us remember that they were well-educated and learned, the scholars of their time. They were critical and sceptical about many things Jesus did. Frequently they would raise objections, which they would present in the form of questions: "Why do you eat with sinners and tax collectors?" (5,30). "Why do your disciples eat corn on the sabbath?" (6,2), "Why do you not wash your hands before the meal?" (11,38). "What authority do you have for acting like this?" (20,2) and many others. "The scribes and the pharisees began a furious attack on Jesus and tried to force answers from him on innumerable questions, setting traps to catch him out in something he might say" (11,53).

It is fascinating to see how Jesus meets the challenge put by these men who lived in their own world of intellectual doubts, queries and arguments. He counters their questions with other questions. "Have you not read what David did when he and his followers were hungry, how he went into the house of God, took the loaves of offering and ate them and gave them to his followers, loaves which only the priests are allowed to eat?" (6,3-4). "Which one of you, if his son falls into a well, or his ox, will not pull him out on a sabbath day without hesitation?" (14,5). "I too will ask you a question. Tell me: did John's baptism come from heaven or from man?" (20,3). "Show me a denarius. Whose head and name are on it?" (20,24). Sometimes Jesus himself challenged them with an unexpected question. "What is your opinion about the Messiah? Whose son is he?" and then "If David can call him Lord, then how can he be his son?" Jesus' questions were so disturbing to the scribes, who thought that by their reasonings they had worked out everything to perfection, that "no one any longer dared to ask him any questions" (20,40).

The scribes often attacked Jesus and, especially during the last weeks of his public ministry, Jesus was forced to assume a position of self-defence. However, this should not make us lose sight of the admiration for, and sympathy with, the scribes' function which Jesus had. In Jesus' eyes it was the scribes' *duty* to ask questions and produce arguments. Very often Jesus must have listened attentively to what the scribes had to say and learnt from their wisdom. Jesus acknowledged their authority because they were "sitting on the seat of Moses" (Mt 23,2). Jesus compared a scribe who becomes a disciple of the kingdom of heaven to a householder who brings out from his storeroom things both new and old (Mt 13,52). Jesus praised a scribe who had given the right answer to a difficult question (Lk 10,28). Most of all, Jesus himself acted like a scribe in many ways: he allowed people to call him 'Rabbi' (Mt 26,25 etc.). By putting forward questions in reply to the questions posed by the scribes, Jesus was not putting on an act. At that moment he identified himself with them; he doubted and questioned and argued like them.

The most striking passage to underline this role of Jesus is found in St. Luke's gospel. Luke narrates what must have been an ancient tradition, namely, that Jesus stayed back in the Temple when he went up for the first time as a boy of twelve years old. He then describes Jesus as follows:

'Three days later, they found him in the Temple, sitting among the doctors, listening to them and asking them questions; and all those who heard him were astounded at his intelligence and his replies'. (Lk 2,46-47).

Jesus listened and asked questions. Surely Luke is not presenting the boy Christ as the omniscient Word of God playing a game with the scribes. No, here we are presented with Jesus 'growing in wisdom' (Lk 2,52) by sharing the searchings of learned men. And as with every mature and educated person, the habit of listening and asking questions must have remained with Jesus throughout his life. Although on many occasions he could teach with authority and act with prophetic determination, on other occasions he knew the doubt of the seeker. "Father, what should I say? Should I say: save me from this hour?" (Jn 12,27). "God, my God, why have you forsaken me?" (Mt 27,46).

The picture of Jesus the communicator that emerges from the above considerations is not the one of a 'preacher' who proclaims the same message on every occasion. The authoritarian model of 'Take it or leave it; this is the Word of God', popularly attributed to Jesus, is not reflected in his way of announcing the message. In every situation

Fig. 9. A questioning Scribe.
Unknown artist, 1500 A.D.

Jesus seems to have had his actions and words guided by the needs of the particular people he met. When he spoke to the ordinary people, he identified with them. He saw their needs. He took examples from their everyday lives and presented parables that would force them to think. When he was in the company of scribes, he listened to their questions, argued with them and raised questions himself. When he was with his disciples or other personal friends, he would share their aspirations and worries and make his instructions respond to these. Just as Jesus himself, the Word of God, was not imposed on mankind from outside, but became one of us, in the same way the word that Jesus spoke was born from his natural relationships with the people; it responded to their needs.

LET THE AUDIENCE SPEAK

If we want to avoid talking in monologues, we have to promote methods by which our audience can speak to us. If we want to escape from the one-sided model of 'preaching', we have to learn how to identify ourselves with the persons we address. Feedback from the audience is essential to any healthy form of communication and it applies also to communication of God's Word.

It goes without saying that, whenever we can arrange our communication on the Bible in the form of a real dialogue or shared discussion, this opportunity should not be missed. In the classroom the teacher can encourage the discussion of topics in workshops or smaller groups. In a eucharistic celebration for small groups, the priest can lead a shared reflection on the readings in such a way that the participants can take a full share in the development of thought.

As this book is specially written for those whose task it is to communicate the Word of God by oral communication in other situations than 'sharing', I will not enlarge on this topic further (see the companion volume *Prayer with the Bible*). For our present discussion we will put ourselves in the position of those for whom such a realistic 'sharing' is not possible.

Let us begin with the realization that, although sharing meets the requirement of feedback to a great extent, it also has its limitations. Sharing is impossible when the group is too big. Moreover, quite a few people are inhibited and do not really open up even though they are invited to do so. A forced situation of sharing may in actual fact leave such a person with more doubts and greater dissatisfaction than when the Word of God has been presented in a straightforward way. Then again, sharing may not leave sufficient room for the role of prophet and teacher to be played by certain persons in the community. Sharing is therefore not the universal answer to our problem, nor the most important one.

Some people have experimented with the so-called 'interview' sermon in which two people ascended the pulpit, one to ask questions and the other to reply. The attempt proved a failure. People experienced it as something that was staged and unreal.

The solution actually lies in making our audience speak in our own presentation. This is what Jesus did in all his preaching. The ordinary people heard themselves reflected in what he said. The scribes saw their own questions and doubts met by the counter-questions posed by Jesus. Our speaking will no longer be a monologue if we allow our audience to speak through our words. The model of the sacred minister 'preaching' to those living in the world will make place for the rapport of a dialogue between the people themselves and the Word of God.

What we have to do, in fact, is never to forget the needs and doubts and queries of our people. Whenever we proclaim the Word of God, we should take our starting point from them. We should ask ourselves what questions *they* ask of God and his words. We should try to determine how Scripture and its message can fulfil *their* desires or allay *their* fears.

We have to aim at verbalising the questions of the audience in our own words. We can present the audience's point of view by introducing a case history. Or we can explicitly pose the questions just as our audience would like to ask them. We should formulate the message of Scripture in the thought patterns and expressions people themselves use. If we do this well, we will, in a certain sense, be acting also on behalf of our audience and thus rendering them a great service. Some of the things we can say on their behalf may be so delicate that people themselves would not dare to speak of them except in a very intimate talk. We should in this way make our monologue into a dialogue: all the time confronting the people's way of thinking with the Word of God.

Experience has shown that we may be more out of touch with our audience than we realise. Even when we try to prepare our communication from a receptor-oriented, rather than source-oriented approach, we may still be far from touching on the actual problems and longings of the people to whom we speak. Before preaching a sermon, it has proved an excellent idea to give our topic a 'test run' in a trial group of people representative of our audience. In the same way teachers could assess the problems that exist in the minds of their pupils by having periodical 'buzz sessions' in which the pupils can express their doubts and queries. Teachers can also get a valuable feedback at the end of a lecture period by allowing spontaneous re-actions and free discussion. The teacher can evaluate the relevance of the presentation by this means and also collect information on topics to be discussed in future periods.

Communicating the Word of God has sometimes been defined as:

1. a verbalised process of learning
2. which puts into words people's problems and aspirations
3. and which introduces the message from Scripture as an important element in fulfilling the desire or solving the problem
4. and which anticipates in words the successful execution of what needs to be done to fulfil the desire or solve the problem.

People's hearts and minds are the soil in which the Word of God has to take roots and grow. As communicators we can do no more than sow the seed, making sure that it touches the soil.

CHAPTER FIVE

THE ALMOND BRANCH AND THE BOILING POT

H. L. Mencken once remarked that the chief contribution of Protestant preachers to human thought has been the massive proof that God is a bore. It looks as if Catholic preachers will be credited by history with a similar verdict. A study done on present-day preaching has brought to light that most sermons are monotonous and have little interest value. Small wonder that audiences are bored. This in turn leads to people avoiding sermons or drawing little profit from them.

In communication, the degree of information value is measured according to the degree of improbability or unpredictability of a piece of news. It is not the intrinsic value of the information, but the unexpectedness that holds attention. The motorist who is killed in a crash gets into the news; the hundreds of thousands of others who get home safely are no 'news' because their safe return is normal and expected. If a cyclone in India kills ten thousand people, it will be considered important news. If, however, the catastrophe continues long enough, its newsworthiness wears off; people get tired of hearing about it.

News need not always consist of things that happen unexpectedly. A good feature article will also attract attention if the topic has not been treated in the same way before. A feature article on the Pygmies in Zaire will be considered to have a high interest value if the information contained in it is specific, concrete and if it highlights unusual features.

The trouble with much of our preaching is that its information value, if measured with an ordinary communicator scale, is practically zero. The preacher says nothing new. Not only the tone and style he uses, but also his vocabulary and the contents of his talk are highly predictable. The typical sermon is full of generalities, discusses fashionable topics and refers to well-known Scripture texts. The information it contains is uninteresting and redundant.

PARTY LINE OR REAL LIFE?

The montony and dullness of the message imparted by many teachers and preachers cannot be ascribed only to their lack of imagination and poor communicative skill. One of the fundamental reasons why the standard instruction fails to interest is that it is seen to propagate an ideology, rather than proclaim a salvific message on behalf of a living God. Many preachers and teachers project the image of being not mystics or witnesses, but party men.

There are historical reasons for this development. The main thrust of theology in the Middle Ages was to establish an overall scheme into which all the truths of reason and faith could be harmoniously brought together. It was the period when the 'Summae' were written. In such a harmonising approach, the stress necessarily fell on general principles, on abstract notions, on universal laws. When the Reformation split the Church, the Roman Catholic part defended its orthodoxy by freezing its creed into a rigid lattice of beliefs and rules. All textbooks followed a uniform pattern. Catechisms were devised in which the whole of Catholic doctrine was spelled out in simple questions and clear-cut answers. Treating doctrine as a set of well-defined truths and duties had its value in a time when poorly instructed Catholic minorities had to hold their own within a hostile religious environment. But the image of christian doctrine being an ideology or party line imposed from above remains as an unfortunate hangover.

For many Christians instruction about the faith is identified with an endless repetition of the same truths. By the stress on dogmatic theses, the reality of living faith is passed by. Sermons and instructions focus on the abstract truths about God instead of presenting him as a real person who wants to meet us face to face. Doctrine only becomes real if it is understood in terms of the mystery of life, its excitement and paradoxes. Salvation cannot be adequately expressed in tenets of the creed formulated in the past tense; it is the search of God for each person here and now.

In the protective scheme of medieval and post-reformation thought, people were sharply divided into distinct categories. Dividing lines were drawn between priests and laity, orthodox and heretic, christian and pagan, true Church and Protestant, between practising and non-practising Catholics, between saints and sinners. These clear-cut divisions don't do justice to what real people are really like. Human personalities are far too complicated to fit any such rigid scheme. The tendency to generalise and categorise kills human interest. People will recognise themselves more easily in such confusing types as the pagan who believes or the saint who isn't orthodox.

Many sermons and instructions still show a tendency to moralise. There is a one-sided stress on the avoidance of sin and the performance of external duties. The preacher sees it as his task to point out to the people which actions are sinful and which are not. That the same information has been given often before does not seem to make any difference. The moralising sermon presents a ready-made table of vices and virtues, thus neglecting to help people in forming their own consciences and arriving at a personal christian maturity.

The old type of christian instruction lays heavy emphasis on authority and establishment. It holds out obedience as the highest virtue. It admires uniformity and rigid organisation. It expects the individual to fall in line with the existing rites and sacramental routine. Insufficient attention is given to the freedom with which Christ has made us free, to the individual growth of every person's spiritual life, to the importance of personal conviction. The life of a christian is judged by his measure of conformity, not by his experience of the Spirit.

The analysis offered here is not meant as an indictment of our teachers and preachers. There is no reason to doubt their good intention or to deny that the system had its merits in certain circumstances. But we should recognise that it has serious shortcomings too. It presents a one-sided and limited view of christianity. It reduces a living encounter between God and man to doctrines and rules. And, as a consequence, it makes christian instruction predictable and boring.

THE FRAYED EDGES OF LIFE

Both theology and the science of communication suggest a remedy in which Scripture, too, can play a role. It can be formulated as a rule; *the more specific and the more concrete our presentation is, the more unpredictable and profound it will be.* Generalisation and abstraction make what we say unreal and boring. Presenting individual persons or events with specific detail, we lay a connection with real life. It is through reflection on real life that we approach closest to the mystery of being and the reality of God.

It is here that the Bible can be of great use to us. For the Bible is essentially made up of real persons and events, of a multiplicity of specific and concrete happenings. In fact, this may be the reason why God did not want to inspire his word in the form of an abstract creed or a logical catechism. Instead he expressed his ideas and his love for mankind through his tangible dealings with individuals in genuine human experiences. The Bible is the ideal medium for communicating the message precisely because it is itself made up of real life.

> In the book of Jeremiah we read:
> "And the word of the Lord came to me, saying, 'Jeremiah, what do you see?'
> And I said, 'I see a rod of almond' (Hebrew: shaqed).
> Then the Lord said to me, 'You have seen well, for I am watching (Hebrew: shoqed) over my word to perform it'.
> The word of the Lord came to me a second time, saying, 'What do you see?'
> And I said, 'I see a boiling pot, facing away from the north'.
> Then the Lord said to me, 'Out of the north evil shall break forth upon all the inhabitants of the land' (Jer. 1,11-14).

This oracle of Jeremiah's always reminds me of the picture of 'Radha in the Kitchen' (Fig. 10). Radha, who symbolises the human soul, is in love with Krishna, the incarnation of God. As she is cooking rice in her kitchen, she thinks of Krishna with great love. Meanwhile Krishna, who in the top right-hand corner of the picture can be seen sitting on the flat roof, listens with interest to a description of Radha's virtues by one of her maids. However, while this intense spiritual and mystic interplay is going on, the earthly realities of the kitchen remain. The artist has underlined this by carefully painting the things one normally finds in a kitchen: a bundle of firewood, a pitcher of water, a basket containing vegetables, piles of brinjals and lotus leaves, a bunch of plantains and various cooking utensils. It pictures the experience of divine love in an everyday setting.

The same seems to be the point of the almond branch and the boiling pot. Jeremiah's mind is full of the things of God. With prophetic foreboding he understands that God will mete out punishment to Jerusalem in the immediate future. While he is cooking his evening meal, his eyes are suddenly opened in a prophetic vision. The almond branch with which he is stirring the pot, which is called 'shaqed' in Hebrew, suddenly sparks off the message that God is standing guarantee, Hebrew 'shoqed', that he will bring about his verdict. The tilt of the pot from the north makes him see in a flash

Fig. 10. Radha in the kitchen.
Chamba painting, India 1800 A.D.

that it is the enemy from the north, Assyria, that will be God's chosen tool. Haven't we all experienced, even though it may be to a much lesser degree, how at the most unexpected moments events or details that are insignificant in themselves, can help our minds switch on to a profound realisation of truth?

Take the story of the two wicked priests, Hophni and Phinehas, who ministered at Shiloh during the early days of Samuel (1 Sam 2). The Bible gives us a vivid description of how they used to give scandal to the ordinary folk.

> The custom of the priests with the people was that, when any man offered sacrifice, the priest's servant would come, while the meat was boiling, with a three-pronged fork in his hand, and he would thrust it into the pan, or kettle, or cauldron, or pot; all that the fork brought up the priest would take for himself. So they did at Shiloh to all the Israelites who came there. Moreover, before the fat was burnt, the priest's servant would come and say to the man who was sacrificing, "Give meat for the priest to roast; for he will not accept boiled meat from you, but raw". And if the man said to him, "Let them burn the fat first, and then take as much as you wish", he would say, "No, you must give it now, and if not, I will take it by force".

Notice in this paragraph of Scripture the striking detail of description. The callousness of the priests is well described by the fact that they do not mind upsetting people's consciences simply because they prefer to eat their meat roasted. The three-pronged fork is a symbol of their greed and selfishness. This is real life and we can recognise ourselves in it. Don't we too at times use our position to profit rather than render service? Does it not happen, for instance, that a priest performs his ministry to get admiration or royal treatment from the people for himself? In such a case God's complaint could also apply to us: "Why do you look with envious eyes on the sacrifice which I receive from the children of Israel? Why do you allow yourself to grow fat on the best part of the things my people offer me?" (1 Sam 2,29).

These illustrations may suffice to show what is meant by the rule that we should be as specific and concrete in presentation as possible. Hophni's servant holding his three-pronged fork or Jeremiah sitting in front of his boiling pot are images from the Bible in which God's word finds expression in very specific and true-to-life forms. Making use of this scriptural approach, we liberate ourselves from generalisations and abstract statements and enter the field of mystery, experience, real life and personal encounter with God.

What we should learn from it is to value whatever is specific and concrete. As I will explain later when introducing narration and characterisation, we should on no account diminish the original force of the text by levelling it off into a more general presentation. At all costs we should preserve that awareness of real life that radiates from the scriptural pages.

RE-LIVING SCRIPTURE IN OUR OWN WORLD

Normally people are very much aware of the inadequacy of their own personal experiences. They feel hemmed in and constricted by the smallness of their own lives: the routine of their daily task, the narrow circle of friends and relatives, the oppression of anxieties and worries. Many try to escape from this prison by giving free rein to their imagination. By seeing films or reading novels, they try to give themselves vicariously the experience of other emotions, exciting adventures, totally different surroundings; I say 'vicariously' because they undergo these experiences by identifying themselves with the heroes of fiction.

To transcend the limitations of our small human lives is a deep-seated human need. It is even a *religious* need. The need is not adequately met by escaping into the realms of fiction, because this doesn't help us to face reality; it postpones problems, but doesn't solve them. The real solution for man lies in a conscious integration of one's own narrow experience into the wider reality of existence. By art, music and poetry we touch on realities such as harmony, beauty, contrast, rhythm. By learning about other people and by sharing their experiences, we make common cause with them and widen the meaning of our own life. By an attitude of listening, of reflection on the mystery of existence, of being open to what reality tells us, we become aware of new dimensions. All this gives meaning to what seems small and insignificant in our own life.

It is in the context of this integration of oneself into the wider reality – in this *religious* context – that the Bible has to play an important role. For the Bible contains the message of God through which the narrow limitations of our lives are torn down in a decisive manner. And this message of God comes to us in the form of human experiences, so that, by identification, we can easily make it our own. To benefit from the Bible in this way, we have to re-live it, in all its richness, so that the experiences recorded there become our own experiences, our experiences today.

Jephthah was a half-caste Israelite, a robber chief, who had been asked by the men of Gilead to lead them in their war against the Ammonites. In his own way, Jephthah was a religious man. At the beginning of the war, he made a vow, "If you will give me the victory over the Ammonites, then whoever shall be the first to come from the doors of my house to meet me when I return victorious, shall belong to you. I will offer him up as a burnt offering". Imagine his distress when, after the victory, it was his daughter who came out first!

"And Jephthah returned to his home at Mizpah. And behold, his daughter came out to meet him dancing to the sound of timbrels. She was his only child. Beside her he had neither son nor daughter" (Judges 11,34).

The story of Jephthah illustrates the kind of tragedy one often meets. The joy of the victory and the happy dance of the daughter are marred by the ugly prospect of death. Jephthah is misguided: God doesn't want human sacrifices (Dt 12,31), but Jephthah doesn't know it. He feels bound in conscience to perform his vow. Don't we recognise the same tangle of blindness and good intention in Christians who burn heretics out of religious zeal, in a father who refuses to take his daughter back home because she is pregnant, in a general who sends a soldier on a mission where he will be certainly killed? To understand this kind of situation, to be able to live with it even if we cannot change people or correct their opinions, we have to approach it the way the Bible does. We ourselves can observe what goes on from a distance; only God can make sense of it.

We have to learn how to make creative use of the biblical material. Real human experiences are so complex that they can spark off different responses in different people. That is why the Bible is so long and so varied. If we were to restrict ourselves to its intellectual content, the scriptural text could have been compressed into at most one-tenth of its present size. But precisely because the Word of God is more than an intellectual idea, because it expresses a living encounter between God and man, exemplified and made real through human experiences, it cannot and should not be reduced in such a manner.

No part of Scripture, therefore, is superfluous. Last century Scripture scholars debated about the wagging tail of Tobias's dog. It will be remembered that young Tobias had gone on a journey to collect some money on behalf of his father. Blind, old Tobit and his wife Anna were anxiously waiting for his return. The Bible recounts the moment as follows:

Fig. 11. Blind Tobit by Rembrandt (1651).

"The dog which had accompanied Tobias and Raphael during the journey, ran ahead and as a messenger of the good news it merrily wagged its tail. Then Tobias's blind father rose and started walking tottering on his feet. Eagerly he stretched out his hands towards his child and so walked out to meet him. He embraced him and kissed him. His wife did the same and both began to weep of joy" (Tob 11,9-11).

The second half of verse 9 (describing the wagging of the tail) is not found in the Greek manuscripts; but it was in the Aramaic text from which St. Jerome made his translation. It shows that the story existed in different forms: at least one of the narrators thought it worthwhile to bring in the description of the dog. Among Scripture scholars a discussion arose as to the role of this verse. Some stated that it is superfluous because it does not contain matter of revelation. Others contended that it could not be inspired because its contents were too insignificant. To me it would seem that the whole discussion took a wrong turn because it started from the presumption that God is interested only in revealing some intellectual truths or moral obligations.

The function of the dog in the story is obvious to anyone who starts from a recognition of human experience. The running ahead of the dog is exactly the kind of thing that will happen at such a home-coming. Because we can visualise the dog with its wagging tail, because we can feel how it radiates happiness, because we can almost see with our eyes the effect it has on old Tobit, the little incident of the dog helps us to experience the story as something real. It is because we omit "the wagging tails" that our sermons and instructions are so dull and dreary.

PART TWO

THE TECHNIQUES

CHAPTER SIX

NARRATION

Kohelet drew his wisdom from everyday life. Observing the "business that God has given to the sons of man to be busy with", he stated: "I have seen everything that is done under the sun" (Koh 1,14). The stuff of life is being busy, action, drama. It is marked by sudden changes. Real life swings between fear and hope, regret and excited expectation. Authors and playwrights have instinctively recognised the frenzy of movement as the core of human life. Shakespeare speaks of life's "fitful fever". G. M. Cohan says we are "hurried and worried until we are buried". It is all "sobs, sniffles and smiles", says O. Henry. And F. W. O'Malley sums it all up by saying "life is just one damned thing after another".

Narration describes life. Good narration captures something of the excitement of real living and so never fails to intrigue. Every speaker knows that telling a story is the best way of captivating an audience. People simply love stories. In their imagination they re-live the events narrated to them. To some extent life and story are interchangeable. Don't we say that life is a fairy tale written by God or that facts are stranger than fiction?

It is hardly a coincidence that more than half of the Bible is narration. The Bible is a book of life in the fullest sense of the word. In this chapter we will discuss the implications of this fact and how we can re-narrate the biblical stories to their best advantage.

As the material is plentiful and its discussion of necessity somewhat drawn out, it may help some readers to have a cursory glance at the sections and what they contain:

"Every story has a purpose" : The meaning of a narrative depends on the reason for which it was composed.

"Hinge of the Covenant" : The Old Testament history of salvation had the purpose of inculcating the Covenant; of teaching God's supremacy and man's dependence.

"Analysing a biblical story" : To understand a biblical story "from within" we should be aware of its component parts : cast of actors, place, time, dialogue, motifs and suspense.

"Narrative force" : When re-narrating a biblical story we should think of describing the setting, introducing the actors, reporting direct speech, using dynamic verbs and descriptive detail, and leading up to a climax.

"Historicity and artistic presentation" : The message of the story is carried by the main statement and by secondary statements contained in details. Audience related and decorative details may need to be transformed through a contemporary presentation.

"Simple free narration" : Some stories can be presented as they are with an explicitation of the "moral" in the course of the narrative.

"Story-Reflection-Story" : Other stories can be used as the frame for instructions on up-to-date topics.

"Some hints from practice" : Suggestions are given regarding the "story-reflection-story" technique.

The ultimate aim of our study is the re-discovery of how biblical narrative could revolutionize our teaching. There will be no harm in our capturing some of the enthusiasm for stories apparent in the old negro song:

"Young folks, old folks, everybody come,
Join the darkies' Sunday School.
Bring along your chewing gums and stick them on the floor.
We'll tell you bible stories which you never heard before".

EVERY STORY HAS A PURPOSE

One day King David was administering justice in the reception hall of his palace. A woman appeared before him who was obviously in a state of great agitation. She wore clothes of mourning. Her hair was dishevelled. She threw herself face downwards on the floor in front of his throne, and cried out, "Oh King! Help me!"

"What's the trouble?" he asked.

"I'm a widow", she replied, "and my two sons had a fight out in the field, and since no one was there to part them, one of them was killed. Now the rest of the family is demanding that I surrender my other son to them to be executed for murdering his brother. But if I do that, I will have no one left and my husband's name will be destroyed from the face of the earth".

"Leave it to me", the king told her, "I will see to it that no one touches him".

She said, "Please swear to me by God that you won't let anyone harm my son. I want no more bloodshed".

"I vow by God", he replied, "that not a hair of your son's head shall be disturbed!"

The woman's story seemed straightforward enough and David thought he had understood it. But actually there was more behind it all, because the woman continued to speak in this way: "Why don't you do as much for all the people of God as you have promised to do for me? Why do you refuse to bring home your own son whom you sent into exile? By making this decision in my case you contradict your decision in the other". Then David understood that the woman had been sent by Joab to plead Absalom's cause. Absalom had killed his elder brother Amnon and had been banished from Israel for it. Now David realised the full purpose of the story. It was meant to make him see that the feud within his own family could better be settled by an outright pardon. (2 Sam 14, 1-33).

This incident in the Bible is highly instructive. It shows that to understand a story one must not only know its contents, but also its *purpose*. The purpose was there all the time, but what it was only became apparent afterwards. Of course, this is an exceptional case. Joab's aim of drawing the king's attention to Absalom was bound to come to light. It was precisely Joab's intention that the king would first understand the woman's story as an ordinary event and only afterwards apply it to his own family. But what we may forget, or overlook, is that *every story* has a purpose, and that we cannot understand the story without knowing what its purpose is.

There was a time when scholars thought that an objective history could be written. Now the fallacy of this assumption is universally admitted. No author can write without adopting a value judgement that will influence his writing. When writing on Henry VIII we may try to stick to facts as much as possible, but we have already made a choice by deciding to write about him. For why should we write about a king? Are kings more important than peasants? Is it because we have more historical records about kings, or is it because we really *know* that he was the most influential person in his time? When analysing this kind of story telling we will see that ultimately the true meaning and validity of the narration will depend on its purpose. A reconstruction of Henry VIII's life and personality from available sources is a legitimate exercise, as long as we realise that this, and no more, is its purpose.

I have gone into this question at some length because it is essential for us to reflect on the purpose of biblical narrative before we can effectively communicate its teaching to others. Some biblical stories have an obvious purpose that can easily be learned from handbooks and commentaries. The books of Jonah, Tobit and Judith are extended parables with the morals heavily laid on. Practically all the other historical books have a unifying purpose, namely the history of salvation. A word about this purpose may be helpful in order to overcome many possible misunderstandings.

HINGE OF THE COVENANT

In the ancient Middle East big nations tried to exercise control over small nations by imposing treaties on them. The right to impose an alliance usually derived from military help which the big nation had provided. Mention of this historical fact in the treaty document became an important element of political practice.

Take the case of the Hittite Emperor Shuppiluliuma who imposed a treaty on Niqmadu, King of Ugarit in the 14th century B.C. The terms of the covenant make clear that Ugarit is being reduced to the status of a satellite state of the Hittite empire. It has to pay tribute. It is subject to the Hittites in foreign policy. It has to cooperate with the Hittite police. The legal document (clay tablets) in which these terms are spelled out, also makes clear why the Emperor could demand this new status of dependence. It points to the help the Emperor has given:

> "When Iturabbi, King of Mukish, Addunirari, King of Nuchash-shi and Afitteshub, King of Ni'i rebelled against their feudal lord, the Emperor, and started the war against him, they brought an army together, cut off the cities of Ugarit, invaded the Kingdom of Ugarit, plundered and destroyed it. Then Niqmadu, King of Ugarit, sent this message to Emperor Shuppiluliuma, 'Please liberate me from the hands of my enemies. I will become your vassal. You will be my feudal lord. I will be enemy of your enemies and friend of your friends. Please help me. These kings are putting me under heavy stress'.
> The Emperor reacted favourably to Niqmadu's request. Emperor Shuppiluliuma sent his grandsons and generals with

soldiers and chariots to Ugarit. These drove all enemy troops out of the Kingdom of Ugarit. They returned to Niqmadu the spoils that had been taken".

Biblical scholarship has shown that the history of salvation had that same function in the covenant or treaty between God and Israel. God was understood to be the Emperor who imposed his rule on the Israelites in the form of an ancient alliance. And, just as in political vassal-treaties, God demanded Israel's subjection on the ground of the many things he had done for his people. When the question arose as to why the Israelites had to keep God's laws, the answer given was not: "These laws are reasonable", or: "God is our Creator", but: "God saved us".

> "When your son will ask you 'What is the purpose of these laws which the Lord our God has given us?' you must tell him, 'We were Pharaoh's slaves in Egypt and the Lord brought us out of Egypt with great power and mighty miracles – with terrible blows against Pharaoh and all his peoples. We saw it all with our own eyes. He brought us out of Egypt so that he could give us this land he had promised to our ancestors. Therefore he has commanded us to obey all of these laws and to be subject to him so that he can preserve us alive as he has until now!' " (Deut 6,20-24).

Once a year the people came together to re-affirm and renew the Covenant with God. On that occasion the prophets and the priests instructed the people anew in all the aspects of their allegiance to God. Their laws would be inculcated again and, where necessary, explained. Through the invocation of blessings, and curses, the people would be reminded of the reward which God would give for loyalty and of the punishment he would mete out for disloyalty. But one important element in the ceremony was to recall the history of salvation. The priest would deliberately recall the past history of the people to remind them of the many ways God had guided and saved them. This was the origin and the function of "salvation history". Beginning most likely with an account of the exodus from Egypt, salvation history gradually began to comprise all the major headings we know from the biblical accounts: creation, the call of the Patriarchs, the liberation from Egypt, the journey through the desert and the conquest of the Promised Land. *The purpose*, then, of salvation history, and therefore of all the main historical books, was to strengthen people's loyalty to the covenant. Clearly it is a *religious* purpose. Tribal stories, secular history, military records and other sources used in the narration are made entirely subservient to this overall purpose.

To be even more specific we might say that the same stories of the history of salvation have two main purposes for us today:

1. They want to teach us about *God*. They want to prove that he is our Master, that he has a right to our submission. They reflect on his strictness, his mercy, his love and his unflinching loyalty to what he has promised.

2. They want to teach us about *our duties*. Being a people party to a covenant, we are expected to be faithful to the obligations imposed by that covenant. The stories will be geared to give examples of how we should act, or how not, and what the consequences of such behaviour will be.

As we will see later, the stories will have to be applied to our own circumstances. At the same time, whenever we take up a bible story for communication we do well to begin to put ourselves into the frame of mind of the original narrators. Putting ourselves back into the covenant situation and feeling how the story helps to inculcate God's rights and man's duties, we will more easily hit upon the particular message contained in the story, and then apply it to ourselves.

ANALYSING A BIBLICAL STORY

Before we can make use of a story, we should read and study it properly. It is, of course, useful to refer to commentaries to see if they have anything special to say about the story in question. But when I speak about study here, I am not first of all referring to a kind of *specialist* study, either of commentaries or even of the text. What I think should be done first and foremost is that we ourselves read and analyse the text carefully, so that we can on our own easily identify the elements of the story.

In the beginning this may seem cumbersome and complicated. It is like anything else we do for the first time. In my experience a personal analysis of a biblical narration can eventually be done in five to ten minutes. What we have to learn is to spot accurately the various elements in the story and so recognise what a particular story is trying to bring out through these elements.

The technique can be learned best by working out a particular example. I have selected for this purpose the story of Ehud (Judges 3, 4-30) not because it contains a deep message, but because it is about the shortest complete story I could find and it lends itself well as an illustration. I will perform the analysis by discussing successively the cast, place, time, dialogue, motifs and suspense. After reflecting on each element in turn, I will try to show the overall results of such an analysis.

vs. 12   When Othniel son of Kenaz died, once again the men of Israel began to do what displeases Yahweh and Yahweh gave Eglon, the king of Moab,   power over Israel because they had done what displeases Yahweh.

13   Eglon in alliance with the sons of Ammon and Amalek marched against Israel and conquered them and took possession of the city of palms.

14   The Israelites were enslaved by Eglon the king of Moab for eighteen years.

15   Then the Israelites cried to Yahweh, and Yahweh raised up a deliverer for them, Ehud the son of Gera the Benjamite; he was left-handed. The men of Israel appointed him to take their tribute to Eglon the king of Moab.

16   Ehud made a dagger — it was double-edged and a cubit long — and strapped it on under his clothes, over his right thigh.

17   He presented the tribute to Eglon the king of Moab. This Eglon was a very fat man.

18   Having presented the tribute, Ehud went off again with the men who had carried it.

19   But he himself, on reaching the Idols of Gilgal turned and went back and said, "I have a secret message for you, O king". The king replied, "Silence", and all who were with him went out.

20   Then Ehud went in. The king sat in the cool retreat of his upper room; he was alone. Ehud said to him, "I have a message from God for you, O king". The king immediately stood up from his seat.

21   Then Ehud, using his left hand, drew the dagger he was carrying on his right thigh and thrust it into the king's belly.

22   The hilt too went in after the blade, and the fat closed over the blade, for Ehud left the dagger in his belly; then he went out through the window.

23   Ehud went out by the porch; he had shut and locked the doors of the upper room behind him.

24   When he had gone, the servants came back and looked; the doors of the upper room were locked. They thought, "He is probably cover-

ing his feet in the upper part of the cool room".

25   They waited until they no longer knew what to think for he still did not open the doors of the upper room. At length they took the key and unlocked the room; their master lay on the ground, dead.

26   While they were waiting, Ehud had fled. He passed the Idols and escaped to safety in Seirah.

27   When he reached the territory of Israel he sounded the horn in the highlands of Ephraim, and the Israelites came down from the hills, with him at their head.

28   And he said to them, "Follow me, because Yahweh has delivered your enemy Moab into your hands". So they followed him, cut Moab off from crossing the fords of the Jordan and let no one across.

29   On that occasion they beat the Moabites, some ten thousand men, all tough and seasoned fighters, and not one escaped.

30   That day, Moab was humbled under the hand of Israel and the land enjoyed rest for eighty years.

The meaning of the story in general is quite clear. It is one more incident to prove that God punishes, but is also ready to forgive. When the people turned back to him, he delivered them from their enemies by raising a courageous and cunning leader. We will concentrate now on the narrative element.

When we consider the _cast_, we find, first of all, some large groups mentioned in general. The two main protagonist groups are: the Moabites and the Israelites. Three persons are mentioned by name: Yahweh (God), Eglon (king of Moab) and Ehud (leader of Israel). Eglon and Ehud are the two main adversaries. Each of them is surrounded by a small group of helpers, who are only referred to in general terms, without names: the men carrying the tribute (vs. 18) and the king's servants (vs. 19, 24,25). If we combine all this information we can draw a simple scheme (see Fig. 12).

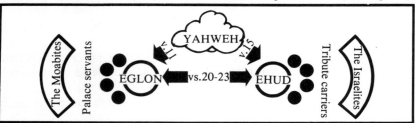

Fig. 12. Protagonists in the Ehud story.
Note the parallelism of the two opposing forces.

Two nations, Moab and Israel, face each other in conflict. The conflict comes to a head in the meeting of their two leaders, Eglon and Ehud, each of whom is surrounded by a small group of helpers.

Next we study *the places* involved. To facilitate matters I have drawn a simple map (Fig. 13). Let us first look at the large movements. The Moabites move from their country (the land of Moab) to the city of Palms (Jericho), where Eglon builds his palace. The Israelites leave their home towns (the hill country of Ephraim) to bring tribute to Eglon at Jericho. After Ehud kills Eglon, he returns again to the hill country of Ephraim, collects soldiers from there, goes back to Jericho and drives the Moabites back into the land of Moab. A few places mentioned on these major routes are the Idols at Gilgal

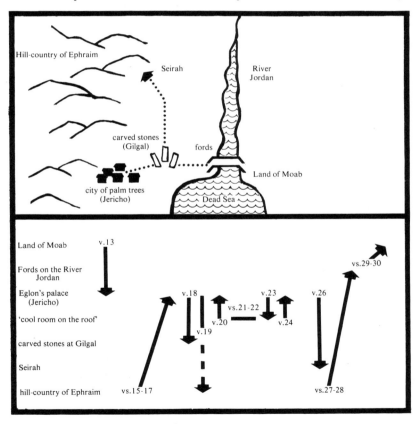

Fig. 13. The top half gives a map of the localities.
Below the movement of the story from one place to another is indicated by the arrow.

and the fords of the Jordan through which one goes to Moab. Some further details of place are given regarding Eglon's palace. The tribute was probably delivered in the reception room downstairs (vs. 18), while the private meeting between Eglon and Ehud took place in the king's private room on the first floor, his upper room (vs. 19). We also find mention of the "inner part of the cool room", which was a toilet adjoining the king's private room (vs. 24). We can express all this in a simple scheme of places (Fig. 13). It is obvious from the scheme that Eglon's palace is the main locality of the story, with particular stress on the scene in the upper room. The other movements converge on this place or move away from it.

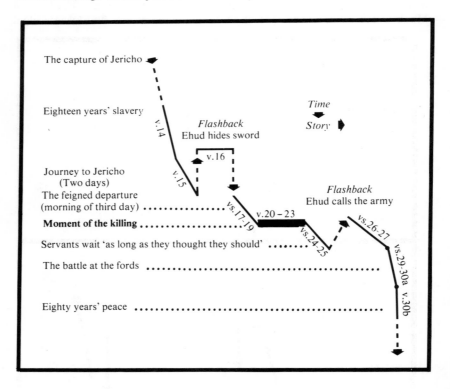

Fig. 14. The vertical column represents the passage of time;
the horizontal one the amount of words devoted to it in the story.

The importance of the scene in the upper room is also confirmed by a study of _the time element_. We feel how the narrator accelerates the time as he develops the story (see Fig. 14). After disposing of 18 years' oppression in one single sentence (vs. 14) he devotes five sentences to Ehud's journey to Jericho which must have taken two or three days. The confrontation between Ehud and Eglon, which probably only took a few minutes, is given another 5 sentences. After this, time gradually lengthens out again. Eglon's courtiers probably wait for one or two hours before taking action (vs. 23-25). Ehud's return to Ephraim to collect an army would have taken at least two or three days. The story ends with the mention of 80 years' peace resulting from this war. In the narrator's handling of time we should also notice his use of "flashbacks". After telling us that Ehud and his companions had sent out to bring the taxes to Eglon, he mentions that Ehud had hidden a dagger under his clothes (vs. 16). Surely the Israelites were searched for weapons before entering the Moabite fortress and Ehud had strapped the dagger on before leaving home! While the king's servants were deliberating what they should do, Ehud *had* already covered a great distance towards the hill country of Ephraim (vs. 26). Such flashbacks help to bring tension into the story.

Dialogue is another means of heightening the sense of drama. The narrator uses only a few quotations of direct speech, but these are well selected. We are not surprised to find that it is the protagonists who speak during their meeting in the upper room which is the climax of the story. Twice Ehud says, "I have a message from God for you" (vs. 19-20). This is not just a ruse to enter the king's presence alone, on the plea that it was a *secret* message. It also expresses the purpose of his prophetic deed. Thrusting the dagger into Eglon's body is an act of judgement performed in the name of God. The other direct speech reported in the narrative expresses human emotion. The anxiety of the king's servants makes them say to one another: "He may be in the toilet" (vs. 24). Ehud's joy can be heard in his triumphant cry, "Follow me because God will give you the victory over the Moabites" (vs. 28). Dialogue helps us to understand both the role of agents and the moments of excitement or emotion in the story. (See Fig. 15).

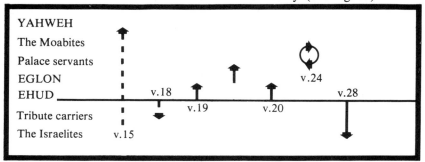

Fig. 15. On the left all persons are listed.
The arrows indicate who is speaking to whom.

Woven through the narrative as a thread are its _motifs_. Motifs correspond to the narrator's personal interest. They are certain themes which the story teller wants to stress and which he therefore refers to whenever he has the opportunity (see also Chapter Eight). In our present story three motifs come to the fore. The narrator is convinced that whatever happens to Israel is ultimately God's doing; God rules history. When the Moabites subdue Israel it is because God wanted to punish his people (vs. 12). Again, it is God who makes Ehud take the leadership in the revolt against Moab (vs. 15). When Ehud kills Eglon it is seen as a judgement from God (vs. 20). The ultimate victory over the Moabites is attributed to God (vs. 28). Another motif is Ehud's cunning and courage. We are told how Ehud is left handed, how he hides his dagger before leaving for Jericho, how he effects an entrance to the king by saying he has a secret message, how he manages to escape by closing the door of the king's private room and

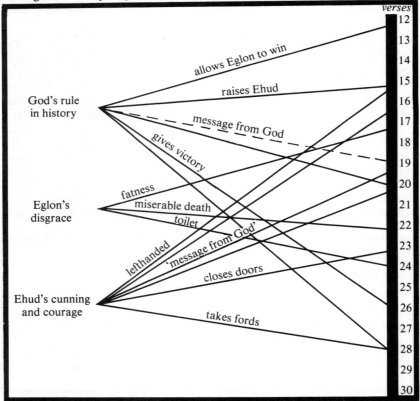

Fig. 16. The scheme shows the verses where the three main motifs recur in the story.

making his exit through a window. All these details help us to admire our "hero", his clever planning and cool performance. Quite the opposite treatment is given to Eglon. We are disgusted with this fat tyrant who receives tribute from poor people (vs. 17). We hear with glee how the dagger kills him, disappears into his fat belly (vs. 21). We laugh with relief when we realise that Ehud can make his escape because the king's servants are used to their master spending long periods in his toilet (vs. 24). Such motifs are better appreciated when we plot their occurrence against the verse numbers (see Fig. 16).

The last element I would like to analyse is the one of *suspense*. Stories usually take their beginning from some problem, some prospect or some conflict that arouses the emotions of the hearer. This 'suspense' inherent in the story is usually brought to a climax, or a series of climaxes, before being resolved. In our narrative the growth of suspense is easy to follow. We are dismayed at the oppression of Israel by Moab. Our hopes rise when we are told that God is going to liberate his people. Guessing Ehud's subversive intentions we share his emotions as he penetrates single-handed into the king's private room. Eglon's death is a climax which partly resolves our suspense, but still leaves us anxious about Ehud's escape. Ehud's successful return to the hill country of Ephraim, and the victory of Israel that follows, finally resolve our emotions and bring them back full circle to peace and satisfaction. (Fig. 17). The suspense in the story is determined by far more than just the contents. It is very much brought out by the style of writing. With the increase of suspense we normally find that sentences become brief and the descriptions vivid. The indications of time and place are more accurate. The narrator introduces more direct speech and uses emotional words. When the suspense is resolved the narrator expresses this by speaking in a more relaxed and general manner.

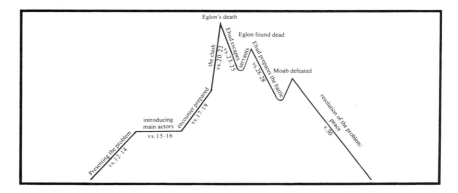

Fig. 17. The rise and fall of suspense.

What do we gain from this kind of analysis? Certainly it will help us see what matters in the story, how the original story-teller viewed and presented his subject. The elements of cast, place, time, direct speech, motifs and suspense are found in every story. Every story has a general background, an overall setting within which it is placed. This overall setting is usually expressed in very general terms: the people are groups, the places are wide, and the period is of long duration. Then the narrator zooms in on a specific scene. This scene is then characterised by its definite locality, a distinctive moment in time, named individuals and the recurrence of reported speech. The whole story is held together by a theme and its dramatic tension. Recognising this inner structure of a story helps us to understand it better and to re-narrate it properly as I will explain in the next section.

It also helps us to get ideas from Scripture itself. In the story we have used as an example, we may be struck by the problem of Ehud's self-understanding. Although he knows himself a person under God's protection who can act in God's name, he realises at the same time that all will depend on his own nerve and skill. Ehud had men under his command, yet at the crucial moment of decision and action, he was on his own. Ehud was troubled by the ethics of his deed. He obtained admission to the king by a ruse, not by telling a lie, thus saving his soldier's conscience. Reflections such as these may well open up fruitful comparisons with other leaders in our own day who have to perform improbable and courageous missions. Or we might be impressed by the central scene itself, the encounter between Eglon and Ehud in the king's upper room. Ehud saved his people by courageously facing the main opponent and by doing this by himself. This might spark off ideas as to how we could solve some problems by tackling them head on. We will discuss further on how such a "message" can be developed in practice. The point I want to make here is that a careful analysis of the narrative elements goes a long way towards making us discover the full riches of God's word.

NARRATIVE FORCE

When we use a biblical story in communicating the message, we do so because we want the message to have a special grip on the audience. This was exactly why the old mediators of the covenant, men wanting to bring out God's supremacy and the people's obligations to him, did not simply enumerate a number of facts, but told their hearers a story.

Telling a story is a powerful means of drawing our audience into our way of thinking. It entices them to pay attention and to share our feelings. Narrative has this special force of its own and as good communicators we should at all costs preserve that force.

There is a big difference between simply pointing back to a story by recalling one or two of its facts, and narrating the actual story itself. For some reason or other many preachers and teachers shy away from straight-forward narration. Somehow they seem to think that story-telling is not sufficiently packed with meaning or is intellectually below their level of speaking. Or it may simply be that they have never really learned how to tell stories. As a result many speakers, if referring to a biblical story at all, will restrict themselves to a brief recapitulation of the event, presuming that their hearers have heard or read the story elsewhere.

They might say something like this: "You will all remember how the prophet Elijah challenged the priests of Baal to decide by a miracle whether Yahweh or Baal is God. Both Elijah and Baal's followers prepared a sacrificial altar. When Elijah prayed, Yahweh responded by igniting the sacrificial wood with a bolt of lightning that fell from heaven. Then the people understood that Yahweh was the true God".

This is not a narrative, but a résumé. The story has been robbed of all its narrative force and reduced to the level of a recorded fact. In other words, the story as story has been ruined. What could have been an excited sharing in Elijah's experience of God has been made as lack-lustre as a death notice. It is good to recognise that it is the attempt to summarise that kills a story. All definite indications of time and place are omitted. No exact descriptions are given. Specific human actions are levelled off into abstract terms and general statements. No dialogue is recorded. There is no build-up of tension, no room for emotion, no climax. All flesh and muscle has been shorn off to leave dead bones.

The function of a relay station is to receive the original signal correctly re-process it and broadcast it again with renewed strength. When we re-narrate a biblical story we have the same task. After carefully reading the story ourselves, we try to narrate it again for our particular audience in such a way that its original narrative force will strike home. This will mean that we should be aware of the elements to be preserved and others to be strengthened or completed. Here are some suggestions that may help us. I will illustrate the various points with reference to the story of Elijah confronting the priests of Baal (1 Kings 18, 20-40).

Whenever we tell a story, our hearers must have *a good visual picture of the setting*. With their mental eyes people must be able to see the place where things are happening. Sometimes a story may have more than one central place of action. Each of these then needs to be described and presented. It often happens that the Bible omits a good description of the place, as it was so well known to its contemporaries. If I say that I met "so and so" while changing trains at Leeds, I need not add a vivid description, because we all have a clear picture of what a railway station looks like. For those belonging to another culture, or a different age, it would be different. The same applies to biblical localities which are so far removed from us in distance, cultural practice, and time. The story of Elijah could begin as follows:

> "Today I would like you to come with me to Mount Carmel in the North of Israel. The time is about 860 B.C. The mountain is covered with forests and jungle, but somewhere near its top we find a wide clearing. We see a lot of people who have gathered from far and wide. It is a huge crowd of hundreds of men, excitedly talking to one another as if something important is going to happen . . ."

Then we have to make sure we *introduce the persons*. People have to have some clear idea who the main actors are, otherwise they will not be able to identify themselves readily with them. In the Bible it is generally presupposed that we know who the persons are. Our audiences are usually not so well informed. Moreover, it is good to remind them of some of the main characteristics that make the actors living and interesting persons to us. To return to our example:

> ". . . Then all of a sudden we see that the people's talking subsides. A great ring is formed. On one side within the ring we see a lonely figure dressed in a brown, camel hair cloak. It is the prophet Elijah. The austerity of his face, and his erect posture as he looks round, command respect. On the other side, facing him, we see a group of priests of Baal, dressed in multi-coloured garments, their faces bright and washed, their beards well-oiled. They stand in small groups, conversing together and occasionally bursting forth into boisterous laughter. Obviously they feel at ease and are sure of themselves. . ."

Direct speech is a powerful element in narrative. We should preserve it when we find it in the biblical text, and, if necessary, introduce
our own. It has an electrifying effect on the audience. It makes our
protagonists real and lends emotional colour to the story.

> "Then Elijah raised his eyes and addressed the people. Looking
> around him with a fierce expression on his face, he said: 'Oh,
> people of Israel, how long do you mean to hobble first on one leg
> and then on the other? If Yahweh is God, be loyal to him. If you
> believe that Baal is God then serve Baal. Well, what is your
> choice? In whom do you believe?' A great silence descended
> upon the people. No one gave an answer. Then Elijah spoke
> again: 'I alone', he said, 'am left as a prophet of Yahweh, while
> the prophets of Baal are 450. Well, I challenge them, here and
> now, to an ordeal. Let two bulls be given us. Let the priests of
> Baal choose one for themselves, slaughter it and lay it on
> sacrificial wood but not set fire to it. I in my turn will prepare the
> other bull, but not set fire to it. You, priests of Baal, must call on
> the name of your God, and I shall call on the name of my God.
> The God who answers with fire is God indeed'.
> The people shouted in response, 'Yes, agreed'."

We should make the most of the *dramatic events* of the story.
Story implies change, a succession of things that happen, a movement
of events as well as a succession of different emotions. The wheels
that make the story of life roll on are the verbs. Our narrative should
be full of dynamic, descriptive and vigorous verbs. The following
section of our Elijah story, in which practically nothing has been
added to the Bible text, shows what action verbs can do.

> "... The priests of Baal took the bull, slaughtered it and pre-
> pared it for the sacrifice. From morning to midday they called
> upon the name of Baal. 'Oh, Baal, answer us!', but there was no
> voice, no answer. They kept on performing their hobbling dance
> round the altar they had made. When midday came Elijah began
> to mock them. 'Call louder', he said, 'for he is a God: maybe he
> is distracted or he is busy, or he has gone on a journey; perhaps
> he is asleep and won't wake up'. So they shouted louder and
> gashed themselves as they were used to do, with swords and
> spears, until the blood flowed down their skins. Midday passed,
> and they ranted on until the time in which the evening offering is
> usually presented. But there was no voice, no answer, no atten-
> tion given to them from heaven ..."

Another element we should not overlook is the *descriptive detail.* The Bible gives plenty of them and we should not omit or abbreviate them. The details give a touch of realism and help to make the event visible. Notice how, in the following excerpts, details such as the twelve stones of the altar, the width of the trenches and the amount of water poured over the victim add to the power of the account.

> ". . . Then Elijah repaired the ancient altar of Yahweh which stood on that place, but which had been broken down. Elijah took twelve stones, corresponding to the number of the twelve tribes of the sons of Jacob with whom Yahweh had made a covenant and with these stones he built a new altar in the name of Yahweh. Around the altar he dug a trench, wide enough to allow two sacks of corn to stand in it side by side. He then arranged the fire wood on top of the altar, slaughtered the bull, cut it up in large pieces and arranged it as a sacrificial victim on the wood. Then he said to some helpers, 'Fill four jars of water and pour it on the victim and on the wood'. This they did. He said, 'Do it a second time'. They poured the same amount of water a second time. He said, 'Do it a third time', and they did it a third time. Water dripped all around the altar and the trench was full of it . . ."

As we are carried along by the story we will, of course, be sensitive to *the build-up of suspense.* With our audience we should live through moments of suspense, climax and happy resolution. There are no exact rules for this; much will depend on our use of intonation, pauses and inflexions of voice. A moment of suspense can immediately be felt in the reaction of the audience. People tend then to become very still and quiet, the interest manifest on their faces. A story-teller will relish the magnificent climax in the Elijah narrative, bringing out how the bolt of lightning did much more than ignite the sacrificial fire.

> ". . . Elijah prayed 'Yahweh, God of Abraham, Isaac and Israel, let them know today that you are God in Israel and that I am your servant and that I have done all these things at your command.' When nothing happened he fell on his knees, stretched his arms out to heaven and called out more urgently, 'Answer me, Yahweh, answer me, so that all these people may know, that you, Yahweh, are God, and that you want to win back their hearts'. There was a moment of anxious silence

(pause) then suddenly the sky rent open and a bolt of lightning sent by God fell down and consumed not only the victim and the wood, but also the stones and the sand, and licked up even the water in the trench. When all the people saw this, they fell on their faces, 'Yahweh is God', they cried out, 'Yahweh is God'."

Telling a story is an art and is something very personal. Each narrator will have his own approach and his own distinctive style. But the elements mentioned above will enter in some form or other in every good narration. It is the prudent and calculated use of these elements that will give our stories the natural force that makes them so powerful in communication.

HISTORICITY AND ARTISTIC PRESENTATION

Children of the scientific age that we are, we are sensitive to the question of historicity. We expect our daily papers to give factual reports of contemporary events. Most of the history books we read are preoccupied with reconstructing past events in an objective manner. "Did it really happen?", "How exactly did it happen?" are the phrases we frequently hear. The scriptural narratives were discredited in the eyes of many when they were found to contain much that is not historical in a strictly scientific sense. This in turn has had a paralysing effect on communicators who have become less inclined to make use of such "untrustworthy material". There are many issues that could be raised here, but I will restrict myself to some practical questions. What *is* and what is *not* historical in biblical narratives? How does this affect our use of such stories?

The answer, in a nutshell, is that narration like any other art of its kind, contains both statement and presentation. When judging what the narrator wants to convey to us, we first try to understand the main statement he is making through his presentation. After this we study the details of presentation and distinguish between: additional statement, audience appeal and decoration. To explain these terms and what they stand for I would like to make use of a painting by Dirk Bouts, a Flemish artist who lived in the fifteenth century. I will later apply the same distinctions to biblical narrative.

If we study the painting (Fig. 18) it is not difficult to establish its *main statement.* The artist presents us with Christ and the twelve apostles at the

Last Supper. The exact moment portrayed seems to be the institution of the Blessed Sacrament when Jesus said "Take and eat. This is my body". Whatever we have to say about the details later on, it is clear from the whole painting that the artist attaches great value to this deed of our Lord. It is as if he says to us: "Never forget the Holy Eucharist which Jesus gave to us when he dined for the last time with his twelve apostles".

However, the painting is so rich in detail that we might, at least theoretically, raise the question: "Did the Last Supper really happen like this?" The artist, who would be horrified at our lack of comprehension, would obviously hasten to give the following reply: "Surely it did not happen exactly like this. For one thing I do not know precisely what things looked like in Jesus' time, neither does it interest me very much. What I have tried to do is to present the institution of the Holy Eucharist in a way that my people can understand and appreciate".

"That my people may understand". Studying the painting again we see that indeed many details are due to the Flemish milieu in which Dirk Bouts worked. The table and the chairs correspond to fifteenth century furniture. The shape of the house, the windows, the doors, the hearth, and the tiles on the floor, reflect the architecture of that age. Many other details spring from his relation to the Flemish audience. Even the personalities of Christ and the apostles have purposely been modelled on the common folk found in Flanders in those years. The realism of many details springs from the artist's desire to reconstruct a scene in which people could recognise themselves and their own situation. We call this aspect of the presentation *audience appeal.*

However, Dirk Bouts also wanted to produce a work of art. He wanted his painting to be beautiful, to be admired for its colours, composition and delicate expression. Many of the details come from this purely artistic concern and have, consequently, a *decorative function.* Some examples of this may be seen in unnecessary objects that were added, such as the statue over the door, the four servants standing to attention, the cupboard standing on the right side and other odds and ends. Like other Flemish painters, Bouts is interested in bringing out depth and distant perspectives. That is why he makes us see a glimpse of faraway scenes through the windows and open doors. Again, like other contemporary painters, the artist shows great skill in capturing the different materials seen in the painting. Just study how one can almost feel the difference between the various surfaces, the tile, the wood, cloth, hair, the metal of the plate and the marble of the pillar. Such details make the presentation attractive, but they do not by themselves add a separate meaning.

Some details, of course, enter for a special purpose. They enlarge the artist's main statement and so I prefer to call them *added statement.* In the painting in question it is no coincidence that the gesture of Christ's right hand corresponds to a similar gesture of the priest at consecration. The round white host, distinct from the loaves of bread lying on the table, and

Fig. 18. The Last Supper by Dirk Bouts.
On view in St. Peter's Church, Louvain.

the chalice, purposely different from the ordinary drinking cups standing about, point to the eucharist. Obviously the artist wants us to see the link between the main celebrant at Holy Mass and Jesus Christ. This I would call an added statement resulting from details of the presentation. Another added statement of this kind concerns the sanctity of the apostles. Innocence, sincerity, love and reverent fear shine from their faces. Judas, in the left foreground, with the grim expression on his face, has been given a different treatment.

If it isn't difficult for us to see the above distinctions in a painting — and I am sure I have exasperated some of my readers by discussing them at length — why on earth do we find it so difficult to apply the same to narrative? Basically biblical narrative is an *artistic* presentation, not a scientific description. Like the painter, the biblical author has a statement to make. He believes in what God has done for his people and his statement expresses this belief. But like the christian artists of later ages the biblical authors were concerned to present the main tenets of salvation history in a form that could be understood and appreciated by their audiences. In one century after another ancient traditions, which often consisted substantially of one or other single fact, were elaborated and embellished by the mediators of the covenant. It is a serious misunderstanding to imagine that they presented the details because they themselves believed them to be historically true. Apart from the main statement and added teaching, most of the details found their origin in the artistic need of captivating the audience.

There is more that we as communicators can learn from the comparison with painting. Dirk Bouts' vision of the Last Supper could inspire his contemporaries with respect for the Holy Eucharist. For christians in a village of the Indian sub-continent, the same picture proves meaningless. Although various items in the painting can be explained to them they will not to be able to appreciate the message on account of the difference in cultural expression and artistic language.

See what fundamental changes in the presentation the Indian artist, A. da Fonseca had to bring about to make the same fundamental statement as Dirk Bouts. (Fig. 19). Now Christ and the twelve apostles are seated on the floor in Indian fashion. They are dressed in the saffron robes of religious men. In short, the whole presentation has been Indianised and we feel instinctively that just as Dirk Bouts did justice to the main "statement" of

Fig. 19. "Khrist prasad" by A. da Fonseca, Bombay.

the Eucharist for his Flemish contemporaries, Fonseca achieves exactly the same through the cultural symbolism of India.

As narrators we have a similar choice. What weighs heavier with us? Strict adherence to written details of the culture centuries removed from our own, or a presentation as expressive as possible of the main statement with details in our own cultural language? Christian theology of the inspired word has always affirmed that it is the meaning, not the external expression, that comes first. The implication for our use of the stories is quite considerable. To be faithful to a biblical narrative and its message we need not worry excessively about stylistic or audience-related written details. Rather we should feel free with the creative vision of the artist, to adjust the presentation in such a way that the message will strike home. It is a practice which skilled catechetical narrators have followed with great success through the ages.

Giving the biblical stories a "modern feel" does not mean that we should introduce manifest anachronisms into our stories. We should avoid extremes that will strike our listeners as odd. Everybody knows that our modern technological facilities did not exist at the time of Christ. An assertion such as "Joseph and Mary caught the bus to Bethlehem", or "Pilate told Herod by telephone that he would send Jesus along", disturb rather than help. But barring such new modern inventions, practically all biblical stories can be re-translated into the every day, human experiences familiar to the people we address.

On the other hand, whatever we do, we should preserve some *local colour*. People are used to hearing about different cultures and other customs. They realise that the biblical stories refer to Palestine 2,000 years ago. A touch of strangeness or oddness in persons, objects and events, makes the story interesting and objective. But any out-of-the-way customs should be explained in terms familiar to our audience and should not dominate the overall presentation. Japanese theatre when presented to a European audience will fascinate at first by its novelty and quaintness. But after ten minutes most people will feel bored and turn away. On the other hand, a film about Japan and Japanese customs, specially made for a Western audience, may well keep people spell-bound for hours.

The final remark related to our re-narrating of a biblical story, concerns the need of *quoting some parts of Scripture literally.*

Usually a biblical narration contains certain passages in which the message of scripture is brought out clearly. While retaining our freedom to extend and enlarge on other parts of the narration for the sake of contemporary presentation, we do well to quote such striking passages in their original form.

In the story of Elijah's confrontation with the priests of Baal, for instance, such passages could be Elijah's prayer "Answer me, Yahweh, answer me that these people may know that you are God". Or, the classic description of how God's fire from heaven consumed the altar as well as the sacrifice. "Then the lightning of Yahweh fell and consumed not only the sacrificial victim and the wood, but also the stones and the soil and licked up even the water in the trench". Such literal quotations of key texts bring our hearers into immediate contact with the inspired word and keep our presentation "biblical" in spite of the trans-cultural alterations we have made in our presentation.

SIMPLE FREE NARRATION

Some preachers and teachers are used to telling a story in two parts. First they will present the narrative itself (and then usually in the "all-bones" fashion, that is: too short, too abstract and without emotion). Then they will indicate the moral which will amount to a long-drawn-out series of applications and admonitions. This approach normally produces the "slump effect" in the audience. As long as the story lasts attention will be riveted. As soon as the moral part begins the audience slumps into distraction. If a teacher at school frequently follows the story-moral sequence, some children may even switch off earlier, while the story is still going on, in anticipation of the repugnance about the moral which they know will come.

In a good story the moral of the story is the story itself. A feature film is not much use if it needs a fifteen minute explanation after the show is finished, to explain what it meant to say. Nor would people want to remain in the cinema for such a purpose. A good novel carries the message in itself, not in an added epilogue. A beautiful church building should speak for itself. An instructive exhibition informs and educates through its exhibits, not by material added on to it from the outside. In other words, whatever a story has to say it should say it as part of the story itself, not as something added on, certainly not as something added as an afterthought when the suspense has been resolved.

The application to our own life, the moral for a particular audience, may need to be made more explicit. But pointing the moral should be done in the course of the story itself. The moral should be interwoven in a natural way, with the events, with the description of the personalities, the dialogues and other details of the narrative. Story and application should be so naturally integrated that the audience experiences the whole presentation as an undivided unity.

Not every biblical story lends itself to this kind of straight-forward presentation. But many stories do, many more than most preachers are aware of. A catechetical instruction in class or a sermon on a Sunday morning might well consist entirely of such a well-integrated narrative. This may seem unbelievable to some. In our experience of sermons many of us have come to identify preaching with moralising, so much so that we use expressions like "don't preach at me", by which we mean, "don't tell me how to behave". A well balanced story, however, can be a very good and effective sermon.

Presenting an instruction from the Bible in this form will be called by me a "simple free narration". Actually it isn't as simple and free as it looks, but it owes its name to the fact that it does not have the deliberate interruptions which we insert when we use the "story-reflection-story" technique that I will describe later on. For a simple free narration we should choose a biblical story that has an obvious message for a certain audience. In presenting the story we do nothing else than re-tell the story in such a way that our audience will take the message home with them.

Let us work out an example. Rehoboam lost half his kingdom because he did not listen to the advice of experienced people (read the story in 1 Kings 12, 1-19). The moral of the story is obvious. The story could well do for boys and girls in high school (a 20 minute conference on a recollection day?), for priests gathered at a clergy retreat (a seven minute homily during concelebrated Mass?) or for a mixed congregation (a 10 minute Sunday sermon?). Our presentation will vary considerably depending on the audience and the occasion, but in all cases it could be in the form of a simple free narration.

In preparation for the event we first read the story carefully. We reflect on what it has to say, or *could* say to our particular audience. With teenagers the main problem centres round what is known as the "generation gap", how to have confidence in all the people who advise us to do things we don't understand or like. With priests our stress will probably lie more on the side of responsibility. Rehoboam as a new king ʾbarged ahead and imposed his authority without realising that the exercise of all responsibility should be guided by the advice of wise men. With a mixed congregation we might, perhaps, draw more on the lasting need of an attitude to learn and to take advice. Reflecting on such applications, we jot them down on a sheet of paper, possibly adding some specific examples from everyday life that illustrate the need of taking the message seriously.

We now have a look at the story as a story. On the lines suggested earlier in this chapter, we analyse the narrative elements and plan our presentation. Here again much will depend on our audience. Priests will need much less explanation than high school children and a more sophisticated form of narration. However, for any audience our story as a story should be good. If we feel embarrassed at telling a story to professional preachers, we might do well to remember that Christ spoke in parables to the first college of bishops!

We now plan our application – going through the story, we look for openings, for small remarks on the side which will imply the application. Suppose I am preparing the sermon for the mixed congregation. The story tells how the people complained to Rehoboam before his enthronement and gave him an ultimatum. "Your father, King Solomon, gave us a heavy burden to bear. If you lighten the burdens he laid upon us, we will acknowledge you as king". Here we could reflect, while telling the story, that people often groan and grumble, but that there is more than once a kernel of truth in what they say. What do *we* do when we hear complaints against ourselves? Do we immediately respond in anger? Rehoboam at least had the common sense not to react immediately. He said to the people's representatives, "Give me three days and then I will let you know my decision".

Again, when in the story we narrate how Rehoboam received different advice from his young companions and the council of elders, we can reflect on the contradictory counsel given us by friends, relatives, the books we read, and the professionals whom we consult. It is a point of wisdom to consider who is giving the advice and why. While narrating Rehoboam's harsh reply, we may dwell a little on Rehoboam's psychological attitude, comparing it to similar experiences we have ourselves when dealing with others. Such reflections and remarks should not be overplayed. They should hardly be noticed as distinct from the story. They should be absent from the last part of the story. The conclusion of the story will automatically make people reflect on the implications for their own lives.

I will add here a fully worked out example of how the story of 1 Kings 12, 1-17 could be used as a simple free narration in an address to priests. I have been asked to give a short homily during the concelebrated Mass. The

Gospel text read during the Mass was Matthew 15, 12-14 where Christ
speaks of the pharisees.

"My dear Fathers,
Christ's warning in today's Gospel that we should not be blind
men leading the blind, cannot be ignored by us priests. There
seems to be some kind of blindness that easily befalls those who
take on responsibility. It may be good for us to reflect again on
the Old Testament story of the blind king.
Solomon had died and a sigh of relief went up all over Israel, for
his rule had been oppressive, his taxes heavy. So when the days
approached for Solomon's son, Rehoboam, to be enthroned as
king the leaders of the people came together and decided to lay
down conditions. We can well picture the scene before us in the
wide valley of Shechem. The tribes had come together. All the
slopes of the hills were covered with tents as far as the eye could
see. And in the meadow near the ancient sanctuary was the
pavilion which had been erected to house the young king, with
his wives, his officials and the servants who formed his court.
There, in front of the pavilion, representatives from the people
met the new king. Their demands were clear. "Your father was a
hard master. We don't want you as our king unless you promise
to treat us better than he did". We can almost see Rehoboam
recoil at these words as we ourselves recoil whenever we hear
words that are unpleasant, that hurt our pride. How do we react
when people criticise the clergy or lay down terms for cooperat-
ing with us?
"Father never prepares his sermon", people say about us. We
are furious but do we take the trouble to find out why our
preaching fails to inspire them?
"Father has his own friends. *We* never see him in our home".
"Father is old-fashioned. He cannot get on well with the young".
"Father looks well after himself. We wonder what he is doing all
day". – They may be hard words for us to swallow. We rise
immediately in self-defence with angry indignation. Why don't
we listen to people first and examine their criticism
dispassionately . . .?
As is usually the case, the people's criticism against the house of
David was justified to a great extent. Had Solomon not imposed
heavy taxes to pay for his costly administration? Scripture tells
us that the daily food requirements for the palace alone
amounted to 195 bushels of fine flour, 390 bushels of meal, 10
fattened oxen, 20 pasture-fed cattle and 100 sheep. Over and
above he needed deer, gazelles, roebucks and chickens, all this

not counting the barley and straw required for Solomon's 40,000 chariot horses and the food supplies for his garrisons all over the country. And had Solomon not raised a levy of 30,000 able-bodied men for forced labour on his royal buildings? Rehoboam sat back and reflected. "Give me three days", he said, "and I will give you my answer". The people retreated with a glimmer of hope. Perhaps, he would listen . . .

Kings were used to confrontation and the next day Rehoboam indulged in this game, playing with what would turn out to be the most important issue of his life. Although asking for advice, he had, of course, made up his mind. He really *knew* what was best. But don't we need the support of those who counsel us to do what conforms to our judgement? Few of us can stomach the people who tell us the truth. Most of us will more readily listen to the advice of people who think like ourselves, who reassure us that we were right in the first place. So we see Rehoboam acting true to form when he seeks advice to his own liking. We see him convoke the council of wise men that assisted his father. He feels important and assured as he puts the royal question, "What do you think I should do?" They reflect. They discuss. Eventually they reach a unanimous conclusion. "Give them a pleasant reply and agree to be good to them. Then you can be their king for ever". It was simple, but it would involve a loss of face. Then Rehoboam turned to his friends, as we so readily do when we feel threatened in our position. Then we go to a man we like, we weep on his houlder, we grumble about our griefs and are consoled by hearing what we like to hear. Rehoboam called together the young men with whom he had grown up. He put the same question to them, "What do you think I should do?" But they gave a different answer. "This is what you must answer", they said: "My little finger is thicker than my father's loins. My father made you bear a heavy burden. I will make it heavier still. My father beat you with whips; I am going to beat you with loaded scourges". It was a classical moment of blind men leading the blind.

Malcolm Lowey, speaking of the misconception that may blind man's mind says in one of his books:

> How many wolves do we feel on our heels,
> While our real enemies go in sheepskin by.

We know the final scene. Rehoboam, feeling sure of himself, hearing the reassuring advice of his friends echoing in his ears, stands in front of the people and assumes an air of authority that was to prove empty. I can see myself holding forth confidently at a meeting and thumping the table.

Rehoboam was a man who thought he knew, but actually he was blind. He took no notice of the people's wishes, the Bible says, and this was a punishment brought about by God. "My father made you bear a heavy burden", he said, "but I will make it heavier still. My father beat you with whips; I am going to beat you with scorpions". Then the people rose in revolt. They shouted insolence at Rehoboam, and said, "Down with David and his house! Let us all go home! Let Rehoboam be king of his own family!" And when Rehoboam sent Adoram, one of his ministers, to pacify the crowd, they stoned him to death. King Rehoboam himself had to flee for his life in a chariot. He became king only over the tribe of Judah". In the name of the Father and of the Son and of the Holy Spirit, Amen.

THE STORY-REFLECTION-STORY APPROACH

Many scriptural stories have a direct bearing on general truths or fundamental virtues which remain valid for all times. God helps us when we pray to him. God is always ready to forgive. Beware of false friends. Respect your parents, etc. Such messages can often be handled by the simple free narrative approach explained above. But what about the many other aspects of our modern christian life? Have biblical stories anything to teach about them? I mean things such as forming a prayer community, the vocation to religious life, loyalty to the church, the forgiveness of sins, the Eucharist, Social Action and the charismatic movement. As our situation is so different from the one presupposed in the scriptural narratives, how can it be made to bear on our present condition?

To meet this requirement, a technique has been developed which I will call "story-reflection-story". The technique consists of inserting two or three major interruptions at well chosen points in the story. The most common pattern followed is: Story – reflection – story – reflection – story. The justification for following such a pattern lies in the fact that our communication contains two distinct and equally valuable parts: the biblical story which provides the motivation and the reflection which carries up-to-date theological thought. Both parts are of equal value. I will need to explain this at a little more length.

In the *City of God* (Book 13) St. Augustine discusses original sin and the mortality of the human race and its consequences. Book 13 is really a treatise on death. In more than twenty chapters Augustine discusses all aspects of death as they were known to him at that time from theology or contemporary philosophy. All men must die. Death is a punishment for man's sin. Death is unpleasant and painful because it involves the unnatural

Fig. 20. Illustration in Augustine's "The City of God".

separation of body and soul. Even those who are saved by Christ have to die, but for them death becomes another means of merit. For St. Augustine all these instructions on death find their roots in the story of man's first sin.

"(Adam's body) would never, in fact, have died, had not Adam by his disobediences incurred the punishment which God had threatened beforehand. Even when driven out of paradise, Adam was not denied nourishment, but was forbidden to eat of the tree of life and so was doomed to die from age and senility . . ."

"By being justly deprived of the tree of life Adam and Eve became subject to that necessity of bodily death, which is now for us innate. For this reason, the Apostle says . . . 'The body is dead by the reason of sin . . .' The Apostle calls the soul 'dead' because it is bound by the necessity of dying . . ." (City of God, 13.23).

In a fifteenth century manuscript of the *City of God* in French, a monk has tried to capture Augustine's thought in a single picture (see Fig. 20). In the background we see the garden of Eden. From a central fountain spring the four rivers that irrigate the whole world. Adam and Eve stand under the Tree of Life while the serpent with a human head offers the apple to Eve. So far the picture is like any other artistic representation of the Fall of man. But notice the two important additions in the foreground. On the right we see the corrupting body of a dead man, symbolising death itself. On the left St. Paul is portrayed holding in his hand the quotation from Romans: "As by one man death entered into the world . . . . ." The artist has thereby presented St. Augustine's thinking in a very graphic and convincing manner. He shows us at a glance, in the same picture, as equal elements of discussion: the story of man's fall, the fact of human mortality and Paul's teaching on death.

It is this same kind of insight: the wish to combine ancient biblical narrative with present-day instruction, that should make us choose the story-reflection-story technique. It proves to be the only presentation that will do justice to both aspects of our topic. To stay with our example of paradise and death, we could put ourselves into the frame of mind of a teacher who wants to explain the christian view of death to sixth form pupils at school. She might begin by jotting down the various points she would like to cover: the experience of death and what it means; that death is not quite the same for animals as for man; that death carries in itself an element of punishment; that on account of Christ's resurrection we won't need to fear death as it leads to heaven; that spiritual death is much worse than physical death, etc. The extent to which such points can be discussed will obviously depend on the needs and abilities of her particular pupils. Being a good teacher she will also bring in illustrations from everyday life, perhaps occurrences in the school, or references to death that would help to enliven and clarify the discussion.

Now she could, of course, at this point, collect all this material and present it to the pupils in some sort of logical order in a straightforward lecture form. But she could say to herself: "Is there a scriptural narrative that could frame and motivate these thoughts on death? Where in the Bible will I find those inspiring images that will help me bring across our christian view of dying?" She might then, quite naturally, think of the story of man's fall (Genesis 2,5 – 3,24). After all, our theology of death derives from this text to a great extent and the themes of life and death are well presented in it.

The teacher should now take her Bible and read the story carefully. She should study the narrative elements, as suggested earlier in this chapter, so that she can make the most of the intrinsic thoughts of this beautiful narrative. She could then compare the points in her lesson on death with the biblical story and bring about a synthesis between the two. This she could do, for example, by planning her presentation in the following way:

Story, first part:	God created the whole world; he filled everything with life; he made man and woman out of love, and made them masters of the created world.
Reflection:	The meaning of life; it means movement, enjoyment and growth; the experience of death with plants, animals and even human beings; some of the questions this raises.
Story, second part:	God planted the tree of life and death and forbade man to eat from it; Adam and Eve sinned by pride; God had to punish them by banning them from paradise and by imposing death.
Reflection:	The experience of evil and sin in ourselves and in the world; pain, suffering and death, while being natural from our point of view, contain in themselves an element of punishment; physical death is not the same as spiritual death; etc.
Story, third part:	God took pity on man and promised redemption; he expressed his love by making clothes for them and he promised heaven through Jesus Christ.
Reflection:	The meaning of heaven; how Christ has overcome death; we need not fear death if we live united to Christ.

Story, fourth part: As a kind of conclusion we give a
vision of paradise to come in heaven;
God will wipe every tear away and we
will finally overcome death.

The presentation suggested above will easily fill a full class period, with
the narrative taking up 40% of the time and reflection and discussion the
remaining 60%.

The biblical story in question needs careful handling. In spite of its containing some central truths about the human condition, it is more of a
parable than an historical narrative. The story may also have other
disadvantages from the teacher's point of view; there may be too heavy a
stress on sin and punishment which may be undesirable when discussing
death with teenagers; they may have heard the story so often before that it
has lost its freshness. The teacher may then decide to turn to another
biblical story to frame and carry her instructions on death. Such stories
could be Jesus restoring to life the son of the widow of Nain (Lk. 7, 11-17),
the raising of Lazarus (John 11, 1-44), Ezekiel's vision of the dry bones (Ez.
37, 1-14) or other similar narratives. While dealing with the same subject
matter, "death", the presentation will take on a new perspective through its
being presented with any of these texts.

SOME HINTS FROM PRACTICE

I know from experience that story-reflection-story can be a very
successful form of presentation for catechetical instructions, conferences and sermons. But having made considerable use of it myself
and having taught the technique to others over a number of years, I
am keenly aware of some of the pitfalls which eager beginners in the
trade are likely to encounter. I hope the reader will pardon me if I give
advice about this in a schoolmasterly fashion.

Do not shorten the story part. Make the fullest use of the
dramatic possibilities offered by your particular narrative. In your
presentation of the story lay a subtle emphasis on those aspects that
prepare the way for what you want to say in the reflection, but clearly
keep them separate in your presentation. The story will be in the past
tense; the reflection will speak about the present. The transition from
one part to the other should speak for itself. "Now let us go back to
our story. We had left Ezekiel in the Valley of Bones, meditating on
death and destruction. Then suddenly he heard a voice. "Son of
Man", it called out . . ."

Make sure that your reflection parts contain up-to-date and
worthwhile instruction. When giving a retreat conference, for

instance, it should contain a real *substance* of illustrations from present-day life, quotations from relevant authors, other scriptural references, and whatever in such conferences provides matter for thought. I have found that some teachers neglect this necessary homework and fill the reflective parts of their presentation with general observations such as anyone could make. As we have seen above when discussing simple free narration, the moral that is implied in the story itself need not and should not be brought out as an afterthought. Doing it makes the presentation exasperatingly boring. Whenever we use story-reflection-story rather than simple free narration we should do so because we have a separate and an equivalent amount of information to convey through the reflective parts.

A frequent question with those who use the technique for the first time is, "How do you compose the presentation? Do you start with the story or the topic?" In theory one could start with either but my experience is that it is more common to start from the topic and then look for the story that can carry it. Topic and story will then mutually complement one another until a harmonious presentation arises.

Some persons have the initial difficulty that they do not see how their topics can be carried by biblical stories. Sometimes this springs from a lack of imagination; at other times from a lack of trust in themselves or an insufficient acquaintance with the biblical texts. To answer these difficulties and to show the possibilities of Bible stories in this field and the many ways in which story and instruction can be interwoven, I will briefly work out five more examples.

In a conference for high school students on anger and reconciliation we could be guided by the story of David and Nabal (1 Sam 25).
(1) We introduce David and Nabal, the difference in their characters, Nabal's feast and David's request for a share (25, 1-8). (R) We explain the psychological differences between people through temperament, education and personal growth. We illustrate the necessity of accepting people as they are.
(2) We then narrate extensively and dramatically how Nabal offended David's messengers and how David in great anger set out to take revenge (25, 9-13). (R) We analyse the reasons for the growth of anger. We see what it does to ourselves and others. We evaluate our relationships from this angle.
(3) We continue the story with the account of how Abigail intervened and made peace (25, 14-42). (R) We discuss the folly of anger and living in

enmity with others. We indicate practical ways in which a person can be a peacemaker.

A Sunday sermon about the communion of saints could be based on the story of the conquest of Ai (Jos 6-7).
(1) We explain how the Jewish people under Joshua conquered the Holy Land with God's help. They vowed that they would give all captured treasures to God (6, 18-19). (R) As Christians we receive God's kingdom at baptism, but in return we vow total dedication to God. We explain the meaning of our baptismal vow.
(2) We narrate how Israel was defeated in the war. Great losses were inflicted because some persons had not kept their vows (don't mention Achan as yet). (7, 2-12). (R) We explain how infidelity to baptismal vows affects the whole church.
(3) We narrate how Achan's sin was revealed and how he was punished (7, 14-26). (R) We point out how God knows every individual's sins. He expects every christian to be holy. We point out the community dimension of confession and the Eucharist.

In a retreat conference for sisters we could speak of religious obedience in the context of Abraham's sacrifice (Gn 22).
(1) God demanded from Abraham the sacrifice of Isaac, an almost impossible demand (22,1-4). (R) We expound the theology of religious obedience as the sacrifice of the will.
(2) We narrate how Abraham and Isaac talked about the sacrifice while climbing the mountain. Isaac was afraid and Abraham full of sorrow. Yet both agree to bring the sacrifice together. We could make use here of Jewish tradition to complete the narrative (22, 5-9). (R) We bring out how obedience is a question of dialogue between superiors and persons entrusted to their care. We quote Vatican II on this and give practical guidelines and examples.
(3) God converted Abraham's sacrifice into a great blessing (22, 10-18). (R) We indicate the advantages of obedience both for one's spiritual growth and for efficiency in the apostolate.

When addressing priests on the competence of the laity to assume church leadership we might refer to the sharing of the Spirit in the desert (Num 11).
(1) The Hebrews in the desert revolted against Moses so that Moses felt inadequate to rule the people all by himself (11, 4-15). (R) We reflect on how since the Reformation, priests have become more and more isolated in their task; the undesirable consequences of this.
(2) God ordered Moses to appoint 70 elders to assist him. These elders

shared in Moses' Spirit (11, 16-17, 24-25). (R) Vatican II stresses the distinctive task and competence of the laity within the church. We work out examples and consequences.

(3) Also two others who had not been present at the function assumed leadership under the Spirit. Moses defended their action when they were criticised (11, 26-30). (R) There are many ways in which we can quench the Spirit. Our priestly leadership should be directed towards encouraging the laity to take initiatives and to exercise their rightful responsibilities.

Suppose we speak to a group of college students on faith. We could take as our starting point Jesus' extraordinary behaviour as described in John 6.

(1) After the miracle of multiplying the loaves Jesus refused to be made king (6, 1-15). (R) The modern world is inclined to worship humanistic values. The Gospel presents a higher set of values that give a new meaning to life.

(2) Jesus walked on the water (6, 16-21). (R) The Christian view of reality transcends the limits imposed on itself by science. The categories of mystery, true freedom and divine love liberate us from a too restricted vision of reality.

(3) Jesus promised to give himself as food (6, 22-58). (R) Faith ultimately means the experience of God who communicates himself to us. It does not need any exterior justification. It is an event that changes our life and thus justified by its results.

(4) Many people left Jesus through lack of faith (6, 59-71). (Brief concluding reflection). Faith is a mature decision which we make in response to our experience of Christ.

CHAPTER SEVEN

BIBLICAL PERSONALITIES

When God chose to reveal himself to all mankind he began by speaking to one nation. In a long history of promise, blessing, threat and punishment he prepared this nation for its part in the plan of redemption. The name of the nation was Israel. God's reactions to Israel's sins and to its virtuous deeds were carefully written down in the books of the Old Testament. Of course, the super-reality of God's nature transcends man's wildest imagination and most profound thought. But for the sake of being understood by man, God presented himself to Israel as if he were a person like us.

We can rightly say that, through all his work and actions, God revealed what he is like, or in other words, that _he revealed his own personality_. In an anthropomorphic and yet profound manner he revealed his likes and dislikes, his intimacy with saints and patience with sinners, his deepest intentions, his desires for mankind, his wish to love and be loved. Israel was the test person for all mankind. As God did with Israel, so will he do with us. The emotions of life, indignation, mercy and anger, displayed by the Divine Majesty towards Israel express his attitude towards us.

Through the incarnation God revealed himself to us as Father, Son and Holy Spirit. Jesus became to us the visible image of the Father, the personal expression of what God is, the exact likeness of God's own being. And in his human life, he expressed more convincingly and powerfully than could have been done in any other way the ideal of human sanctity.

God's influence on Israel produced saints and heroes, men and women who proved their character and virtue in their lives. These persons were meant to set a concrete ideal to be followed by all. David was held out as a model which Solomon had to follow. "Walk before me with innocence of heart and in honesty, like David your father", (1 Kings 9,4). Paul enumerates many persons who gave an example of heroic faith (Heb 11). The Gospels and Acts record the personalities of followers of Christ with whom we can easily identify.

The inspired Scriptures also record the sins and transgressions of those who refused to accept God's graces. Those too serve a useful purpose in the recorded history of salvation, because they set an example of how we should not act. They constitute a lasting warning on how a man can fail. David's fall and its consequences will not be forgotten. Jesus speaks of sinners in some of his parables. Ananias' and Sapphira's greed and punishment "made a profound impression on the whole community and on all who heard it" (Acts 5,11). Something of every sinner can be recognised in ourselves.

The Bible contains the self-revelation of God and the human picture of virtue and sin. It focusses intentionally on many personalities. It pronounces an inspired judgement on many of them: praising some men and criticising others. In this way, the Bible provides us with a real "mirror of life" complete with practical warnings and detailed advice. Biblical examples should be more precious to us than examples taken from other sources. Profane examples may clarify and illustrate; they may even inspire to heroic action. They can never claim the inspired judgement contained in genuine biblical examples. A biblical example shows us what God thinks of persons who acted and spoke before us; we know from this how he will look on us if we act in the same way.

BIOGRAPHIES IN SCRIPTURE?

Human history is of necessity a record about people. For nineteenth century historians history described the achievements of kings and great leaders. C. Carlyle states confidently, "No great man lives in vain. The history of the world is but the biography of great men". R. W. Emerson caps this statement, "There is properly no history, only biography". Such sweeping assertions are easy to make. The truth is that biographies, in our sense of the word, were rarely written in the past. About most great leaders we have plenty of history, but little biography.

Biography in its fullest sense tries to recreate the life of an individual. It means much more than presenting facts and dates in a chronological order. It means an attempt to make the individual recognisable to us as a human being, so that we may know the traits of his personality and understand the motives for his actions. Good biography starts with psychological insight and produces the illusion of a life actually being lived. In the words of Sir Edmund Gosse it paints "the faithful portrait of a soul in its adventures through life".

The Bible does not contain this kind of biography. Not even the Gospels in spite of their outspoken intention to focus on Jesus Christ can be called biographies. For although they present valuable material on the personality of Jesus, their main purpose was to proclaim him as the saviour, rather than reveal his inner personality. In this respect John comes closest to a revelation of Jesus' inner life and even he is preoccupied with the experience of Jesus in the life of the Church. The modern preoccupation with biography, recreating "the earthly pilgrimage of a man" for its own sake, did not find its way into the Bible.

But there is no reason for despair. For the Bible abounds with "character sketches", the illustrious literary ancestors of our modern biography. Such sketches were written of Pericles and Sophocles by Ion of Chios in the fifth century B.C. In ancient China Ssu-ma Ch'ien (145-85 B.C.) published his "historical record" in the form of short characterisations of living persons under various headings such as "maligned statesmen", "rash generals", and "assassins". Such chapters which are full of anecdotes, lively descriptions and a lot of dialogue, are rightly regarded as forerunners in the art of biography. For they give us a glimpse of the human personality, sufficient to afford us an insight into what made the person tick. The Bible too presents such character sketches.

The account of Gideon (Judges 6, 1-8,35) is a so-called "brag" story. Various scattered traditions about Gideon, about his call to leadership, his first conflict with the followers of Baal in his home town Ophrah, his victory over the Midianites and other exploits, were bundled together into one hero saga. Sagas had a social function. By boasting about past leaders and glorious victories they taught the nation courage and self-respect. In spite of its briefness and ragged composition the brag story about Gideon contains a real character sketch of him as a person.

The story of Gideon is totally centred round the figure of Gideon himself. The whole development of events is recounted from Gideon's point of view. We are looking at things from his angle. We may therefore say that the story does in some way convey a reflection of Gideon's psychology. We are made to imagine Gideon's state of mind and to understand how Gideon slowly changed from being an ordinary, timid man into a courageous leader.

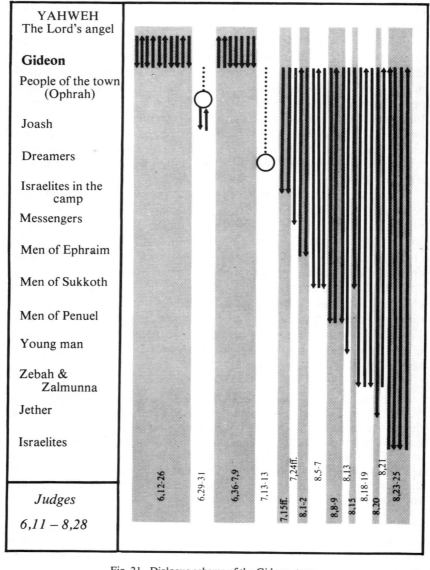

Fig. 21. Dialogue scheme of the Gideon story.
The arrows indicate who is speaking to whom.

This psychological approach to Gideon can be demonstrated in a brief analysis of the dialogue scheme in the story. (See Fig. 21). The story has many different dialogues. In all of these Gideon is either the person who speaks or the person addressed! Only two conversations are reported in which Gideon is not one of the speakers. But even in these cases the conversation is about Gideon and Gideon is present as hearer. The two Midianite soldiers talk about their dream, but Gideon overhears them (Judges, 7,13-15). Gideon's father refuses to let the townspeople enter his house, while Gideon is obviously listening inside the house (Judges 6,29-31). Gideon is consequently the psychological centre of the story.

This also emerges from the narrator's obvious interest in Gideon's motives and attitudes. Gideon basically has a timid character. He is beset by doubts. He cannot believe that God will help so he hides himself in a wine press (6,11-13). After cutting down Baal's altar he does not have the courage to face the infuriated townspeople himself (6,29-31). Before venturing Israel into battle he requires three signs from God, two with a fleece (6,36-40) and one through a dream (7,9-14). But God teaches Gideon how to be courageous. Dealing patiently with him he forces him into a heroic role. When Gideon is made to reduce the number of his army first from 32,000 to 10,000, then to 300 soldiers only, we can almost feel the psychological stress building up in Gideon. But he responds admirably. Gideon grows into a competent leader. His surprise attack on the Midianite camp is a gem of military tactics. He wins the support of the Ephraimites with diplomacy and by ruthless determination overcomes all obstacles encountered during the pursuit of his enemies.

The information about a man like Gideon remains sketchy. Yet the picture we have of Gideon's character is vivid enough to serve us as an example. Many leaders today go through crises similar to those experienced by Gideon. They too are beset by doubts and tempted to put their trust in the number of allies. They too have their moments when they hide themselves, or ask for a sign, or the moments of high decision when a man commits himself to a course of action that may make or break him. Hopefully leaders in our own days will also share Gideon's feelings of humility when he was offered kingship by his companions. "It is not I who shall be your king", he said, "nor my son. God alone must be your master". Here was a small man who on the crest of victory remembered his true position.

VISUAL IMAGES

A visual image is a great help in building up a personality in the eyes of others.

Politics and advertising know this well. When Dwight Eisenhower was elected President of the United States in 1952 it was not on the strength of his political views, but almost entirely on account of the "personality" of "Ike" that had been carefully built up by a communication drive. Ike was presented to the American electorate as a father-figure with all the qualities admired by Americans. His public image was carefully planned. Whenever he appeared before the camera he received special make-up. He was told how to smile and how to look sincere in his dealings with the people. To present him as an energetic person he was mainly shown in the context of work; as addressing a crowd, as signing important papers, as travelling by car or presiding over a meeting. His family was drawn in because of its publicity value. As one of the campaign planners put it, "Just as we sell a product on the market, so we sold the President to the public. Just as most shoppers buy an article not for its own worth, but for the glamour of the package, so the President was elected not because of the policies he had, but on account of the image of his personality".

Perhaps we feel disgusted at the way people are tricked into accepting what advertisers or politicians tell them. However, what we can learn from these "children of the world" is the enormous influence exercised by visual images. Just think of the position occupied in the minds of youth by pop singers and film stars. Man's psychology is made in such a way that norms, ideals and values are most easily understood in the form of living persons. We like to project our wishes and expectations on to personalities. We easily understand abstract ideas if they are presented to us in the guise of human beings.
  Jesus himself understood this human need and made skilful use of it in his preaching. Remember the personalities which he created through his parables: the good Samaritan, the unforgiving servant, the good shepherd, the father who welcomes his devious son, the Pharisee and the publican, and so many others. How powerfully does he contrast rich and poor in his parable of Lazarus.

"There was once a rich man who dressed in purple clothes and lived in great luxury every day. There was also a poor man, named Lazarus, full of sores, who used to be brought to the rich man's door hoping to fill himself with the bits of food which fell from the rich man's table. Even the dogs would come and lick his sores" (Luke 16,19-21).

When a personality is presented to us, we either identify ourselves with him or reject him. We either sit with the rich man at the table or lie on the floor with Lazarus. Jesus presents the personality of the rich fool who dies on the night that he scores his greatest success (Luke 12, 13-21), in order that rich people among his audience may identify themselves with this person and take steps to reform. No one can hear the parable of the talents without realising he has to identify himself either with the servants praised for their hard work or with the negligent overseer. The persuasive force and pastoral use of such personalities in the teaching of Jesus is obvious.

But let us not stop here and miss the point. We can learn a lot from Jesus on how to present such personalities. Jesus understood that man thinks visually and knowing this he preached through *visual* images. He wanted us to *see* the rich man in his purple clothes and the poor man covered by sores and surrounded by dogs. How did Jesus achieve this effect in his description? What makes an image stand out? Modern research has demonstrated that among all the component elements of a visual picture it is especially colour, outline and movement that make the deepest impression on our minds. Jesus made skilful use of all these elements.

He often painted *colours* with a stroke of his brush. He characterized man's helplessness by saying that he cannot even make "one hair white or black" (Mt 5,36). If we can judge the weather – "red sky at night" – why can't we see the signs of the Kingdom? (Mt 16,2). Hypocrites are like white-washed tombs and those who sin against charity will be thrown into a red-hot fiery furnace. The mention of the colour helps us to have a clear picture in our minds.

Experts tell us that our mind does not retain all the lines that we see but only *the outline*. That is why we will remember a fat man because of his bulky outline or a tall man because of his long silhouette. It is amazing to note how Jesus too does not stress the so-called component parts of his visual pictures but the outlines. He constantly finds images that can be easily "silhouetted", such as a sheep carried on the shoulder of the shepherd, a narrow gate, a measure of corn that is overflowing, a lamp on the lamp stand, and people standing up and praying with out-stretched hands. It is this kind of image that remains anchored in our memory.

Sense perception is activated by the *movement* of its objects. It has been proved that if we were constantly to see the same unmoving picture, our eyes would not be able to distinguish clearly what they saw. Movement and action help to characterise the specific properties of different realities. In other words, we have a special liking for moving images and record them better. Jesus presents us with quite a few in the gospels. Just think of such dynamic pictures as a man "shaking off dust from his feet", or calling out the latest news from his housetop, a farmer pulling up the wheat and tying it in bundles, and an angry person hitting someone else on his cheek. The action is graphic and dynamic.

Sociologists have tried to determine what influences us most when we judge other people. Surprisingly enough, it proved to be *the clothes they wear*. From a man's clothes people deduce his social status, his view of life and even his character. Small wonder that Jesus often refers to clothes when characterising people. The austere dress of John the Baptist is contrasted by the fancy clothes worn by wordly courtiers (Mt 11,8). The hypocrisy of the Pharisees can be read from the size of the containers of Scripture verses dangling from their foreheads and the length of the prayer hems of their cloaks (Mt 23,5). The splendour of flowers in the field is compared to Solomon's robes (Mt 6,29). It is because "clothes make the man" that Jesus instructs his disciples to wear a simple tunic with "no money bag at the belt and with no sandals on their feet" (Mt 10,9).

As in our own verbal communication, so Jesus too had mainly to rely on words when trying to evoke mental images in the minds of his audience. This verbal approach brings with it special limitations that require extra skill from the communicator. Many things that can easily be shown in a film cannot be so clearly communicated through a radio broadcast. Visual impressions can only be partly translated into sounds and words. Here again, research has been helpful – this time through the literary sciences – to show how language can help to build a mental image. Of special interest to us here is the function of dialogue. We have already met dialogue as an element of narrative. It also plays a role in characterising a person.

Words spoken by a person help us to get an insight into his nature. Dialogue is, as we know, the main medium of drama and stage performance. Our Lord shows great skill in making use of *quoted speech* to characterise persons or situations. The attitude of the repentant tax collector is so well summed up in his words: "Oh God, have pity on me, a sinner". Compare this to the pharisee's boastful prayer: "I thank you, God, that I am not greedy, dishonest or immoral like everybody else". People who worry are characterised by what they say: "From where will come my food? or drink? or my clothes?" God's invitation is expressed as a call to a wedding: "My feast is ready now; my steers and prize calves have been butchered and everything is ready, come to the wedding feast". Jesus' complaint is contained in what the children say on the market place: "We played wedding music for you but you would not dance! We sang funeral songs, but you would not cry". The dramatic force of these expressions makes us feel we are in contact with real living persons.

HOW TO MAKE A PORTRAIT

It may be helpful to put together the various elements that go into the building up of a portrait.

Our task is similar to that of a public relations officer who has at his disposal a lot of information about an important person, and who is given the job of introducing this person to the general public. Or, we may compare it to the work of an historian who tries to conjure up in the imagination of his hearers a correct and living picture of the person whose life he describes. I have always found it useful to imagine myself standing on a stage addressing a large audience, stretching out my hand to the famous person standing next to me whom I am supposed to introduce. The point I want to make is that if we want to do justice to our task of introducing another person, whether as his public relations officer, his director, or host, we must think about the kind of elements that our portrait of the person should contain. For the sake of illustration I will refer to Absalom throughout this section (1 Sam).

Of course, there is the need for *visual presentation* to the extent this is possible. People know a person better if they can see his face, his eyes, his hair, his gestures, the characteristics of his dress, or his way of walking.

Absalom, we know, had a stately figure: "In the whole of Israel there was no man who could be praised for his beauty as much as Absalom. From the sole of his foot to the crown of his head there was not a blemish on him" (14,25). Absalom also wore long flowing black hair that fell in heavy tresses on his shoulders. He must have been an impressive person to look at in spite of being the dandy he was.

We normally identify a person by his *bio-data*. By this we mean the common facts that somehow fix his origins: his name, the place where he was born or educated, his language and culture, his father and mother, his job, his age and his previous history.

The Bible informs us that Absalom was the third son of David, that he was born at Hebron (around 1000 B.C.). That his mother was Maacah, daughter of Talmai, the king of Geshur (3,2). When he was forced to leave Judah, he fled to the royal palace of Geshur.

A person reveals his true mind by his *attitude towards others*.

In spite of David's love for him, Absalom had absolutely no regard for his father. Not only did he undermine David's authority and stage a major revolt against him; when he entered Jerusalem he expressed his contempt for his father by having a tent pitched on the flat roof of the royal palace, ordering his father's concubines to be brought there and entering the tent "in the sight of all Israel". (16,20-22). Later he pursued David with a large army, firmly determined to kill him. Such an attitude clearly gives us an insight into his personality.

People's attitudes often become clear by what they say. *Direct speech* reveals a person's deepest motivations and intentions.

The Bible records how Absalom used to stand outside his father's palace to court the goodwill of important people in the kingdom. "Absalom would say, 'Look, your case is sound and just, but there is not one official of the king who will give you a true hearing!' He would then go on to say, 'Oh, who will appoint me judge in the land? Then anyone with a lawsuit or a plea can come to me and I would see to it he had justice' and whenever anyone came up to do homage to him, he would stretch out his hand, lift him up and embrace him" (15, 2-5).

A man's attitude of mind is also revealed by his *habits*. Dr. Johnson, writing about biography, once remarked that the small habits persons have in their daily lives may be more important in understanding a person than major events. He complains that many biographers "have so little regard to the manners and behaviour of their heroes, that more knowledge may be gained of a man's real character by a short conversation with one of his servants, than from a formal and studied narrative, begun with his pedigree and ended with his funeral".

About Absalom, for instance, we hear that he had the custom of cutting his hair once a year. He would make a public show of it. He would have the hair weighed which might amount to "200 shekels of the king's weight" (about 2½ kgs). We also hear that Absalom liked to show himself in public driving a chariot drawn by horses, "with fifty men to run ahead of him" (15,1).

Information on a person's character also flows from *his deeds*, from the way in which a man deals with a difficult situation.

When Absalom's sister Tamar had been raped by Amnon, Absalom was furious and decided to avenge his sister's honour. But he did not say anything about it to anyone. He bided his time until a good opportunity arose. This came when Absalom arranged a banquet to which all the king's sons, including Amnon, were invited. Absalom travelled specially to Hebron to invite Amnon. When Amnon was intoxicated with wine, Absalom ordered his servants to kill him. He then fled away to Geshur. The whole episode showed him to be a cunning, hypocritical, scheming and cowardly person.

A final norm for evaluating a character is the way a person is accepted by others. The emotions and *reactions of contemporaries* indicate to some extent the favourable or unfavourable sides to a person's character.

We know that Absalom must have had very good qualities because he was loved by his father, David. Quite a few people admired him. Perhaps, we learn most about Absalom from the reactions of Joab. Joab was Absalom's friend. He interceded for Absalom with David on more than one occasion. But when Absalom's treason became clear, Joab broke with him and did not hesitate to kill him as he hung helplessly from the tree, caught as he was by his hair.

It is not always possible, necessary, or even desirable, to give all such details about a person. But it is good to realise that it is this type of element that presents a person more than abstract words. When giving a portrait we should be on the look-out for these elements and interweave them into a harmonious description of the person.

To conclude this section, I will give a short portrait of David which contrasts favourably with that of Absalom.

"When we turn to King David, we meet a totally different person. David had always been a great warrior. He had fought a lion with his bare hands. He had taken up the challenge of

Goliath when no one else dared to step forward. But on this day when Absalom with his rebellious troops are converging on Jerusalem David shows an inner strength of character that is of even higher quality than his leadership in war.

We see David leaving the city with all his court, walking on foot. The flight is his decision. He takes some practical measures that will strengthen his position in the inevitable conflict with Absalom. In spite of the unexpected treachery, he does not act in panic. He leaves his foreign Gittite troops the option to stay out of the civil war, if they so desire. He refuses to take the ark of the covenant with him so as not to endanger this sacred object. His overall attitude is one of resignation. "If I find favour in the eyes of God, he will bring me back and let me see both the ark and its temple. But if he says 'I have no pleasure in you', behold, here I am, let him do to me what seems good to him".

David was a humble man. He knew his own sins and weaknesses and so he could understand sin in others. When Shimei cursed David outside the city gate, David did not resort to violence. "Let him alone and allow him to curse", he said "for it must be that the Lord has told him to curse. It may be that the Lord will look upon my affliction and the Lord will repay me with good for this cursing of me today". David showed true greatness of mind by being ready to forgive. After defeating Absalom he granted pardon to Shimei. David's love for Absalom was of a similar quality. In spite of the injustices dealt to him, he instructed his troops to spare his son's life. And when he heard that Absalom had been killed he mourned for him, "Would that I had died instead of you, oh Absalom, my son, my son!" In David we recognise the greatness of a humble man."

PORTRAIT – REFLECTION APPROACH

Man is in need of living examples after which he can model his life. Our presentation of a biblical portrait should be such that it corresponds to the needs and aspirations of our audience. The portrait should be highly visual, congenial to the group we are addressing and reflecting qualities or virtues desired by it. The portrait should be such that it can easily "catch on" in the imagination of the audience so that it can become a model for future behaviour.

The history of devotion to St. George may serve as an illustration of the psychological processes involved. In the early centuries of the Church George was an ambiguous historical figure. In the West he was remembered as a soldier-martyr who died for the faith. In the East he was linked to the mythological Perseus of Joppe who was supposed to have killed a man-eating monster to save the virgin Andromeda. The St. George figure as we know it today arose when the knights of the early Middle Ages were in need of a saint who would represent their ideals. When the crusaders heard of St. George in Palestine, he was suddenly discovered (about 1000 A.D.). In a very short time a portrait of St. George became universally accepted in which eastern and western traditions, past events and contemporary thinking were blended into the "Ideal of the Knight". Richard Lionheart claimed to have seen St. George in a vision during the Crusades. St. George became patron saint of England. Thirteen militant orders were dedicated to him.

Fig. 22. Statue of St. George by Donatello (1386-1466).

At times, for short homilies, a simple portrait of a biblical character may have sufficient punch to stand on its own. This applies to all such considerations of character universal to man and remaining valid for all times. A simple presentation of Absalom's or David's character, possibly both by way of contrast, does not need much by way of a message added on from the outside.

But often we will find ourselves in the same predicament that we faced in the story-reflection-story approach: we have two separate and distinct sources of communication. On the one hand we would like to present the portrait of a biblical person that can serve as an example. On the other hand we have definite things to say to our audience that result from our experience about life today. The portrait-reflection presentation would seem to provide an answer to this problem.

I have to give a conference to a group of sisters about spiritual direction. Reading up some books about it and noting down from my own experience what seems important to me, I end up with a worksheet that contains points such as the following:
* In *Christian Perfection* Rodrigues describes how important a spiritual director is for progress in the spiritual life.
* Many skills cannot be learned from books, but must be handed on by persons. (Note the story of the groom at St. Albans who taught his son how to rub down a horse).
* According to Indian tradition a disciple learns about God from direct contact with his Guru. Note the words of Bahina Bhai "A tree that comes into contact with a sandalwood tree becomes exactly like it. So if one comes in contact with a saint, one naturally becomes a saint. The little rill that flows through a village, when it finally mingles with the Ganges water, takes on the form of the Ganges through association with it . . ."
* Spiritual direction can be given by various people in various ways. Notice: the novice mistress, superior, confessor, retreat father, companions in a prayer group, etc. Enlarge on each.

When the worksheet has grown sufficiently in content so that I have a rough picture of what I could usefully say to the sisters about the topic, I search for a biblical personality that could carry and deepen the message. After some seeking I come up with the Queen of Sheba as the best candidate. She was, after all, a person who came from far to consult Solomon about God and the meaning of existence. She had all the qualities of a distinct personality. She showed both independence of mind and willingness to learn. So I turn to 1 Kings 10 and read carefully what the Bible has to say about her. I compare this with the notes of my worksheet. I discover that I have overlooked some important aspects of the question, such as the search for wisdom so important in the biblical text. I regroup and complement my points in harmony with the shape her portrait takes in my mind. Eventually I come up with the outline of my conference which to my mind combines the message of the biblical text and the practical remarks of spiritual direction in one harmonious presentation. In short, it might amount to this:

Portrait, Part 1:	I introduce the Queen of Sheba. She must have been a very capable person to ascend the throne in an Arabian kingdom. Being queen meant acting as supreme judge, as general and as mistress of life and death for all her subjects. Apparently she was also a philosopher and a religious seeker who understood that the search for widom should be the first priority in her life.
Reflection:	Wisdom in Old Testament terms is a combination of insight and holiness of life. It expresses the fullest realisation of our human potential. I read and explain Wisdom 7, 22-30 in this context. I reflect on our own desire to attain self-fulfilment, how perhaps it has waned in the course of our religious life. I introduce Bahina Bhai, the Indian Guru, who was born in 1628 at Kolhapur but who fled from her home to become a Hindu saint because she felt irresistibly drawn to God and the spiritual life. I quote from some of her works.
Portrait, Part 2:	In spite of her independence of mind and her capable leadership, the Queen of Sheba is also an example of someone understanding the need for guidance. She undertook a long journey to have the chance of asking Solomon many questions about the world, the meaning of life, and God. I dramatise the scene of the Queen of Sheba learning from Solomon. Sitting at his feet she benefited from revelation and Solomon's personal intelligence.
Reflection:	No one can make progress in his path to God without the help of other people. I explain the rule of having a spiritual guide, a rule begun by the fathers in the desert (Rodrigues). I give the example of learning a skill from a master, pointing

out that much in the spiritual life is a matter of experience. I quote once more the Indian saint Bahina Bhai, how she herself learned to pray from Tukaram and what she says about the use of the spiritual guide. I indicate some of the practical ways in which we can get spiritual help: from superiors, our confessor, our companions, and so on.

Portrait, Part 3:   I conclude by stressing some of the unusual features of the Queen of Sheba. She was an Old Testament, non-Jewish saint, who became the type of a true religious seeker. Christ praised her and saw that people like her would play a role at the last judgement. Although she was a pagan she will put many of those who heard the Gospel to shame.

I believe that the similarity to and difference from the story-reflection presentation will be clear from the above example. When we have *a story* we move from one event to another. One division of the story into parts will be dictated by the inner dynamic tension of action within the story. When we present *a portrait*, however, our description will be static. Instead of saying, "he did this, then that", we will be saying, "he was like this, he was like that". The different parts of the portrait will be based on the distinct qualities of the personality that we describe, the one after the other.

I have found that some people, when attempting this approach, are inclined to present their biblical personality in what may best be called a brief chronological biographical description. What I mean is that they try to take us through a person's life from birth, through childhood and youth, to adulthood and old age. The presentation of David is then divided into three parts: David as a boy, David as a young man, and David as the mature king.

In my experience such an approach proves unsatisfactory. First of all, the rapid sweep through a person's life usually degenerates into an enumeration of small facts and events, instead of elaborating individual scenes or powerful descriptions that can well be imagined. Secondly, there are few biblical personalities about whom we have such a complete range of information. Thirdly, when presenting a person in a portrait our stress should not fall on the time element in his life, but rather on an aspect of his personality that inspires us. To my mind we reach our purpose better if, for instance, we present

David as a strong leader (part 1), then as a sinner (part 2), and finally as a man of prayer (part 3). Each of these three aspects of David should be documented by referring to incidents that happened throughout his life.

The distinctive characteristic of true biography is the change in a person, the growth of character, the development brought about by fortune, and so on. Saul, for instance, began as a humble and devout leader, but slowly became proud and self-reliant. The change in his personality is part of the message. However, even in this case, it is not necessary to recount this change by moving through Saul's life in a chronological order. The contrast between his earlier humility and later pride can be brought out by a portrait of the proud Saul with biographical flashbacks to the way Saul used to be. In general it is advisable to portray the person at a definite moment in his life, with references when required to what went before or what was to come afterwards.

THE RIGHT CHOICE

Personality protraits have their impact because the hearer tends to identify himself with the person described. To make the most of this process we should choose personality examples suited to our audience. When speaking to women, our best model will be a woman. Usually, audience, topic and situation will go hand in hand to fix our choice.

When addressing a group of Women, good personalities to present might be: Judith (leadership in society), Sarah (preparation for marriage), Ruth (bridging social and cultural gaps), Hannah (guiding children to God), Jezebel (influence over the husband for good or bad), Esther (the tension between one's private life and a social function) and Deborah (the matter of emancipation).

However, we should not exaggerate this stress for a 'mirror-person' to suit a particular audience. Any human being, whatever his status, age or background, can identify himself with any other human person. Sometimes too great a similarity between the portrait and the audience results in a negative reaction. We should not give children only examples of children. Children like to identify themselves with adults, as we can see from children's games, and they feel underrated if we do not present examples from adult life. Whatever our audience, our portrait should be presented to them in such a way that they see its relevance for their own lives. This is not so difficult as human nature is basically the same for everyone and people quickly enter into another person's life. H. V. Morton rightly says in *Women of the Bible*, (London, 1940 page 4):

"The more we know of our fellow men, and the more closely we study the lives of those who have gone before us, the more clearly do we realise that the strings of the heart are numbered, and that the harmony or the discord that life draws from us is the same old tune that has been running through the world since mankind was born to sorrow and joy. The changes, the inventions, the fashion which are the keynote of our time, are perhaps apt to make us forget that men and women have not changed much since the age of Genesis."

This leads us on to another point. There are some persons about whom the Bible gives a lot of information, such as Abraham, Jacob or Joseph, the Viceroy of Egypt. They appear in the limelight of salvation history. Our attention is easily drawn to them. But there are other persons who play a rather secondary role, who appear on the scene for only a short time. Yet these too may have a valuable message through their personality. By an ingenious use of the often scanty information offered by the Bible, by our knowledge of the general background situation and a lot of poetic imagination, we can draw a fuller picture of such personalities that will not fail to make an impression on our audience.

Suppose that you want to speak on the Holy Eucharist. Your sermon is meant to be delivered during the "Family Eucharist". Going through the Gospel passages dealing with the subject, you will come across the boy who gave the five loaves and two fishes that Jesus was to multiply (John 6,9). What do we know about him? He was introduced to Jesus by St. Andrew (John 6,8). He was among those following Jesus in admiration for his teaching (John 6,2). The rest we can reconstruct from other Gospel texts and a little imagination. The boy was attracted to Jesus. Perhaps he used to help the apostles, or he came along with his father to listen to Jesus. When there was a shortage of food, it was he who happened to have some bread and fish with him. Gladly he stepped forward to lay this food – all he had – in Jesus' hands. Perhaps he expected that Jesus and the twelve would eat it. Then imagine his surprise when Jesus worked the miracle. *His* bread and *his* fish never came to an end under the breaking touch of a smiling Jesus! So, we too, in Eucharist, offer ourselves, however small we are, to see our offering multiplied infinitely by its becoming Jesus' own sacrifice.

Or, you may wish to discuss compassion. It may be that the penitent David, St. Mary Magdelene, the sorrowful St. Peter or the good thief, have been presented by you on other occasions. Why not take, for a change, the interesting case of one of the sons of Jacob, Judah? It was Judah who was mainly responsible for selling Joseph to strangers (Genesis 37). But his heart was touched by God's grace. Without recognising the Viceroy of Egypt as the brother he had injured, he made in his presence a sincere confession of his sins, and he irrevocably offered his own life for that of Benjamin (Gen 44, 18-34). He was thereupon granted forgiveness by Joseph and by God (See the Messianic promise in Gen 49,8-12). He became a model of true conversion.

Again, we might wish to stress the Gospel teaching about helping a person in need. The parable of the Good Samaritan may have been read as the Sunday Gospel and we do not want to bore our audience by unnecessary repetition. Why not spend some time on Pharaoh's daughter, who saved Moses' life (Ex 2,5-10)? From Egyptian history we can reconstruct quite well the kind of life such a princess lived, her riches, pleasures, distractions. The Bible's words about her, "The baby wept and she had compassion", shows that she was a tender, kindly and brave person. At considerable risk to her own security she saved a person who needed her help. Race or religion did not matter to her; she was moved because she heard the child weep and realised its danger. What better parallel can we find to what Jesus meant when he told the parable of the Good Samaritan?

SOME DO'S AND DON'TS

The question may arise as to how far we can use our imagination in filling in details we require to present our portrait. Are we not doing an injustice to Scripture by exerting ourselves to find more in it than we actually do? The answer lies in keeping a sense of proportion. Wherever possible, we should try to remain faithful to the biblical text, making the fullest use of the details actually given in the Bible. Usually much more material is provided by the scriptural account than we at first realise. It is a good piece of advice, therefore, to read the scriptural text more than once and to take careful note of what is given before we start enlarging the picture with other means. It is a good idea too, to use the actual words of Scripture wherever this proves feasible.

When the information provided by Scripture remains deficient, we should not be afraid to use our poetic imagination in order to ensure that the portrait will achieve its purpose. After all, it is not the details themselves that count, but making the overall message of the

Bible understood and accepted by our audience. We would not be faithful stewards of God's word if we were to neglect its substance by anxiety over immaterial details. Moreover, when we apply our imagination we can indicate this to our audience so that they can distinguish between the hard facts of Scripture and the imaginative touches of our own presentation.

Here follows a small example of how this could be done in practice:
"Elijah, the new Moses, was truly the image of a man of God. He wore a cloak of camel's hair and a loin cloth of leather (2 Kings 1,8). *We may well imagine* that he had a long beard. His face showed the sharp features of a man used to fasting and penance. He ate twice a day. His simple meals consisted of a piece of bread in the morning and some meat in the evening (1 Kings 17,6). *He surely must have been* of a robust physique for we are told that on one occasion he ran faster than the horses of Ahab's chariot (1 Kings, 18,46). Moreover, we are told that he took an active part in executing the 450 prophets of Baal (1 Kings 18,22,40). . ." (The references to scripture verses are only given to show which details derive from Bible texts).

Another matter we have to dwell on is the need to maintain some kind of consistency in our portrayal of biblical personalities. In the course of our preaching, giving conferences or teaching catechism, the same personalities will occur again and again. People retain what we have told them before, and being presented with a series of conflicting images about the same person confuses and upsets.

Popular presentation has a tendency to over-simplify character. In "popular" films the main characters are classified as either very good or very bad. The world is divided into two camps: the innocent heroes on the one side; the rogues on the other. If we want to be true to the Bible and remain consistent in our presentation of it, we will have to learn to shade our examples, not to paint our portraits either too white or too black.

David can be held out as the model of a good and familiar friend of God with the gift of profound personal prayer. He possessed courage and faith. On the other hand he also committed serious sins on various occasions and was not allowed to build the temple because he was "a man of blood". Are we going to present him as a "good" or "bad" character? The answer is that, from whatever angle we present David we should somehow leave room for both his positive and his negative qualities.

Inexperienced preachers are sometimes tempted to adduce many examples in the same sermon or conference. Speaking about the enormous influence of good political leaders they might refer to Hezekiah, Josiah, and Mattathias to prove their point. Usually the attempt fails. The audience is confused and not really convinced because it does not know the biblical text sufficiently well to see the force of all these examples. The moral is clear. It is better to present one well worked out, powerful portrait than ten badly presented ones. It is the quality of involvement rather than the quantity of models that determines success.

THE ONE-POINT EXAMPLE

So far we have been discussing how portraits of biblical personalities help us to put across a scriptural message. There is another kind of Scripture text, related to personality, that contains a message in a different way. I mean the one-point example. This refers to the many incidents narrated in Scripture where a certain person made the right or the wrong decision. The action itself and its consequences contain a lesson relevant to us today. One-point examples are good material for short homilies or for illustrations in the course of longer expositions. I will mention a few to indicate the kind of text I mean.

Joshua was deceived by the Gibeonites. He believed they came from a far country and made a covenant with them. He made this mistake because he had neglected to consult God (Jos 9,1-18). We should ask God for guidance even when we think we know what is right.

Elisha offered to Joash the victory over Aram. Joash only responded half-heartedly. If he had had more confidence and determination he would have been given a complete victory (2 Kings, 13,14-19). We receive only small favours from God because of our own lack of confidence.

Jonathan knew that he was dealing with a devious man when he went to talk to Trypho. Yet he was deceived by Trypho's hypocrisy and so lost his own life and those of 3,000 companions (1 Mac 12,39-53). When dealing with treacherous people we do well to be extremely prudent.

When Nehemiah was rebuilding the walls of Jerusalem his enemies tried to distract him from the task. But Nehemiah knew where his priority lay. "I cannot come down to meet you. I am engaged in a great undertaking" (Neh 6,1-3). Nothing should keep us from our main task in life, such as looking after our own spiritual welfare.   ▪

Eleazar refused to eat pork, even though secretly other meat had been substituted for it. He knew that his example would strengthen the resolve of his fellow-Jews and would help many others be faithful to the Law. He died a martyr's death for his convictions (2 Mac 6,18-31). We are not allowed to give a bad example to weaker brethren even if our actions are excusable in themselves.

When Naaman had been cured of his leprosy, Elisha's servant Gehazi asked Naaman for a financial reward. He was punished for his greed. He contracted the leprosy which Naaman had lost (2 Kings 5,20-27). Greed may bring us material wealth, but it also brings the misery such wealth entails.

Such one-point examples can sometimes be presented best by the defect-example-moral sequence. First, we point out the defect in us which we illustrate from experiences known to our audience. We then present the one-point biblical example, indicating how its moral teaches us how to overcome the defect. Priests who always find an excuse to miss their annual retreat (the experience of the defect) may be inspired by the determined stand of Nehemiah to reconsider their attitude. One-point examples are like small darts that may prick our conscience into action.

CHAPTER EIGHT

MOTIFS AND THEMES

When the UNCTAD met in New Delhi in 1974, the French delegation rejected a certain draft because it incorporated the term, "gentleman's agreement". The French said, "We don't know what that means. We don't have that word in our language". At the time many people scoffed at the French objection which they thought absurd. But I maintain the French were right. If we don't have a word for something in our language, that reality does not exist for us. The idea of making a "gentleman's agreement" includes a wealth of notions that are interconnected and that make the idea work: a person's code of honour, mutual trust, an attitude of give-and-take that is opposed to legal formality. When we translate terms like these, or transfer them to another culture, there is bound to be confusion. The result is that a term like "gentleman's agreement" is retained in its Anglo-Saxon form even when it is used in other languages.

I began with this example because there is considerable confusion about terms regarding the topic of the present chapter. The phenomenon we will discuss may, according to standard dictionaries, be designated by the proper English terms "theme" or "motive". But on account of the many other connotations these terms have in present-day English, I prefer to follow the example of modern English writers and employ the term "motif" (pronounced moteef; from the French), or "leitmotiv" (pronounced light moteef; from the German). As these terms originated in music and the fine arts, we had better begin with some comparative study.

MOTIFS IN WORKS OF ART

The Philistines settled on the Gaza coast around 1150 B.C. Their precise country of origin remains uncertain. What we know is that they came by sea, tried to enter Egypt but were defeated and driven out by Pharoah Ramses III. Wherever they came from then, the Philistines brought their distinctive art and culture with them. A remnant of this Philistine civilisation has been uncovered by archaeology. According to its findings the Philistines used a kind of pottery not found elsewhere in Palestine. Philistine earthenware flasks, wine containers and beer jugs have a characteristic shape of their own. The yellow-grey ground is usually covered with paintings of black and red geometrical figures, the space between the bands and spirals has often been filled with carefully painted swans. (See Figs. 23 and 24). The swans are normally depicted according to a fixed design. The swan turns its head back, apparently to smooth out its feathers. The wings are slightly lifted up, the tips pointing downwards.

Fig. 23. Philistine jug.

W. F. Albright remarks that the wing resembles nothing so much as a crumpled up bolt of lightning. The swan is sometimes varied by other figures such as a fish, but without any doubt the swan is the most frequent design. The swan occurs on the pottery of many different settlements. We find it again and again on pottery that can be dated over various centuries. Artisans must have copied its design from one generation to the next. Customers must have liked to have the design on the pottery they bought. Obviously some importance must have been attached to this particular figure. The most likely explanation is that the swan, like other animals that are related to water, was considered a symbol of fertility, wealth and prosperity. Having the swan on a jar was a mark of good luck, a blessing, a painted prayer.

The design of the swan is a "motif" of Philistine art. We may call it a "motif" because:
   (1) it is a feature that frequently recurs in the work of art; and
   (2) it expresses an important idea of the artist.

Fig. 24. A Philistine wine container.

Both elements are essential for the complete understanding of the term. At times one finds the term used loosely for any pattern, figure or design as in "the curtain was covered with gold embroidered animal motifs". But this is a weakened and derived use of the word. In its original meaning "motif" is: a predominant idea of the artist which governs all the details of his work; a feature, design or figure that prevails in varying forms throughout a composition; a recurring salient thematic element or feature of a work of art.

The motif need not be a particular object or recognisably different design. It can be a picture, an element, an aspect of something else. It may be contained in the way another object or reality is expressed.

Fig. 25. Two typical Dorian sculptures from the 6th century B.C.

To illustrate this the reader should study Figures 25 and 26 which show some samples of ancient Greek sculpture of the 6th century B.C. A remarkable characteristic of this sculpture is that both human and divine persons were always protrayed with a smile. It has been called the "archaic smile" as it disappears as a feature in later classical Greek art. Portraying gods and men with a smile on their face was a very deliberate practice. The smile has been delicately carved, not only in the carving of the lips, but also in the expression of the eyes and the rest of the face. How unusual this smile is can be seen best in the statue of the Dying Soldier (Fig. 26). Although the statue is extremely realistic in all other details, in the position of a body thrown to the ground, in the tension of the muscles and so on, the face has been given the expression of a smile!

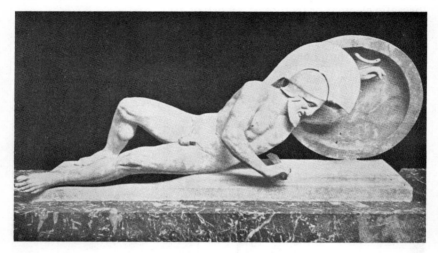

Fig. 26. The Dying Soldier (480 B.C.)

C. W. M. Verhoeven, who has made a special study of this feature, explains it as a particular early Greek interpretation of human and divine life. The smile was purposely added, he says, to liberate the work of art from everyday life. Statues were not made to record living persons, but to bring out the greatness, the other-worldliness of extraordinary beings. The gods and goddesses are portrayed in human form, but by the smile of transcendence on their faces they are marked off as persons free from our mortal world. Statues were also made of kings and heroes but only after their death. On their faces too the smile of transcendence indicates the new status of immortality they have acquired. This explains the paradox of the Dying Soldier who smiles. The smile on his face marks him as a hero who has gained immortality.

For the ancient Greeks the smile was a self-evident symbol. For us it is not. We first need to recognise it as a motif and this we do because it occurs so often. If only one Greek statue from the earlier centuries had been discovered, we would probably not have been able to interpret the archaic smile correctly. We might have thought it no more than a realistic trait of the person portrayed. We would have ascribed the smile to happiness or kindness in the individual depicted. But once we have recognised it as a motif, our interpretation of the smile will greatly differ even when judging one particular statue.

Elusiveness is the amazing characteristic of a motif. Whenever it occurs it implies a special interpretation for a work of art, or an individual part of it, but before we can make such an interpretation we have to study the motif as it occurs throughout a culture or a whole piece of art. It slips from our grasp until we have got a firm grip on it.

MOTIFS IN SCRIPTURE

Tradition tells us that St. Luke, the author of the third Gospel, was a citizen of Antioch in Syria. He became a christian around the year 45 A.D. A few years later he joined St. Paul at Troas to assist him in his mission among the Greeks in Macedonia. As far as we know, Luke stayed in the Greek town of Philippi for six years, helping to build up the christian community there. St. Luke wrote his Gospel for young Greek converts, trying to show them, from authentic sources of the life of Jesus, how his message fulfilled their highest aspiration.

If we read St. Luke's Gospel we are struck by the number of times he stresses that Jesus brings us joy. At Jesus' birth the angel announced, "I have good news for you which will bring great joy to all the people" (2,11). A similar tiding of joy accompanies the announcement of the coming of John the Baptist (1,14). Our Lady called out "Rejoice, rejoice, my spirit, in God my Saviour" (1, 48). Such joy runs as a motif throughout the Gospel. The 72 disciples returned to Jesus in great joy (10,17). "All the people rejoiced over every wonderful thing Jesus did" (13,17). Jesus too preached about the joy of conversion when he said, "There will be more joy in heaven over one sinner who repents than over 99 respectable people who do not need to repent" (15,7). The Gospel ends with a remark about the joy of the apostles after Jesus' ascension. "They went back into Jerusalem filled with great joy" (24,52).

This explicit stress on joy is a peculiar trait of Luke's Gospel. Matthew, Mark and John speak of it too, but not to the same degree. The joy which the early Christians shared as a community in the Holy Spirit was an experience of the greatest importance to Luke. He often records in the Acts the immense joy and happiness of the communities after conversion: at Jerusalem (2,37), at Samaria (8,8) at Antioch of Pisidia (13,48.52) and elsewhere (see 8, 39). He describes the joy in the Holy Spirit resulting from receiving encouraging news (11,24: 50,3: 15,31, etc.). He mentions the paradoxical Christian joy of being thought worthy to suffer for Christ (5,31). We hear an echo of St. Paul's injunction, "Rejoice in the Lord always, I say it again, rejoice!" (Phil 4,4). Knowing this background, the frequent mention of joy in the life and message of Jesus takes on a deeper dimension.

Joy in St. Luke's Gospel is a motif in the full sense of the word because it is a recurring factor arising from a predominant idea of the author. The implications of this from a scriptural point of view are far-reaching. When we discover a true motif, we are certain that the author was interested in the idea it conveys, that it was part of his deliberate teaching. It is something the inspired author wanted to put across and so it is an element covered by inspiration. A true motif always contains a message worth meditating about and communicating to others.

Every author has a number of motifs that he wants to convey through the way he composes his writing. This is the reason why we have four Gospels instead of one. Each of the four evangelists presented the life and message of Jesus for a particular audience and with special aims in mind. As they could not and would not alter the substantial traditions available, the evangelists would bring out their specific interests by a process of selection, emphasis and interpretation.

To stay with St. Luke, we find this evangelist bringing out such motifs as the central role played by Jerusalem (a new thing for non-Jewish converts); the universality of Christ's mission (to contrast Christianity with Jewish proselytism); and the distinct contribution of women (as women were more emancipated in the Greek world).

ZOOMING IN AND WEEDING OUT

How do we discover the right motifs? It is possible to make frightful mistakes. Before we may confidently regard a motif as truly biblical we should not only be able to answer the question, "Does it occur often in the text?", but also "Does it represent an idea in the mind of the author? What was the predominant interest that gave rise to the motif?" Bible dictionaries and at times even books on so-called "Bible themes", may misguide us. The simple repetition of a word or an idea does not make it into a motif.

The reader will pardon me for giving some examples of spurious motifs that I have actually come across. To punish mankind God sent his rain in the deluge (Gen 6-9). God rained fire and sulphur on Sodom to destroy it (Lk 17,29). So whenever God sends rain it is a sign of punishment for sin (sic!). If we read that the Father "sent his rain on the honest and dishonest alike" (Mt 5,45) we should understand it as meaning that all alike suffer under his punishments. The rain that shakes the house upon the rock and brings down the house built on sand (Mt 7,24-27) is God's punishment that strikes all alike. The particular preachers in question, who belonged to an ultra-conservative evangelical group, even added that the increase of rain in the past years manifestly expressed God's anger about the spread of sin in modern society.

Less disastrous, but still questionable from a scriptural point of view, is a sermon based on all the occasions when Jesus said, "O woman". "Great is thy faith" (Mt 15,28); "O woman, you are free from your sickness" (Lk 13,12); "O woman, what is there between you and me?" I Jn 2,4); "O woman, this is your son!" (Jn 19,26) and "O woman, why do you weep?" (Jn 20,13). At first sight the attempt seems intriguing but then we realise that "O woman" is not a true motif. It was simply the ordinary way in which one would address a lady respectfully. Seeing a profound significance (a part of the inspired message?) in its repeated use is as out of place as discovering a sinister undertone in a person's daily "Good morning" at breakfast.

Another danger besetting us when we want to communicate a motif is the temptation to adduce too many instances in which the motif is found. Some motifs are so strong in the Bible that we can be almost overwhelmed by them.

Take, for instance, the motif "God's word". It comes back hundreds of times throughout the Old and New Testaments. We find it at Creation, throughout the history of salvation, through the Prophets, in the Wisdom books, the Gospels, the letters of St. Paul, Acts and Revelation! Trying to do justice to such a motif requires a course of thirty lectures or a book of 200 pages. Attempting to present this motif in its entirety in a conference or sermon (as I have experienced from one speaker) is as futile as trying to pour the ocean into the proverbial hole on the beach.

The only way of dealing satisfactorily with such a motif is to be extremely selective in the material and to present the few passages chosen in a very thorough manner.

We could, for instance, take the Old Testament notion that God rules history by his word. There is a constant motif, that occurs more than twenty times in the historical books, "All this happened according to the Word that Yahweh had spoken". From among these texts I could choose three important ones, such as Joshua's evaluation after the conquest: "You know that not one thing has failed of all the good things which the Lord your God promised concerning you" (Jos 23,14-15); Solomon's prayer at the consecration of the temple, "Not one word has failed of all the good promises which God uttered by Moses his Servant" (1 Kings 8,56). I would join to this the passage from 1 Corinthians where Paul says that God keeps his promise and will not allow us to be tempted beyond our power (10,13). If we work out at some length what the first two passages mean, how the Jews experienced God's presence during the conquest and the attainment of prosperity culminating in the building of the temple, how they experienced God's fidelity to his promise through these events, we will understand better why St. Paul can appeal to God's fidelity.

Not every motif, however authentic, lends itself equally well to effective communication. Some motifs are rather abstruse or general or abstract. They are usually expressed in polysyllabic, heavy, ponderous words of Romanic origin. I think of words like gratitude, providence, humility and others. Some preachers seem to have a predilection for this type of motif, forgetting that their audience is badly in need of something more definite, something tangible and visual to fix its mind on. Motifs that are expressed in objects or things that can be seen, touched or smelled in one's imagination, are much to be preferred. They capture the mind more easily, and, surprisingly enough, are not less profound in thought.

Consider the virtue of humility. The term means something all right, yet it is vague and abstract. When we study Jesus' teaching on humility, we find that he employed expressive examples. One example that kept recurring as a true motif in Jesus' life and teaching was "taking the lower place". Jesus spoke of this when Peter and James wanted to have the best places in his Kingdom (Mt 20,20-28), when he rejected the pride of the Pharisees (Mt 23,5-12), and when he addressed the guests at the dinner party (Lk 14,7-11). Jesus himself took the "lower place" when he was born in a stable (Lk 2,7), when he wanted to be baptised by John (Mt 3,13), when he washed his disciples' feet (Jn 13,3-17) and so on. Instead of speaking about "humility" as the connecting thread in our exposition we would do well, therefore, to take *this* motif from Jesus' life. With a little explanation of the Jewish preoccupation with precedence in the synagogue, at banquets and in public meetings, and some reflections on what "taking a lower seat" would mean for us today, it would probably come across as a very inspiring and thought provoking message on humility!

We may summarise this section by noting the following practical guidelines. We should check our motifs for their biblical validity. From among the many passages in which the motif occurs we should select a few representative ones and present these well. We should give preference to the kind of motif that is visual and expressive. This will involve a good deal of weeding out of irrelevant material and zooming in on a limited, but attractive motif that will capture the imagination.

MOTIF-INSPIRED EXPOSITION OF A TEXT

Although the direct exposition of a motif may often prove quite satisfactory, experimenting with a variety of methods and techniques has convinced me that one particular way of presenting usually proves the most satisfying from many points of view. I call this mode of presentation "the motif-inspired exposition of a text". I will try to explain how it is built up and why this approach has certain advantages.

It is a well-known rule in communication that we should not present our hearers with an amorphous mass of information. For the sake of simplicity and to aid concentration, we need to give our audience a foothold, a fixed point in our discussion on which they can focus their minds.

Rembrandt knew this well. In all his later paintings we find a patch of light on the main subject of his picture. The surrounding figures and the background will be purposely left in a less well-lit area, or even in a shade. On account of this so-called "chiaroscuro" effect, Rembrandt makes it very easy for the observer to grasp the painting in one glance.

In oral communication too, there is a need for such a unifying factor. Instead of speaking about a motif in general and moving from one text to another, it seems much better to focus attention on one particular Bible text (which contains the motif) and then deepen its meaning by reference to other passages where the motif occurs.

Another advantage deriving from this manner of presentation in sermons is that it fits in better with our present arrangement of the liturgy. Following ancient tradition we have three readings in the Sunday liturgy, the first from the Old Testament, the second from St. Paul's letters and the third from the Gospels. Preachers rightly prefer to stay close to the subject matter referred to in these readings, particularly to what was said in the Gospel passage. Now we know that in our up-dated lectionary the first reading of every Sunday has been chosen to fit the Gospel message of that Sunday. From a liturgical point of view therefore, it would be handy if we could focus attention on a phrase found in the Gospel text of that day and explain this phrase with reference to the first reading and other Bible texts. In other words, if we find a motif in our Sunday Gospel text, the motif-inspired exposition fits in beautifully with the structure of our liturgical readings.

How exactly do we set about composing a sermon of this kind? On the sixteenth Sunday of the year (cycle 3) the first reading from Genesis 18 records how Abraham gave hospitality to God. The Gospel text contains the episode of Mary and Martha (Lk 10,38-42). We scan the Gospel passage carefully and meet a genuine Lucan motif in the very first line: "A woman named Martha welcomed Jesus into her house". We remember how throughout Luke's Gospel importance is attached to this act of welcoming Jesus into one's home. It is the turning point in the life of Levi (5, 29-32). Jesus states that the sinful woman who wept over his feet gave him a greater welcome than his host (7, 44-47). Zacchaeus is converted by receiving Jesus into his home (19,1-10). The disciples of Emmaus are rewarded with the eucharistic bread when they invite Jesus: "Stay with us" (24,29). We could therefore select "making Jesus welcome in our home" as a good motif to guide our sermon. Reading the Gospel text once more, and especially our Sunday reading of Mary and Martha, we ask ourselves: "What message does this have for my congregation?" It may well be that in our Christian homes, in spite of much goodwill and many laudable customs, there is too little time given to prayer, meditation and spiritual reading, too little "sitting at Jesus' feet", with too much stress on external things. We then have the material for our sermon.

A motif-inspired exposition of the text will then follow this sequence of presentation:

We begin by drawing attention to the central passage we have chosen. In this case we refer to the phrase in the Gospel: "A woman called Martha welcomed Jesus into her house".

We give a visual description of the motif from general background knowledge.

We describe how Jesus travelled from village to village and so was dependent on the hospitality of people. After a long day's journey along the hot and dusty roads of Palestine a hearty welcome given in a particular home would be greatly appreciated. For Jews, as still with the Bedouin in the desert today, inviting a person into one's home and eating and drinking with him was the highest expression of friendship.

We now elaborate on the motif with other texts of scripture.

We recount how Jesus sought intimacy and closeness when allowing himself to be someone's guest. We illustrate this with reference to some Gospel passages that we must elaborate on sufficiently for people to appreciate the motif; perhaps Jesus' words on hospitality (7,44-47), his reception in Zacchaeus' home (19,1-10) and his revelation to the disciples of Emmaus (24).

We reflect on the meaning of the motif for us.

Here we discuss how Jesus could be made welcome in our Christian homes. We give some practical advice. We adduce examples from everyday life.

We close by referring again to our central text.

In this particular case I would conclude the sermon by a summing up of what the whole passage of Mary and Martha signifies. Martha wanted Jesus to feel at home in her house, but she missed the point when she thought that food and drink were the most important gifts she had to offer. Although Jesus appreciated Martha's care and concern, Mary had chosen the better part because she gave time to prayer and reflection.

On the same Sunday, the 16th of the year, (cycle 2), the Gospel reading mentions that Jesus "had pity on the crowds because they were like sheep without a shepherd" (Mk 6,34). The first reading is from Jeremiah and contains the promise that God himself will raise shepherds to look after his flock (23,1-6). Basing ourselves on the motif of the shepherd (Ps 23; Ex 34; Jn 10) we could make this our starting point for a good sermon on the need for fostering vocations to the priesthood.

The motif inspired explanation of the text also lends itself to conferences or religious talks on occasions outside church. A meditation on our Christian duty to help the poor in underdeveloped countries could well be centred on the biblical motif of "growing fat". Our focal text could be "Woe to you who have your fill now" (Lk 6,25). We can elaborate the motif by the parable of how Israel, the adopted son, became disloyal to God when it had grown fat on all God's gifts (Dt. 32-7-15); with the story of how the sons of Eli fattened themselves at the expense of God's honour and the good of the people (1 Sam 3, 12-13) or with the description of evil-doers as those who fatten themselves while the poor go hungry (Ps 73,1-12). Each of these three Old Testament texts add a different dimension to the motif of "growing fat". The motif might have a special meaning in the context of advocating the family fast day.

AND WHAT ABOUT BIBLICAL THEMES?

The word "theme" is quite misleading in English. Although dictionaries assure me that it *can have* the same meaning as that which I have constantly referred to as "motif", the fact remains that in everyday parlance a "theme" stands for any subject of discussion, any topic. There is a world of difference between a motif and a topic. A motif is a pattern, an emphasis, that frequently recurs in a work of art because the artist wanted it to be so. A genuine motif reveals a predominant idea in the *artist's* mind. A "topic", however, is any subject that *I myself* may choose to speak or write about.

The presence of gargoyles on the outside of Gothic cathedrals is a genuine motif. But general subjects, such as "Gothic architecture", "Gothic cathedrals", "Gothic architects", or "Gothic gutters", or anything like it, are topics. They are generalisations chosen by myself and reveal *my* way of interpreting reality, not the original artist's way.

Fig. 27. Gargoyle on the tower of the Notre Dame at Paris.

We should be aware of this when talking about "biblical themes". It is useful, and even necessary for reasons of study, to consider general topics regarding the Bible. Whole books may be devoted to subjects like "Old Testament Morality", "Sacrifice in the Temple of Jerusalem", "Prophetism in Israel", and so on. These are "themes" in the strict sense of the word. By carefully collating all the available information from scripture and from extra-biblical sources, we obtain a clearer picture of the reality discussed. But we should always remember that it is *our* way, our twentieth-century way of synthesising and interpreting that information. By presenting such a theme we are presenting our own interpetation and so we are hardly justified in calling it a "biblical" theme.

There are good reasons why we should take this word of caution seriously. We are the first-fruits of a new biblical movement in the Church. Essential to this movement is the recognition that there is nothing that should stand between ourselves and the Word of God. During the past centuries one obstacle between many christians and the Bible was precisely thematic theological synthesis which was considered superior to the Bible text. The Bible was not studied in itself but only as an auxiliary branch of dogmatic theology. Whole generations of priests and religious went to their graves without ever having read the whole Bible. Children at school learned an outline of the Bible in "Bible history class" without direct reference to the scriptural text. The intention was good, but the effect disastrous. The living biblical text can never and should never be substituted by abstraction and generalisation. We are justified in demanding a high standard of "biblical" themes. To be biblical they should speak for the Bible itself.

Speaking on "themes" also requires examination from the point of view of our role in communication. Scriptural themes or topics are, properly speaking, the preserve of the scripture class, the academic lecture. The thematic approach is therefore legitimate whenever we instruct students on the science of Scripture. But whenever we communicate Scripture in a pastoral context, whether it be a sermon, a spiritual talk, a retreat conference, or a catechism class, we are engaged in a different kind of work. Here it is not information about the topic, but the Word of God itself and its message that should come first. There is a big difference between talking about the Temple of Jerusalem as a topic, and pointing to the motif of the Temple in John's Gospel: how Jesus foresees that his own body will be the Temple (2,19-21), how he announces the Temple of the heart (4,20-24).

SERIALISED EXPOSITION OF A MOTIF

Some valuable and important Bible motifs are so rich that they cannot be sufficiently covered in a short homily or in one conference. If we have the opportunity of addressing an audience regularly, we could well spread the motif over a number of separate occasions. I call this a serialised exposition of a motif, because we deliberately plan the whole presentation as a series of separate talks.

A good illustration of what the finished product should look like is the "Dance of Death" produced by Hans Holbein the Younger in 1538. Holbein was court painter to Henry VIII but this book was published by him at Lyons in a French edition. The structure of the book is simple. Holbein selected 41 scripture passages speaking about death. He applied each particular text to a different category of person: kings, priests, monks, nuns, astrologers, physicians, etc. to cover all ranks and classes in society. He illustrated each Bible passage with a small woodcut and a four-line verse, both applied to the Scripture text and the category in question. See the text and illustration regarding the Old Woman (Fig. 28) and the Miser (Fig. 29).

THE OLD WOMAN

Death is better than a bitter life or continued sickness. *Ecclesiasticus xxx, 17.*

THE MISER

Thou fool, this night thy soul shall be required of thee: then whose shall those things be which thou hast provided? *Luke xii, 20.*

The love of life has ceased in thee,
Who long hast known this suffering strife;
Then come along to rest with me,
For Death is better now than life.

This very night shalt thou know Death!
To-morrow be encoffined fast!
Then tell me, fool! while thou hast breath,
Who'll have the gold thou hast amassed?

Figs. 28 & 29. From Holbein's "Death of Death".

Holbein's interpretation of some scripture passages is questionable. His application of these passages to specific categories of persons is arbitrary. Yet the overall outcome is a very convincing and true picture of the biblical message. He achieves this by doing two things at the same time: by taking care to make each unit an interesting section that could stand on its own, and by achieving a closely knit unity between all the sections. He makes his work all of a piece by the systematic enumeration of forty categories of persons (thus underlining that *all* men must die) and by repeating in each woodcut the figure of death. In fact, reading the booklet one sees how death dances its way through the world, sparing no single human being.

A serialised exposition of a motif should have the same qualities. There should be something new, something interesting in itself in every talk, while preserving the effect of overall unity within the whole series.

This may not be as difficult and complicated as it looks at first. Suppose you are celebrating the Eucharist for a small congregation on weekdays. You have six short homilies to prepare, each lasting approximately three minutes. Why not take as the overall motif "the gift of the promised land", as we find it in the book of Deuteronomy? For us the promised land is the Kingdom of Heaven, our spiritual life, our communion with Christ and his followers. A serialised exposition on this motif could be broken up as follows:

Monday: The land God promises is a good land (main text Dt 8,7-9).
Tuesday: The land is not acquired by our own strength but as a gift (main text Dt 6,10-12).
Wednesday: The land God gives is a holy land which we may only inhabit if we are worthy of it (main text Dt. 1,34-36).
Thursday: Enjoying the fruits of the land is a measure of God's blessing (main text Dt. 7,13).
Friday: God's holy land had to be kept undefiled (main text Dt. 21,22-23). This is, incidentally, the reason why Christ's body had to be removed from the Cross before the Sabbath day. Jesus thus became a 'curse' for our sakes (Gal. 3,13).
Saturday: Even though Moses could not enter the land himself, he was granted a vision of the Holy Land (Dt 34,1-5). The full realisation of God's Kingdom will only come in heaven.

St. Matthew highlights important moments in the life of Jesus by associating them with the tops of mountains. Through this motif he seeks to underline new beginnings, turning points that mark off Christianity from the Old Testament religion. A series of five conferences on the newness of Christian life could follow this motif.

Mt 5-7:   Sermon on the Mount. The Christian's code of sanctity contrasted with the decalogue proclaimed on Mount Sinai.
Mt 17,1-8:   Jesus' transfiguration on the mountain. In Jesus God is continually present among us. Our Christian life should be transformed by the experience of his presence.
Mt 21,1-9:   Jesus' triumphal entry from the Mount of Olives. Jesus accepts his salvific mission through suffering and crucifixion, thereby setting a norm for our understanding of life. The function of suffering and death.
Mt 25,31-46: Verdict of the last judgement (presumed to be on a mountain as it mentions God's throne). The supremacy of fraternal charity is proclaimed. God is loved in our neighbour.
Mt 28,16-20: Ascension scene on the Galilean mountain. As Moses saw the promised land from the Nebo so Jesus sees the world Church that is to begin.

Such conferences would obviously need to be worked out very well to justify such an extensive treatment, but if handled properly they could give an interesting panorama of Christian life in some of its more distinct aspects. At the same time this approach would correspond closely to what Matthew had in mind when he placed these scenes on mountain tops.

A SERMON ON EATING AND DRINKING WITH GOD

This sermon, addressed to a Teachers' Guild on a recollection day in Lent, illustrates the technique of a "direct exposition of a motif".

Easter is approaching. The austere Lenten Liturgy dominates our ceremonies: the violet vestments, the absence of flowers, the thoughtful tone of our hymns, the insistence on penance in prayers and sermons – all these remind us of death and sinfulness. With the Church we feel the need for conversion and redemption. We want to prepare ourselves, through reflection and self denial. We want to feel happy and free from sin when the Church in a few weeks' time will burst out with joy in the Paschal Celebration!

What will Easter mean for me, and for those whom I must lead and guide in this preparation? Will Easter be merely a series of external festivities? Or, will it mean a joyful reaffirmation of our Faith, a renewed change of heart, a more intimate union with God through Holy Eucharist? How should we prepare for that great moment of the Easter communion? It is no waste of effort to reflect on the meaning of Easter. We must take time to absorb and understand its message, so as to live it and spread it around us. What benefit would we and our students or families derive from wearing new clothes or eating Easter eggs if the deep significance of Easter escaped us?

Most of our feasts such as Easter are marked by festive meals, by a lot of "eating and drinking". It may be helpful to remember that Easter means our privilege of being allowed to "eat and drink" with God. I will trace this motif through some of the most important parts of Scripture.

At the Last Supper, Jesus told his disciples that he would not eat and drink with them again until the Kingdom of God were set up (Lk 22,16-18). In other words, the next time he would eat and drink with them was to be at Easter, when the Kingdom of God had been inaugurated! This gives a good starting-point to our reflection:

Jesus at Easter.

To the Jews, "eating and drinking with someone" meant being someone's intimate friend. One ate only with close relatives and near friends. No, it meant more: in the time of the Patriarchs, eating and drinking with another implied that one ratified a pact of friendship. Isaac and Abimelech concluded their covenant of brotherhood by "eating and drinking together" (Gen 26/30). Jacob and Laban similarly celebrated a lasting agreement with such a meal taken in common (Gen 31,45-54). According to Sacred Scripture, the sharing of food and drink expresses a mutual bond of friendship and brotherhood, a very intimate relationship. We read how God sent a lion to kill a negligent prophet, because he "ate and drank" with the sinful people of Bethel! (3 Kings 13,1-32).

In Paradise Adam and Eve were God's Guests. In this garden of delight God had planted many trees "pleasant to the sight and good for food" (Gen 2,8-17). What does Scripture indicate with these words? It implies that Adam and Eve were allowed to eat God's own food and drink from his river. It wants us to understand that God made men his intimate friends, that he accepted them as his own children, giving them his own life (sanctifying grace).

We all know how sadly mankind disappointed God, symbolized in the sin of our first parents. They disobeyed their father and master by transgressing his command. They greatly offended their generous host by eating of the forbidden fruit. God had to punish them by sending them out of Paradise, away from the tree of life. No longer were they allowed to eat and drink at God's table; in the sweat of their brow they were to work for their own bread (Gen 3,17-24).

Mankind was in sin. Man was separated from God. But in his infinite goodness Almighty God was already planning salvation. He wished to bring men back into his household and make them his own children again. He would send his own Son to bring about this reconciliation. To prepare the way for this Redeemer, he chose the Jewish people and revealed his purpose to them.

God's gesture of friendship took the form of a Covenant with the Jewish people. This pact of alliance was concluded with a sacrificial meal. Moses and Aaron together with seventy elders from among the people were allowed to share in this banquet on Sinai: "They ate and drank" in the presence of Almighty God (Ex 24,9-11). Year after year this Sacrifice of the Covenant was repeated and celebrated on various occasions. At the pasch each Jewish family would offer a lamb in sacrifice and then join in a holy meal, to partake of the offering (Dt 16,1-7). In such ways God began to realise his desire to call men and invite them back home. The new friendship he opened to them was still very imperfect. It was more like a picnic in God's presence than a real sharing of food with him! But it prepared the way.

God eventually did send his Son to redeem us. As Jesus Christ, he became one of us. Adam and Eve had sinned by wanting their own food and spurning God's will. Jesus Christ, the representative of all mankind, made it his food "to do the Will of the Father" (Jn 4,31-34) and, at the hour of trial expressed his determination to "drink the chalice" of painful obedience (cf. Jn 18,11). Where men had sinned through disobedience, Jesus in their name offered the sacrifice of supreme obedience. The highest expression of that total obedience and that deepest worship was his death on Calvary. The triumphant sign that God had accepted this sacrifice, was the Resurrection of Jesus Christ at Easter!

The significance of Easter is the success, the victory of Jesus' sacrifice. Through this sacrifice we are all entitled again to be God's children and to sit at his Table as his intimate friends. Can we be surprised, then, that Jesus chose a sacrificial meal as the way of celebrating victory? At the Last Supper he instituted the most wonderful banquet the world has ever witnessed! Under the species of bread and wine his sacrificial Body and Blood were to be made present. By attending this consecration and giving their assent to its meaning, his followers for ever after would join themselves to his supreme sacrifice. And – more wonderful still – through the eating and drinking of his Body and Blood they were to share his own inner life, his own Love of the Father manifested in his sacrifice. Could Jesus have realised the "eating and drinking with God" in a more profound way than this?

"Take and eat. This is my Body that will be handed over for your sake".

"Drink of this, everyone of you; for this is my Covenant-Blood that will be shed for the sake of many with a view to forgiveness of sins" (Mt 26,26-28; Lk 22,19-20).

At Easter we joyfully celebrate the victory of Jesus' sacrifice over death and sin. Through him we are invited to sit at God's table. As God's intimate friends, as his own children, we can eat and drink with him. We know that in the same way as Jesus Christ has risen and is now gloriously present at God's right hand, so we too shall one day rise with our bodies and be eternally happy in God's presence. Our "eating and drinking with God" will not end here on earth: for all eternity we shall share in God's love and happiness. During the Paschal celebration the Church exults with joy over those consoling truths.

In preparation for this feast the Church urges on us the practice of fasting. She wants us to fast not only from material food, but from our attachment to self, to pleasure, to material goods. The Church expects us to make our own the sentiments of Christ, to join him in his rejection of sin, in his love of God and self-sacrifice. This is why the Church desires that we solemnly re-affirm the obligations we took on ourselves at Baptism. During the Easter night she makes us repeat those promises of friendship with God, first uttered when God gave us his life through the flow of water.

But, most of all, the Church wants us at Easter to partake of the Eucharist in a very special way. As a good mother who urges even her reluctant children to take what is good for them, she enjoins on us the Easter communion as a grave obligation. But whoever has grasped the meaning of Easter will not see this as an "obligation" but as a "need"; if at any time of the year, then certainly at Easter each believer has to share fully in the sacrifice of Jesus by "eating and drinking" of his Meal!

Yes, the unspeakable privilege of "eating and drinking with God" at the sacrificial table of the Eucharist urges us to go every Sunday and share in this celebration. This is the deepest reason of our Sunday obligation as well as of the "Easter communion". If we understand what Easter means, every Sunday will be appreciated as a small Easter of its own.

MEDITATION ON FRIENDSHIP AND RECONCILIATION

A prayer service for high school students has been dedicated to the theme of friendship. After a reading from the Gospel (Jn 15,11-17) and the singing of an appropriate hymn, the following text is given as a "meditation". The text is to be followed by shared, spontaneous prayer.

It is an ordinary Sabbath day in the month of Tammuz of the year 160 B.C. We are visiting Jerusalem and have heard about the great teacher Jesus ben Sirach. We have attended the Sabbath service in a nearby synagogue and are just entering the living room of Sirach's house.

There he sits on a low couch, his yellow talith over his shoulders, a black skullcap on his head, and a long flowing white beard covering his chest. Keen students have already taken their places on the mat in front of the teacher. The room is low and dark. The light from a small window in the wall is strengthened by the shine of some flickering oil lamps placed here and there in the apartment. Those who have come to listen to the master greet him and speak with one another in low murmurs.

Jesus ben Sirach is not an ordinary teacher. He has great experience. He has tasted the realities of life. For some time he has worked in a government office. He has helped his brother run a prosperous business. He has fought in a war and has seen famine and destruction. He has travelled to many countries and knows people from all ranks of society. Yes, Jesus ben Sirach is a knower of men. He knows their weaknesses, their ambitions and their struggles. He realises that it is his duty to explain God's law in such a way that people can put it into practice in their everyday lives. Today we will listen to his instruction.

Sirach fixes his eyes on the eager faces around him and begins to speak: "My dear children, today I would like to speak to you about friendship. All of us need friends. Whether you live by the work of your hands, whether you are a governor ruling the people, whether you are a priest employed in the temple or a scribe studying the law, you will need some good friends to help you stay on the right path.

> A faithful friend is a sure shelter,
> whoever finds one has found a rare treasure.
> A faithful friend is something beyond price,
> there is no measuring his worth.
> A faithful friend is the assurance of life,
> and those who fear the Lord will find one.
> Whoever fears the Lord makes true friends,
> for as a man is so are all his friends.
>
> (Sir 6,14-17).

Of course, everybody likes to have friends. We like to have people with us who are kind to us and help us. But many people lose their friends after some time because they do not trust them. It may be a friend is doing something we had not expected. It may be that someone else reports on his actions to us. I once knew a merchant who cut off a good friendship because he thought, without sufficient reason, that his friend had cheated him in a business deal. When his friend tried to explain the real facts the merchant did not even want to listen to him.

> Do not find fault before making thorough inquiry.
> First reflect, then give a reprimand.
> Listen before you answer,
> And do not interrupt a speech in the middle.
>
> (Sir 11,7-8).

Some people can be so angry about the faults of their friends that they turn their feelings into resentment and hatred. Two friends I knew became deadly enemies in this fashion. Although they brought sacrifices to the Lord at the same altar, they would not even speak to one another. I cannot understand how such people can pray to God with a clear conscience. God disapproves of such disposition of mind. We should be ready to forgive our friend whatever he may have done against us.

> Forgive your neighbour the hurt he does you,
> and when you pray, your sins will be forgiven.
> If a man nurses anger against another,
> can he then demand compassion from the Lord?
> Showing no pity for a man like himself,
> can he then plead for his own sins?
> Mere creature of flesh, he cherishes resentment;
> who will forgive him *his* sins?
>
> (Sir 28,2-5).

Sirach sighs and continues his instruction:

Now suppose you have reason to think that your friend has done something against you. It may look as if he has betrayed one of your secrets. He may have spoken evil of you. He may have broken an agreement. He may have acted in a way that seems contrary to your interest. What should we do in such a case? Many people simply keep silence. They bury it in their heart. They act externally as if everything is all right, but in their heart they harbour a suspicion. This is not wise, my children. No friendship can last in that way. The best thing to do is to speak about it directly. Ask your friend, and usually you will see that your reason for suspicion was unfounded.

> Question your friend, he may have done nothing at all,
> and if he has done anything, he will not do it again.
> Question your neighbour, he may have said nothing at all,
> and if he has said anything, he will not say it again.
> Question your friend, for slander is very common,
> do not believe all you hear.
> A man may sometimes make a slip, without meaning what he says,
> And which of us has never sinned by speech?
>
> (Sir 19,13-17).

When I was a boy, two of my aunts started to quarrel with one another. I remember it all very well. It began with some minor misunderstanding about who was to be allowed to go to the market place to do the necessary shopping. In the end the quarrel became so serious that they came to blows and my father had to separate them by force. How silly people can be. Even if there has been a misunderstanding, it can be solved so easily by reconciliation. Anybody will be ready to forgive if you honestly say, "I am sorry I have offended you". The only thing that ruins friendship forever is pride and unwillingness to humiliate ourselves.

> If you have drawn your sword on a friend,
> do not despair: there is a way back.
> If you have opened your mouth against your friend,
> do not worry: there is scope for reconciliation.
> But insult, arrogance, betrayal of secrets, and the stab in the back —
> in these cases any friend will run away.
>
> (Sir 22,21-22).

It is a wise man who can keep his friends. But what a blessing if we do so. There is nothing so consoling in life as friendship of many years standing. It is something we should treasure and try to preserve at all costs. It will be one of the reasons for our joy in old age. It will give us hope in times of despair and courage when we feel depressed.

> Do not desert an old friend:
> the new one will not be his match.
> New friend, new wine:
> when it grows old, you drink it with pleasure.

(Sir 9,10).

CHAPTER NINE

PERSPECTIVE, IMAGINATION, MYSTERY

I want to reflect on abstract art and deduce some principles that will prove useful in our task of oral communication. Before 1900 the fine arts in Europe were generally dominated by realism. This meant that in portraying objects or events the artist tried to express more or less what could be seen by the human eye. Even though the artist would transcend the reality he portrayed by giving stresses and by using light, colours and composition to express his artistic interpretation, the resulting object of art corresponded to what existed or, at least, to what *could* exist. Sculpture, painting and drama were naturalistic.

At the turn of the century, a revolution suddenly took place. It was as if artists had suddenly discovered a new dimension in reality. Wassily Kandinsky, a Polish painter of that period, describes how one evening he entered his own studio and saw a canvas he had not seen before. It did not represent anything. It was nothing but colours and forms. But Kandinsky stood struck by its "indescribable beauty". It turned out to be one of his own works, but inadvertently put on its side! So, Kandinsky discovered that something beautiful can be expressed in a painting through colours and forms without conforming to a naturalistic representation of reality.

The Hungarian Constantin Brancusi (1876-1957) made the same discovery in sculpture. When portraying an artistic object he refused to be so overwhelmed by its realistic details so as to overlook the major characteristics of the objects that fascinated him. Rather than trying to capture an image of reality, Brancusi decided to try and express his artistic emotion, his feeling about the object, the thought that held him spellbound. Consider, for instance, his marble head called "Mlle Pogany" (see Fig. 30). I imagine that he took his inspiration from an actual person. However, when trying to express her beauty, Brancusi concentrated on the main forms, rather than on detail. The whole sculpture is a beautiful structure of curved spaces. It is graceful and pleasing to the sight. It somehow holds our attention. But it is no longer a portrait of Miss Pogany. It is rather some kind of artistic dream of the sculptor, an impression about her which he gave solid

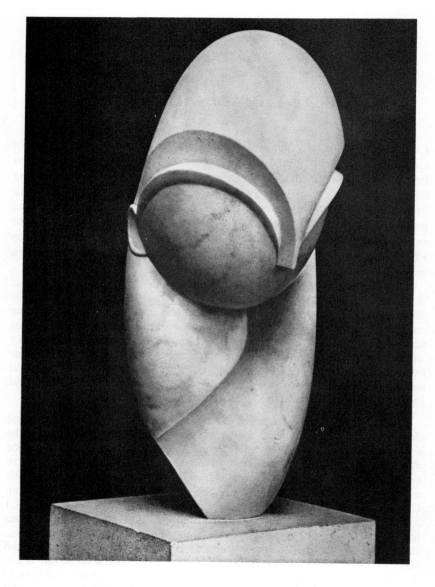

Fig. 30. "Mlle Pogany" (1931) by Constantin Brancusi.

form in marble. A similar idea in stone is Brancusi's "Bird in Space" (see Fig. 31).

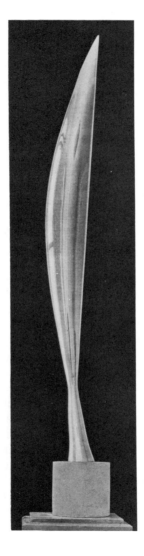

Fig. 31. (Brancusi), "Bird in Space".

Perhaps it is something of our age that this kind of art has now become very popular. We find abstract art in war memorials, stained glass windows in our churches and illustrations for our books. Apparently the modern mind needs such flashes of the imagination, such dramatic flights of fancy. Or is it that through our high-pitched tensions and ever more demanding pace of life, we have become impatient with the placid portraits and pastoral landscapes of the past? Could it be related to our twentieth century disregard for secondary things and accidentals, our preoccupation with substance and priorities? One thing is certain: abstract art is in. Somehow or other it seems to reflect a particular gift, or twist, of our modern mind.

I believe that this observation has great consequences for our communicating Scripture. Although there are still many occasions when the more traditional forms of narration, presentation of portraits, elaboration of themes and other approaches can be used, we may sometimes be called upon to do in communication exactly what abstract art has done for painting and sculpture. We may have to depart from the ordinary, realistic way of presenting themes and indulge in a more imaginative and creative form of presentation.

In a realistic presentation, just like in ordinary life, we have to keep such details as persons, times, places and the order of events carefully distinct. If we follow a kind of "abstract art" approach the exact boundaries between such categories collapse. Objects and persons which are quite separate in everyday life merge and become one reality. Past, present and future may be mixed up. Different faces may blur into one picture. The point is that we relentlessly pursue one particular line of thought at the expense of such naturalistic detail: it is the inspiration that counts. We sacrifice realism in order the better to communicate the vision we have conceived.

It is obvious that no exact rules or guidelines can be given about such an approach. My contribution can only lie in drawing the reader's attention to the possibilities which this approach may offer to him. I have put together some examples of approaches that belong to this category and shall describe them in the hope that they may spark off an individual and creative response in each communicator. As we will be walking on the dividing line between madness and genius, between utter nonsense and artistic brilliance, I hope that the following sections will be read with a good amount of tolerance and critical evaluation. Let everyone try the recipe for himself and taste the stew.

THEOLOGICAL PERSPECTIVE

Classical theology recognised that some Old Testament persons were "types" of Christ. Events that happened in ancient history could prefigure the realities introduced in the New Testament. Remember what Peter wrote about baptism.

"Now it was long ago, when Noah was still building that ark which saved only a small group of eight people 'by water', and while God was still waiting patiently, that these spirits refused to believe. That water is the type of baptism which saves you now, and which is not the washing off of physical dirt, but a pledge made to God from a good conscience, through the resurrection of Jesus Christ" (1 Pet 3,20-21).

It is interesting to note that "type" and later reality are mixed in their presentation. For Peter the people who went through the flood with Noah were saved by baptismal water. Or, inversely, a person who is baptised today enters the ark and is saved through the flood from complete destruction.

Let us consider another example. The sacrifices brought by Abel, Melchizedek and Abraham were types of the sacrifice brought by Christ. Abel's because he brought a sacrifice that was pleasing to God; Melchizedek's because he brought a sacrifice of bread and wine; and Abraham because in it a father gave up his only-begotten son. In the Roman eucharistic prayer we find the following supplication:

"May your face be pleased and serene as you look upon these gifts. May you take them up as you took up the gifts of your servant Abel, a just man; the gift of Abraham our Patriarch; and that which Melchizedek set before you, a holy sacrifice, a victim without blemish".

Regardless of their being separated in time and space these three types were thus presented in one glance.

We find the same simultaneous presentation in a sixth century mosaic at St. Apollinare in Classe near Ravenna (see Fig. 32). Abel, Melchizedek and Abraham stand round the altar as if they are concelebrating. Each of them brings his characteristic gift, which prefigures Christ. Abel holds up his lamb. Melchizedek makes ready to take the bread and wine and Abraham brings his son Isaac. From an historical point of view putting these three persons together is absurd, yet it makes sense to us. For we immediately grasp the unifying idea of the sacrifice with all the details pointing to Christ.

Why could we not do the same in oral communication? Suppose I were to address a community gathered today for the Eucharist in the following terms:

Fig. 32. Mosaic in St. Apollinare at Classe near Ravenna (7th cent. A.D.)

"As we are gathered here today let us remember that we are Abel, facing our Creator. Humbly we bow down before his majesty offering the simple gift of our lamb, an expression of our total submission to his will. Again, we are Melchizedek, we carry in our hands the bread and wine which the God of heaven and earth has given us. Reverently we stand in his presence and thank him. We are Abraham, bringing his beloved and only son Isaac. We bring him to Mount Moria, to express by this terrible loss of what is dearest to us, that we love God above everything else and that we are ready to give up all other things to please and serve him. Today we will witness the miracle whereby our lamb, our bread and wine, our dearest son Isaac, will become Jesus Christ himself. This is the sacrifice we are bringing today".

It will be seen at once what we have done. We have telescoped into the present reality the ancient scenes of the three types. While looking at today's events (in Eucharistic celebration), we see the other sacrifices that prefigured it within the same perspective. This is why I call this approach "theological perspective". Past and present merge. I identify myself so much with the ancient story and its protagonists that I become part and parcel of it. That is why I don't say, "I am doing now what Abel was doing then", or "I am like Melchizedek", but simply "I am Abel, doing this. I am Melchizedek himself".

Having experimented with this approach myself on various occasions, I can testify to its possibilities. When properly prepared and brought with the right kind of flair, it is able to deliver a very strong message. On the other hand, I have also found that there are some limitations that have to be kept in mind. The approach presupposes that the audience is familiar with the scriptural text on which it is based. If people have never heard of Abel or Melchizedek our words will make no sense. They should know the biblical passage in question so well that a single reference to them is enough to remind them again of the scene involved. In other words: we can only use this approach regarding bible texts or biblical persons that can be presumed to be known. Or, if the passage is not familiar we could only speak about it in this way after it had been read out.

The approach also requires that the audience is sufficiently mature and sophisticated to appreciate the unusual presentation. It would not do to confront children with this kind of presentation. Moreover, a preacher should not use this kind of presentation too often. From the point of view of communication "theological perspective" is rather heavy and becomes indigestible if offered too frequently or in too large quantities. In some ways it resembles Christmas pudding which can be delicious if not served every day or in over-large chunks.

Here are some scripture passages that lend themselves to theological perspective:

Is 2,1-4:   Mount Zion is the Church; Yahweh is Christ; the peace of the New Jerusalem is the peace of Christ's kingdom.

Dt 6,4-9:   Loving God is the first commandment of Jesus' kingdom. The details refer to details of our life.

Is 11,1-4:   The whole passage is applied to Christ, joining Gospel incidents to the Old Testament phrases.

1 Kgs 19,9-14:Elijah's experience of God is transferred to the stages of our own mystical experience of God through Christ.

Tob 4,7-11:   Almsgiving is transferred to the dedication of one's life in a religious society.

Gen 6-8:   Salvation by the ark means salvation through baptism.

Jer 31,31-34: Our Christian life is the new covenant of sanctity opened up by the prophets. We are the house of Israel. Egypt is our life of sin. His law in the heart is the Holy Spirit.

Jdt 14,18-20: Our Lady is the new Judith who saved her people from death.

Ex 17,9-13:   The battle with Amalech is the fight of the militant Church on earth. Moses' raised arms are the intercessions of the faithful.

3 Kgs 8,1-14: The inauguration of the temple is an ordination to the priesthood. As God filled the temple so he fills the new priest.

IMAGINATIVE ELABORATION

Another way of presenting Scripture in a non-realistic fashion is to take one element and work it out to its fullest extent. I call this approach "imaginative elaboration". Something in a Bible text strikes us. It opens a whole vista with unsuspected implications. It makes us see other texts in a new light. So without bothering too much about safe-guarding other elements of the text, we work out this particular element in such a way that its over-riding importance is brought out.

Once, when Christ was exasperated by people's lack of faith he complained "Now, to what can I compare the people of this day? They are like children playing in the market place. One group shouts to the other, 'We played wedding music for you but you would not dance. We sang funeral songs, but you would not cry!' " (Mt 11,16-17). Christ complains. He wanted to dance, but his contemporaries refused to dance along with him. This text was elaborated by Sidney Carter in his famous song, *The Lord of the Dance*. Notice how the motif of the dance is extended to all aspects of

Christ's life and how eventually Christ himself is identified with the Dance (life) itself. It is a good example of imaginative elaboration.

What has been expressed in this song could equally well have been put forward in a short homily. The bold application of the same motif to all kinds of circumstances and events takes us by surprise. It throws a new interpretation on the life and person of Jesus. The novel idea of considering our Christian life as a dance led by Jesus floods us with unexpected emotions of joy and happiness. Working out the concept is not difficult. What we need is the imagination to grasp the potential of a metaphor such as Christ's complaint about the dance.

A master of this kind of approach was Attar of Nishapur. This Sufi teacher of the 12th century, who wrote 114 treatises, was a genius in teaching through fables, maxims, apalogues, allegories and illustrative biographies. Much of this material he made up himself. One example that will interest us concerns Jesus. Attar apparently had been struck by Jesus' injunction that the apostles should pray for their enemies and that they should not carry gold or silver in their purses. Starting from such passages, he constructed a beautiful anecdote.

"Some Israelites reviled Jesus one day as he was walking through their part of the town.
But he answered by repeating prayers in their name.
Someone said to him: "You prayed for these men, did you not feel incensed against them?'
He answered: 'I could spend only of what I had in my purse'."

With our respect for the actual Gospel passages, we Christians would not easily make up such a story. But surely there would be nothing against it, if we introduced the story with words such as: "Our purses are so heavy with the gold of our pride and the silver of our imagined personal honour. Isn't this the currency we constantly use in our dealings with others? But this morning I let my imagination have its head. I saw Jesus walking in Palestine. Some Israelites reviled him as he was walking through their part of the town, etc. With such an introduction the story would be recognisable as having been made up by ourselves and yet would give the unexpected, powerful message that is implied in the Gospel: "I could spend only of what I had in my purse".

In the first book of Kings we are given three different pictures of Elijah. When he fled from Jezebel and despaired of his life, he lay flat out on his back under the juniper tree (19,4). After the ordeal of Mount Carmel Elijah waited anxiously for the promised rain. With nervous expectation he bowed down to the earth, putting his face between his knees (18,42). But when the rain had come he jumped up with joy and ran in front of Ahab's chariot as far as the city of Jezreel (18,46). These three basic postures express rather well the different frames of mind we may be in from time to time, the changing moods we pass through. An interesting conference could be devoted to recognising our own postures and the ways in which we can tackle our moods. The passing moods of lying on our back, of crouching and running should make place for a serenity of standing in the presence of God (19,11).

Samson wore long hair. It had never been cut, for Samson was a person dedicated to God's service by a vow and his uncut hair was an external sign of this (Judges 13,5). Samson's long hair gave him extraordinary strength. When he allowed his hair to be cut, his strength was gone (16,19). It only returned when his hair had grown again to the same length (16,22). Samson's long hair was his particular secret, the sensitive sign of his relationship with God. Each one of us has a similar sign, a secret, a delicate part of our personality that we should never allow to be mutilated. This is *our* long hair related to our particular strength.

Example: A Sermon for Mission Sunday.

As I was preparing for this sermon and wondering what I should say on Mission Sunday, I suddenly became distracted. In spirit I was taken twenty-eight centuries back to Bethel in the kingdom of Samaria. I found myself in a large square, right in the middle of the temple. On the one side I saw the gates through which many people were entering with their sacrificial gifts. On the other side I saw the altar with the tabernacle of the covenant.

In a corner of the large square I noticed a lean man, dressed in ordinary clothes, who was speaking to the people around him in an excited manner. Many came flocking around him to listen to what he was saying. Just at that moment a rich lady entered the temple gates. She was carried in on a palanquin and surrounded by many servants.

The lean, excited man, whose name I learned was Amos, pointed an accusing finger at her and said: "Listen to this word, you rich women of Samaria, you fat cows of Bashan. You, who oppress the needy and crush the poor. You, who say to your husbands: 'Give us more comfort, buy us more wine'. The Lord Yahweh swears by his holiness: The days are coming when the city of Samaria will be destroyed. You will be carried out on fleshhooks as chunks of meat are carried by butchers. It is the Lord who speaks".

Then Amos turned to the people around him and said: "Why are you trampling my courts to bring me your useless sacrifices? Worship is to no purpose if you don't practise justice. It is the Lord who speaks".

While Amos had been speaking, a small group of persons had emerged from the priest's house. A big, fat fellow, dressed in priestly robes and with a great plate on his chest led the group. People told me his name was Amasiah. He was the priest and the people with him were the temple guard. Amasiah pushed his way forward through the crowd and confronted Amos.

"Get out of here, prophet," he said. "Useless seer of visions. Go back to the land of Judah. Earn your bread there. Do your prophesying stunt in your own country. We want no more prophesying in Bethel. Remember this is the king's sanctuary, the temple belongs to him".

Amos turned to Amasiah. His face had become white as a sheet. He said: "I am not a prophet. I do not belong to any prophetic school. I am an ordinary shepherd, I assure you; and from time to time I look after fig trees as well. But Yahweh the Lord himself took me away from herding the flock. He told me: 'Speak in my name to the people of Israel'. Therefore you say, 'Get out of here and don't prophesy'. Very well. This is what Yahweh says: 'You too, Amasiah, will see the exile. Your own sons and daughters will beg for their food in the streets. You yourself will die on foreign soil'. It is the Lord who speaks".

At this moment the temple police had moved forward and taken hold of Amos. Overcoming his resistance they dragged him towards the gate of the temple square and threw him outside.

I had really become very much interested in this man Amos. So I slipped out of the temple gates myself and ran after him.

"Amos, Amos", I said, "Did you say you are *not* a prophet?"

Amos turned round. "Certainly I am not a prophet. Didn't you hear that priest's insinuation about my 'earning my bread by a prophesying stunt'? I am not doing this as a job! I feel I *have* to do it".

"Well, Amos", I said, "Don't take me wrong. I am not on the side of that pharisee Amasiah. I like what you were saying about the rights of the poor and that people should help them. But all the same I have some problems. After all, you don't belong to the kingdom of Samaria. Your own country is Judah. And you yourself admit that you are only a shepherd who hasn't made any special studies. How can you presume to come so far from your own country and tell these people here what is right or wrong? On what authority are you doing these things?"

Amos said to me: "It's not on my own authority I assure you. The Lord sent me. He told me to go. It wasn't my own idea. I can't help it that God picked on me to do this task".

"Now look here, Amos", I said. "Be reasonable. It is an easy thing to say that God told you to speak. Anyone can make such a claim. But if God spoke to you, how did he actually do it? Did you hear his voice? Did he appear to you in one or other form?"

Amos looked me up and down. "This is a strange question", he said. "No one has ever asked me this kind of question before".

Feeling a little uncomfortable I said, "You should know I belong to the twentieth century after Christ. We like to analyse the psychology of people. We would like to know what makes a prophet tick. Can't you explain how God spoke to you?"

"I wonder", Amos said. "It's difficult to speak about such things. Well, as I was going about my job, looking after the sheep, I kept hearing different stories about all these injustices committed against poor people. I really got worked up about it. I realized that God is angry about this too. And then suddenly the Spirit of the Lord came upon me and I knew that I had to speak in his Name — You can't say No when the Spirit comes upon you like that. Have you ever heard the roar of a lion? When a lion roars you can't help but feel afraid. If God speaks to you, you have to prophesy!"

"That must be a wonderful experience", I said. "It must be a wonderful thing when the Spirit of God gets hold of you like that and can make you speak and act in his Name".

Amos looked at me the way you look at a person who doesn't understand a thing. "I don't know if it is so wonderful," he said. "I tell you, it hasn't made life much easier for me. Just wait, it may happen to you too one day . . .". Then he turned round and walked away.

As I watched him go, I thought about the mystery of this individual, this ordinary man, Amos, who was transformed into being a prophet by the Spirit of God, a shepherd appointed to be ambassador of Almighty God, this missionary from the land of Judah.

And I thought about how closely mission and Spirit are related. I remembered how Jesus himself after his Resurrection had stood in the midst of his Apostles and had breathed his Spirit upon them. How he had said: "As the Father sent me, so I am sending you".

And it struck me that this is perhaps the meaning of World Mission Sunday: that there are still many people like Amos today; that the Spirit of God still stirs in the hearts of many; that as the Spirit of the Father moved and made Jesus, so the Spirit of Jesus moves many men and women today to preach his Gospel of salvation.

I said to myself: "This is truly a surprising thing – worthy of celebration".

MYSTERY RAMBLE

The human mind is an exceedingly complex computer. And it works fast. Consider, for instance, the activity implied in understanding speech. An ordinary person's passive vocabulary in any language involves a minimum of twenty thousand distinct words. For every word we hear in conversation, this entire vocabulary must be scanned before we can pin down its meaning. If we remember that in ordinary conversation the mind may have to digest as many as two hundred words per minute, we may somehow realize the speed and efficiency with which our mind must work. Add to this that while we are listening the mind is simultaneously engaged in a number of other tasks, such as interpreting what we see with our eyes, recalling persons or events related to our present experience, preparing a reply and so on. The mind can travel a long distance in a few seconds.

When we meditate on scripture the mind will follow the erratic path inherent in human thinking. As associations come to us, we will move backwards and forwards from one consideration to another. Our focus of attention will be like an electric spark running round a circuit, lighting now this, then another area of our brains. Our thoughts are like monkeys jumping about among the branches of a huge tree. The sequence of our thoughts will be bewildering to an outsider, but for ourselves it has a logic of its own, the logic of the mind's free discovery of associations.

Sometimes it may be helpful to other people if we "think aloud", if we make them share in the seemingly haphazard, yet compelling turns of thought experienced during meditation. What results is a string of associations based on a Gospel text and presented as they came to mind. For lack of a better name I will call this a "mystery ramble". It is a "ramble" because it lacks the structure of a topic that is presented systematically. I call it "mystery" ramble because by the helter-skelter presentation of worthwhile ideas it does seem to touch more easily on the mystery of God and ourselves.

The main characteristic of the mystery ramble is its total lack of inhibition. Hieronymus Bosch was such a fascinating painter because he painted exactly whatever lived in his artistic imagination (see Fig. 33). In the mystery ramble everything is possible. The events of the past become realities in our own lives. Plants and animals can speak. They may address God, or persons, or things, just as we like. We may combine flashes of imagination with present-day experience or visions of the future. Yet, a mystery ramble should be more than just a wild run of fancy. Because it is concerned with the mystery of existence, the chain of associations will be held together by the search for truth, by the desire to get at the root of things.

A mystery ramble usually turns out to be a rather intensive kind of communication. It lends itself better to a short homily, rather than to a lengthy instruction. Because it resembles human thought which comes in short flashes, rather than in a continuous flow, the presentation should be deliberate, with plenty of pauses to prepare for the unexpected turns of thought.

By way of example I will reproduce here the complete text of a short homily by Rev. A. Rabou. It is a small masterpiece of the mystery ramble approach. The readings during the Mass had been Wisdom 12,21-26 ("God overlooks men's sins and hates nothing he has made") and Luke 19,1-10 (the story of Zacchaeus.)

"It is an awful thing to be small like Zacchaeus . . . Do you still remember many years ago . . . when Mass had finished . . . then you walked out of church between all these grown up people, everybody towering high above you, your eyes at a level with your dad's knees. It was dark and warm and somehow upsetting . . . it is a terrible thing to be small . . . then you want to move up. 'Zacchaeus, was that the reason that you climbed the tree?'

And yet, all of us are small . . . everyone has his own smallness . . . we try to hide it behind the walls of our home, behind our attitude, behind our silence . . . we are afraid that it may show up . . . it might compromise us . . . it wouldn't be so bad really if everyone else were not constantly seeking to put the spotlight on that weak spot we have . . .

'Is that why you climbed that tree, Zacchaeus?'

Fig. 33. The paintings of Hieronymus Bosch (1450-1516) are full of 'mystery'.
In this 'Vision of Tondal' he put on the canvas the weirdest associations of thought,
just as we experience in our own reflections.

It is a pity that people can nail us on just a small part of our existence without looking any further. It is something you may hear at times in a hospital. A nurse standing next to your bed . . . "this is an appendicitis, doctor" . . . Do I look so shrivelled as to merit such a remark? "He is red . . . he is a marxist", they say, but they don't see that he has a heart of gold. "She is a whore", they say, but they forget that she is called Mary of Magdala, a woman longing for true love . . . "He is a thief, an extortioner", . . . and they forget that he is Zacchaeus, a man of infinite desires.

'Was that the reason why you climbed the tree, Zacchaeus?'

And Zacchaeus explains: "I want to escape from all that narrow-mindedness, away from the short-sightedness and pettiness of people. I am fed up with their world. I want to be on the look-out for a man who does not nail me on account of the one weakness I have . . . who does not condemn me . . . who gives me space to live in . . . who says to me: 'Hello, Zacchaeus, happy to know you'. And to whom I could then say: 'Do you know, there is one thing that upsets me. I am a thief, an extortioner . . .' And who then smiles at me. Is there nobody like that in the whole wide world?"

If you are looking for such a person you have to climb very high, Zacchaeus, you have to look very far, for such persons are hard to come by.

"To allow someone to have his weakness because we see so much good in him" is an attitude we rarely meet. The opposite is frequent: "Not allowing someone to enjoy his happiness because we keep reminding him of his weakness". If I were you, Zacchaeus, I would climb a lot higher. Just to make sure.

Just by chance Jesus happens to pass that tree. If I understand the Gospel properly, Jesus seems to have a hobby . . . he always looks at fig trees. He curses them if he doesn't find any fruit in them . . . "Cut that tree down", he says . . . He enjoys it if he finds the figs he is looking for . . . And today he finds in this fig tree an enormous fruit . . . that infinite desire of the man up there . . . who wanted to see Jesus. And he understands that man . . . well, yes, he is aware of his shortcomings . . . but he overlooks them. They are immaterial in his eyes. No, he is concerned about the human person, about that individual with his infinite desires . . . "Come down . . . it is you I was looking for . . . I would like to stay with you".

Congratulations, Zacchaeus! You made a good impression on Jesus. You are a man who can make the heart of God beat quicker . . . by nothing else than your great desires. And Jesus enters his house. Nice for Jesus, to find some consolation while he is on his way to his Passion in Jerusalem. Consolation from this extortioner.

"Jesus, if you were to walk around in our city today, do you know what our reaction would be? We would certainly not kneel down in adoration . . . we would say to one another: it is absurd to see what houses he enters . . . it is unbelievable what kind of people he makes his friends . . . Jesus, you have to be more careful . . . This will lead to gossip, you know". That is what we would say and then you might turn towards us and reply "Cut this tree down for from such a frame of mind Christianity cannot expect any fruits".

You do not pay attention, oh God, to the sins of man. You do not abhor anything you have created.

CHAPTER TEN

READING SCRIPTURE TO OTHERS

The public reading of Scripture in our liturgical services, at prayer meetings or on other occasions is one of the most important, and most under-estimated, opportunities of communicating the scriptural message to others. Although most people today can read and write, they are "illiterate" in the sense that their personal reading is very restricted. For many who have not acquired the habit of reading the Scriptures for themselves, the public reading of select passages has become their only immediate contact with the inspired word.

There are also good theological reasons for treating the public reading of Scripture with respect. It is not correct to think of the Bible as a collection of ancient writings, recorded thousands of years ago in languages that are now extinct. The Bible is the *living* Word of God. It is God's Word to us *here and now*. That is why the Bible becomes truly alive, becomes God's living Word in a special way whenever it is proclaimed in the Christian community. Scripture and the Church are inseparable. Just as the Church never grows old but in every community of the faithful age after age remains fresh and youthful, so the sacred Scriptures remain relevant and alive by their proclamation in every new community.

Christ promised that he would remain with us until the end of time (Mt 28,20). Christ was not only thinking of his continued presence through the Spirit he

Fig. 34. Christ with the Gospel. Sculpture known as "Le Beau Dieu" in the Cathedral of Amiens.

would impart to his followers, through the Holy Eucharist or the sacramental powers he invested in the Apostles. Christ was also thinking of his Word, of which he said, "Heaven and earth will pass away; my words will never pass away" (Mt 24,35). He knew his Gospel would be preached all over the world (Mt 26,13). He realized too that the resounding of his Word in every new generation would require the combination of a handing down of exact wordings ("Remind them of everything I told you"; Mt 28,20) and of the interpretation of living guides ("Who hears you, hears Me"; Lk 10,16). The Second Vatican Council touches on this mystery when it states: "In the liturgy God speaks to his people and Christ is still proclaiming his Gospel" (Liturgy 33).

If the reading of Scripture makes Christ present in his Word, it follows that the reader does much more than mechanically reproduce in sound what he finds written on paper. The reader has to be personally involved. He cannot transmit the text as a living word unless he himself first understands it. It is not without significance that the ministry of the lectorate has been given a new status by the Church in recent years. In the new installation ceremony the Bishop prays over the new Reader with these words: "God, bless this brother of ours who has been selected for the office of the lectorate. Grant that he may unceasingly meditate on your Word; that doing this he may be both profoundly enlightened by it himself and faithfully announce it to his brothers and sisters. Through Christ our Lord. Amen".

In this chapter I will introduce two forms of reading which I feel every Reader should know: simple guided reading (in which the reading is preceded by a key message) and commentated reading (which is a mixture of text and explanation). However, before we can discuss these techniques in themselves we need to go into some of their component elements: translation, decoding, formulating the key message.

THE NEED OF TRANSLATION

When we speak to others there is something we want to convey. We call this the message or the meaning. Everything in communication is subservient to this meaning. The sounds, the words, the sentence constructions, the expressions on our face or the gesture of our hands, the intonation of our voice, all of them aim at making the other person understand what we want to say. The same is true of the Bible. Because it is God speaking to man, the Bible has to follow in this regard the same fundamental law of all human communication. What matters in the Bible, what it was inspired for, is the message, is the meaning of what God wants to say. Everything else is of secondary importance. The scrolls on which the sacred text was written, the pens or quills the sacred authors used, the languages they expressed themselves in, their vocabulary, their idiom and style of writing, and whatever else was needed to make a book a book, had no other purpose than to convey the meaning of God's inspired Word to us.

This is why the Word of God can and should be translated for every new human community. If inspiration were to reside principally in the Hebrew idiom of the Old Testament or the Greek constructions of the New, modern versions of Scripture would no longer be the inspired Word of God. But such is not the case. The same meaning can be translated for different cultures and through different languages in a variety of ways. And although the external expression may vary, the meaning of a text can reach us in a modern language as effectively as in the original tongue.

When I am speaking of "meaning", I am not restricting this term to some intellectual truth we want to convey: the term should be taken to indicate everything that is transmitted in a human communication. It involves the transmission of ideas, the expression of emotions, the definition of relationships and a giving of one's self. It is this complex "meaning" that is the outcome of genuine human communication.

As "meaning" is so fundamental in our communication of Scripture, we need to study it in a little more detail. Where exactly do we find meaning in a text? Where does it reside? Some people think meaning resides in words (because we think that the word 'city', for instance, *means* a 'conglomeration of many houses'). Others think meaning is contained in a complete sentence. But neither of these two opinions is correct. Meaning can only result from a total unit of communication, from everything that was said by a person in a particular context.

Jesus stated: "A city built on a hill-top cannot be hidden" (Mt 5,14). What is the meaning of this statement? Of course, we have to begin by identifying what the individual words, such as "city", "hill-top", etc. stand for. Then we can study the combination of these words and understand their mutual relationships. If a town is constructed on the top of a mountain it can be seen from afar. But is this the *meaning* of Jesus' statement? Is this what Jesus wanted to teach? Was he giving advice to town-planners? Was he worried about the landscape or the pros and cons of a high location? Surely not. Jesus used this statement as an example, almost as a proverb. The *meaning* of what he said is clear from the whole context, namely that if we live in communion with God, the effects of it will be visible to others in our lives. We should not try to hide the light that shines in our hearts.

Many of us have been misled by our study of languages with its stress on the "meaning" of words in those languages. Unconsciously we may have allowed ourselves to become literalists. We may have come to think that words "contain" a meaning, almost like the old scholastic philosophers who believed that objects were somehow grasped by notions inside the mind. Such an understanding of language often leads to the idea that a word-for-word translation is to be preferred. A little reflection will show the fallacy of this idea and the obstacles it could put in the way of clear and effective communication.

Words do not contain objects, they refer to them. Words are like handles by which we get hold of a certain experience. Different languages may use different handles to refer to the same experience.

If we walk in the rain and we want to keep ourselves dry, we may carry a small imitation-roof over our heads. In English we call the object "umbrella" (from the Latin word "umbra" which means "shade"). The French speak of "parapluie" (which means "against rain"). The Germans call it "Schirm" (which stands for "protective cover"). In the South Indian languages the terms used, such as "godugu" in Telugu, are related to the word for "gift" as there is a popular belief that the invention was presented by the gods to give relief to mankind. The Malay word "pajong" seems to derive from the shape. These terms are obviously related and may at times refer to the same experience (so that we could substitute one term for another in translation). Yet they do not cover one another fully. In English we can say that some congress was organised "under the umbrella" of this or that institution. When talking about a "Schirm" the Germans may also refer to a parachute. When speaking of a "pajong" Balinese may refer to a ceremonial umbrella unknown in Europe. Words are labels attached to objects and experiences. Translation requires that we first identify the object or experience meant and then search for the label in the receptor language by which the same object or experience can be expressed.

A WORD ABOUT VERSIONS

People who make a scientific study of the Bible may prefer to have a translation that is as near to the original languages in construction and style as possible. We call this a "source-oriented" translation. Such a translation of the Gospels, for instance, tells us a lot about the original Greek in which the Gospels were written. But for most people the unusual vocabulary, the strange constructions and outlandish style of writing, become an obstacle to their understanding of the meaning. For them a receptor-oriented translation, that is a translation using the very words, expressions and idioms the receptor would use, is absolutely essential. It follows from this that when we read the Bible to others, we do well to choose the version from which we read according to the needs of our audience.

The *Revised Standard Version* and the *Douai* are source-oriented and cannot be recommended for pastoral use. *Knox* is appreciated in literary circles: its heavy style and archaic expression may put off the younger generation. The *New English Bible* and the *Jerusalem Bible* will be easily understood by the ordinary, adult, well-educated member of any parish community. *Today's English Version* (of which the New Testament is called *Good News for Modern Man*) has succeeded in making the meaning more accessible for many people. It employs very simple and straightforward language in which difficult words and complicated constructions have purposely been omitted. It also lends itself well for reading to children or to those for whom English is not their first language.

To see what difference a translation can make to understanding the meaning, we will here compare two renderings of Colossians 1,24-28. Following the Greek closely RSV has only *three* sentences; TEV breaks them up into *seven* normal English sentences.

Revised Standard Version
Now I rejoice in my sufferings for your sake, and in my flesh I complete what is lacking in Christ's afflictions for the sake of His Body, that is, the Church of which I became a minister according to the divine office which was given to me for you, to make the Word of God fully known, the mystery hidden for ages and generations but now made manifest to his saints.

To them God chose to make known how great among the Gentiles are the riches of the glory of this mystery, which is Christ in you, the hope of glory.

Him we proclaim, warning every man and teaching every man in all wisdom, that we may present every man mature in Christ.

Today's English Version

And now I am happy about my sufferings for you, for by means of my physical sufferings I am helping to complete what still remains of Christ's sufferings on behalf of his Body, which is the Church.

And I have been made a servant of the Church by God who gave me this task to perform for your good.

It is the task of fully proclaiming his message, which is the secret he hid through all past ages from all mankind, but has now revealed to his people.

For this is God's plan: to make known his secret to his people, this rich and glorious secret that he has for all peoples.

And the secret is this: Christ is in you, which means that you will share the glory of God.

So we preach Christ to all men.

We warn and teach everyone with all possible wisdom, in order to bring each one into God's presence as a mature individual in union with Christ.

At times we should not hesitate to use a paraphrased translation such as *The Living Bible* if we find that it proves the best version for a meaningful proclamation in particular circumstances. A good paraphrase may actually turn out to be exactly what needs to be done to make people grasp what the Bible is trying to say. According to RSV, Peter says to Simon the Magician: "Your silver perish with you!" (Acts 8,20). The paraphrase of P. B. Phillips comes much nearer when it makes Peter say: "To hell with you and your money!" (*The New Testament in Modern English*).

Carle Burke, a Chaplain in a County Jail in New York, tried to translate some parts of the Bible in the hip language used by the people entrusted to his care. I consider the following version of Psalm 1 published in his book *God is for Real, Man,* as a model of what translation should do. Notice how not only the words, but the constructions and the sequences of thought have been adapted to the New York brogue. Yet the text conveys accurately the *meaning* of the Psalm.

A guy is pretty smart
  If he don't hang around with hoods
    And do what they tell him.
He is smart too if he don't poke fun
  At people who try to do the right thing.
He is always happy 'cause he knows for sure
  That he is doing the right thing.
In fact it makes him feel so good
  That he thinks about it day and night,
    And that don't do no harm either.
He feels good 'cause this is God's way of doing things,
  And you can't beat that.
This guy is sort of like a tree
  In Humboldt Park
    That grows by the lake.
It don't get looking like a droop
  'Cause it gets plenty of water
    And things to live from.
But the hoods are not like that —
  They are like the dust that blows down the street
    And all over the place,
      And ya hate it.
So they won't stand a chance,
  When the day comes to figure out the score
    They will just get wiped up
      And they won't be where the good guys are —
        And that's for sure too.
That's 'cause God knows the way
  People are
    Down inside of them,
      And you can't give him a snow job.
A hood may be on top now,
  But it won't last.

DECODING

Even if we are making use of a reasonable translation, it may be that
we come across words or constructions that will be difficult to
understand for the particular audience for which we are reading.
Since it is our task to convey the meaning of the text as accurately as
possible, we may then have to "de-code" the words or constructions

in question. This means in practice that by a little explanatory addition, by substituting a more commonly used word, or by breaking up some difficult sentence, we make the text easier to understand. The listener is constantly trying to break the code of the text that is read out to him. By "de-coding" some difficult parts, we help him understand the text better.

In one of his books on journalism Rudolph Flesch narrates an incident which I will freely adapt here to illustrate decoding. The plumber of a big hotel found himself constrained throughout winter to mend pipes burst on account of freezing. He wondered whether he could use some chemical (which I will call "decalicarboacid") to melt the ice in frozen pipes. He wrote to a laboratory in Washington asking for guidance. When he received a telegram with the contents: "Decalicarboacid causes negative transmutation steel aggregates deterioration consequent", he was puzzled about its meaning and asked for clarification. The second telegram stated: "Rapid erosive deterioration steel plating incumbent on friction with decalicarboacid compound". In disgust the plumber sent a telegram himself: "Blast your big words. What does it mean?" This time he received a lucid answer: "Don't use DCC acid. It eats the hell out of your pipes!"

Suppose we have to do the first reading in a Eucharistic celebration for children (or attended by many children). It is the eighteenth Sunday of the year, year 3 according to the liturgical cycle. In a lectionary which follows the Jerusalem version, the text will read as follows: (Eccles 1,2; 2,21-23):

"Vanity of vanities, the Preacher said. Vanity of vanities. All is vanity!

For so it is that a man who has laboured wisely, skilfully and successfully must leave what is his own to someone who has not toiled for it. This, too, is vanity and great injustice; for what does he gain for all the toil and strain that he has undergone under the sun? What are all his laborious days, his cares of office, his restless nights? This, too, is vanity".

The text has an important message. Yet its meaning will not be perfectly clear to the ordinary English speaker of today, and certainly not to children. One reason for this obscurity is the term "vanity". In ordinary English "vanity" indicates a character trait. It implies self-praise, smugness, conceit, a certain amount of ostentation. We call a person vain when he or she spends half an hour combing his (or her) hair and admiring his (or her) own beauty in a mirror. This is not its meaning in the scriptural text. Here the term refers to something being "useless", "to no purpose". We still meet this in everyday language when we say something is "in vain". The inspired writer wants to say that all we do in life, all our hard work and ceaseless efforts, seem to lead us nowhere. Everything we do, we do in vain.

When we proclaim this Bible text to others, especially if they are children or if we cannot presume a classical education, we will have to decode the term "vanity"; otherwise we run the risk of allowing many people to miss the message. We can do this decoding in two ways. Either we can give a brief explanation of its meaning before we start the reading (as we do in "simple guided reading", see below). Or we may substitute a more up-to-date expression for the ancient term. In that case we might change the first line of the reading in terms such as these: "Utterly useless, the Preacher says. Utterly useless! Everything is useless and in vain".

If we use another lectionary, such as the one based on the *Revised Standard Version*, we will need to do a lot more decoding in our reading. Often the Gospel Reading begins with "And he said to them . . .", leaving the listener guessing as to who is speaking to whom. Our duty to decode such ambiguities will require that we clarify the situation by stating more explicity "And Jesus said to his Apostles" or "And Jesus said to the Pharisees", etc. In communication we should avoid guesswork and leave nothing to chance. A slogan for broadcasters is, "the meaning of the message is in the hearer". What meaning our message carries should not be judged by what we intended to put into it, but what the listeners managed to get out of it.

FORMULATING THE KEY MESSAGE

As I have pointed out before, the meaning of a particular text does not arise from individual words, nor from stray sentences, but from a whole unit of communication. Restricting ourselves to the Bible, we observe that such units may be long or short; they may consist either in a whole chapter or in just one paragraph or a number of paragraphs. The natural units of the Gospel, for instance, are Our Lord's parables, his miracles, his sayings on various occasions. Paul has some lengthy arguments on certain theological matters; other topics he deals with in just a few sentences. Normally when we select a passage for reading we choose a natural unit that conveys one overall message. The selection of readings in the lectionary has also followed this rule.

In order to do justice to the passage we are reading, we ourselves should first have a good idea of its overall message. For the sake of clarity we might call this message the "fundamental assertion" of the passage. It amounts to the main teaching the inspired author wanted to convey through this unit of writing. Studying the text in preparation for our reading it to others, we should try to be clear ourselves on what its fundamental assertion is. We then think of our audience and try to formulate what the fundamental assertion of this particular Scripture text means to them. This formulated fundamental assertion I call the 'key message'.

To understand what is meant by the fundamental assertion and what by the key message, and why it is useful to distinguish between them, we could not do better than study some actual scriptural examples.

On the third Sunday of Lent, year 1, the first reading of the lectionary is from Exodus 17,3-7:

> 'Tormented by thirst, the people complained against Moses. "Why did you bring us out of Egypt?", they said. "Was it so that I should die of thirst, my children too and my cattle?"
>
> Moses appealed to the Lord: "How am I to deal with this people?", he said. "A little more and they will stone me!"
>
> The Lord said to Moses, "Take with you some of the elders of Israel and move on to the forefront of the people; take in your hand the staff with which you struck the river, and go. I shall be standing before you there on the rock at Horeb. You must strike the rock and water will flow from it for the people to drink". This is what Moses did in the sight of the elders of Israel.
>
> The place was named Massah and Meriba because of the grumbling of the sons of Israel and because they put the Lord to the test by saying, "Is the Lord with us, or not?"

The fundamental assertion of the passage is that the Hebrews in the desert made a mistake when they lost confidence in God. God was present among them. He was able to supply them with water to drink even in the middle of a wilderness of sheer sand and rock. But what does all this mean for my particular audience in this liturgical celebration? What do I need to highlight to make my listeners take the message home?

For an ordinary parish congregation we may want to link the reading to the Gospel which speaks about the water of eternal life that Jesus will give (Jn 4,5-42). Our key message could then be: "God gives us the water of life". If the Mass is celebrated for a community of nuns, the key message could be: "Never despair. Never put God to the test. God can make water flow from rock!" In a Mass for children we might say: "Just as God gave water to the Jews when they were thirsty, so God will grant us the spiritual things we need!"

Announcing the key message before the reading is a great help in making people understand the passage. People need such a help because the reading is usually a small extract, lifted out of its scriptural context, couched in a way of speaking removed from our own. In modern communication, this technique of introducing a text with a key statement is now common practice. The essential content of a newspaper report is announced in the caption. When the news broadcasts a statement by a government spokesman, it first gives the gist of the statement before quoting the actual text. In the complex mass of information they have to digest people soon get confused. A 'key message' given before the actual text eliminates vagueness and ambiguity.

It is worth studying how the BBC handles the efficient transmission of highly complex information. The following is a fictitious example given to illustrate the technique.

"Dr. F. L. Falstaff of Exeter University, who conducted a study on horn-billed ducks, has come to the conclusion that their eggs are not fit for human consumption (key statement).

In his research report, he states: 'In some parts of England the eggs of the species are still considered a rare delicacy. When served as omelettes the eggs have a characteristic taste that will be instantly recognised by any connoisseur. But chemical analysis of the eggs' content has raised serious doubts about the advisability of using them for nourishment. The second, inner membrane contains a dacty-pyro-phosphate combination that may prove intoxicating and injurious to human cell formation'."

If the gist of the doctor's declaration were not given beforehand in a 'key statement', many people would miss the meaning of what the doctor is trying to say. The same applies to many biblical texts.

The key message is not a 'summary' of the text that is going to follow. It does not try to cover all the details of the text or enumerate its various elements. The key statement limits itself to the overall teaching of the whole passage for a particular community.

Suppose our reading is the parable of the talents. The key statement should not try to re-tell the parable in a shortened form, by saying for instance: "In this parable Our Lord compares three men. One received ten talents and he produced another ten. The second one five talents and he produced another five. But the man with one talent produced nothing. The first two were rewarded to show us that we must produce results according to the gifts we have received". This is *not* the correct way of formulating the key statement.

We do not need to mention the talents at all, or how the parable develops its teaching. Our key statement could simply be: "God will judge us according to the gifts we received". Or: "God expects each one to produce fruit according to the gifts he received".

My experience in formulating key messages and in checking those formulated by others has led me to draw up the following six guidelines which, in my opinion, indicate that a particular key message is the right one. The ideal key message should:

(1) be a statement or exhortation (it should be formulated as a sentence; a noun or 'title' is not half as effective);
(2) be short;
(3) express the main teaching;
(4) be worded in every-day language (it should not contain unusual biblical phrases or anything that reduces the directness of the statement);
(5) be meaningful to the audience (and the occasion);
(6) address them directly (the statement should not be phrased in too general terms; it should normally include words such as 'we' or 'you').

The key message should be formulated in a language that is relevant to our own day. We should keep out all scriptural or theological jargon. We have to tell our audience bluntly, in their own every-day language, what the particular text means to them.

> The key message to Mt 17,1-8 should not be "Jesus was transfigured before his disciples", but "Jesus gives a glimpse of his true self".

As Scripture is basically an event in which God communicates himself to man, the key message will reflect the aspect of encounter. What I mean is: in the key message we should not present the message of Scripture as if it is speaking about a third person, about people far away and distinct from ourselves. Scripture is always trying to say something to *me*, to *us* as a community, God's people listening to his word.

> When we read that Jesus chides the scribes and pharisees (Mt 23,13-22), we might be tempted to formulate a neutral key

message, such as: 'Jesus condemns the pharisees for their hypocrisy'. Here the aspect of encounter is missing. We should rather say: 'Jesus warns us against hypocrisy', or 'Jesus wants us to be absolutely straightforward and sincere'.

SIMPLE GUIDED READING

'Simple guided reading' is one way of presenting a reading as clearly and effectively as possible. The technique consists essentially in having a very brief introduction before the reading of the actual text. The short introduction contains the key message. It may occasionally also include a few words of 'decoding', whenever such decoding cannot be done in the course of the reading itself. Normally, the introduction will be just the key message and nothing else.

On the tenth Sunday of the Year, Year 2, the first reading during Mass is from Genesis 3,9-15. In the RSV lectionary, the text runs as follows:-
'The Lord God called to the man and said to him, "Where are you?" and he said, "I heard the sound of thee in the garden, and I was afraid, because I was naked; and I hid myself". He said, "Who told you that you were naked? Have you eaten of the tree of which I commanded you not to eat?" The man said, "The woman whom thou gavest to be with me, she gave me fruit of the tree, and I ate".
Then the Lord God said to the woman, "What is this that you have done?" The woman said, "The serpent beguiled me, and I ate".
The Lord God said to the serpent, "Because you have done this, cursed are you above all cattle, and above all wild animals; upon your belly you shall go, and dust you shall eat all the days of your life. I will put enmity between you and the woman, and between your seed and her seed; he shall bruise your head, and you shall bruise his heel".'
The fundamental assertion of this passage is the promise of an ultimate victory over the powers of evil. The passage was obviously selected for that Sunday to fit in with the Gospel text in which Jesus discusses how Satan can be overcome (Mk 3,20-25). If the reading is for an ordinary parish congregation the key message could be formulated as follows: 'God promises that the powers of evil will eventually be overcome by Jesus Christ'.
When we read the text as it is given in our RSV lectionary, we notice some archaic words that may not be understood by everyone in our congregation. During the reading we can decode them by substituting modern equivalents for them. For this reason we may decide to read 'you' instead of

'thee' in vs. 10; to read 'God said' instead of 'He said' in vs.11; to read 'deceived' instead of 'beguiled' in vs.13; to read 'offspring' instead of 'seed', and 'crush' instead of 'bruise' in vs.15.

As this is a difficult passage, it may also be necessary to remind people of the biblical context. To get the meaning, they will have to realise that the excerpt is from the paradise story. They will have to know the roles of the man, the woman, and the serpent. This decoding may have to be done in the introduction.

The whole presentation of the reading could then take the following shape (note that the words in the text that are printed in italics are those substituted for the archaic expressions found in the lectionary):

'The sin of Adam and Eve symbolises the sin of all mankind. But God does not allow his plan for mankind to be thwarted by sin. He promises the ultimate victory over all powers of evil in Jesus Christ. The reading is from Genesis 3,9-15'.

(Pause for a short while)

'The Lord God called to the man, and said to him, "Where are you?" and he said, "I heard the sound of *you* in the garden, and I was afraid, because I was naked; and I hid myself". *God* said, "Who told you that you were naked? Have you eaten of the tree of which I commanded you not to eat?" The man said, "The woman whom *you gave* to be with me, she gave me fruit of the tree, and I ate".

Then the Lord God said to the woman, "What is this that you have done?" The woman said, "The serpent *deceived* me, and I ate".

The Lord God said to the serpent, "Because you have done this, cursed are you above all cattle, and above all wild animals; upon your belly you shall go and dust you shall eat all the days of your life. I will put enmity between you and the woman, and between your *offspring* and her *offspring*; he shall *crush* your head and you shall *crush* his heel".'

Suppose that in a catechetical instruction we have spoken about death. We want to end the lecture with a reading from Sir. 38,16-24. By way of introduction we may say:

'In this text the Bible teaches us the correct attitude when one of our dear ones has died. It is natural for us to feel great sorrow and we should observe the normal custom of mourning. However, we should not be so upset about it that it would spoil the rest of our life. Instead, we should use our common sense and learn the lesson that we too will have to die one day'.

'My son, shed tears over a dead man,
  and intone the lament to show your own deep grief;
bury his body with due ceremonial,
  and do not neglect to honour his grave.
Weep bitterly, wail most fervently;
  observe the mourning the dead man deserves,
  one day or two, to avoid comment,
  and then be comforted in your sorrow;
for grief can lead to death,
  a grief-stricken heart undermines your strength.
Let grief end with the funeral;
  a life of grief oppresses the mind.
Do not abandon your heart to grief,
  drive it away, bear your own end in mind.
Do not forget, there is no going back;
  you cannot help the dead, and you will harm yourself.
Those who died tell us:
'Remember my doom, since it will be yours too;
  yesterday was my day, today is yours'.
Once the dead man is laid to rest, let his memory rest too,
do not fret for him, once his spirit departs.'

COMMENTATED READING

It happens at times that the text we want to read to others is some-what involved or is so replete with meaning that a simple reading of it will not do justice to its contents. We may then need to follow some other technique through which the full meaning of the text can be brought out. Commentated reading essentially consists in enlarging the text with little explanatory phrases that are introduced wherever they may be required.

At times we are asked to open a meeting 'with a little prayer'. We are given eight to ten minutes for this purpose. A small, but powerful commentated reading from Scripture will usually prove an excellent way of starting off. We may then follow the 'commentated reading and prayer of response' approach. The approach has four parts: a small reading from Scripture which we intersperse with com-mentaries, a second reading of the same text without our personal enlargements, a brief pause for personal reflection and finally a short spontaneous prayer (called 'prayer of response' because we both respond to the Word of God and to the situation in which we speak the prayer).

Suppose a one-day meeting has been called on 'peace and justice'. Apart from improving the exchange of accurate information, the meeting will also consider programmes of action that have been proposed. When I am asked to open the meeting 'with a little prayer', I suggest that it may be worthwhile to begin with a short reading from Scripture and that altogether I will need about ten minutes for this purpose. The actual presentation then could be as follows: (commentary is in italics).

'Dear friends, we want to invoke God's blessing on our gathering today. All our discussions should ultimately spring from our being sensitive to his demands. Let us therefore begin by listening to what the Word of God has to say to us in Isaiah 51,1-3.

"Listen to me, you who pursue integrity,
   who seek Yahweh
— *The prophet in this text addresses especially those who seek to further the cause of justice. His words will be of special relevance to us* —

Consider the rock you were hewn from.
— *We should never forget we belong to Christ* –
The quarry from which you were cut.
Consider Abraham your father
and Sarah who gave you birth. For *Abraham* was all alone when I called him, but I blessed and increased him.
— *In other words, when pursuing the cause of justice we should remember that our strength is our faith and that God can increase the fruit of our labour, if we live from faith as Abraham did* –
Yes, *God* has pity on *Jerusalem, that is God is concerned about the situation of mankind.*
has pity on all her ruins;
God will turn her desolation into a *paradise,*
her wasteland into the garden of Yahweh.
— *We are here given a vision of the ultimate happiness and welfare to which God destines all mankind* –
Joy and gladness shall be found in *Jerusalem,*
thanksgiving and the sound of music."

I will now read the text without my reflections. After this, we will pause for a short while to meditate in silence and then I will formulate a short prayer on behalf of us all.
'Listen to me, you who pursue integrity,
   who seek Yahweh.

Consider the rock you were hewn from,
the quarry from which you were cut.
Consider Abraham your father
and Sarah who gave you birth.
For he was all alone when I called him, but I blessed and
    increased him.
Yes, Yahweh has pity on Zion,
has pity on all her ruins; turns her desolation into an Eden,
    her wasteland into the garden of Yahweh.
Joy and gladness shall be found in her, thanksgiving and
    the sound of music.'
        (Pause a short while)
    'Almighty Father, bless this assembly of ours which is
dedicated to furthering the cause of justice among all men. Fill
our hearts with your concern and pity for every human person
whom, we know, you created out of love. Help us to think and
act like men of faith, true to Christ, the rock from which we have
been cut. Let our proposals be inspired by your vision of joy and
happiness for all. We make our prayer through Christ, your
Son, our elder Brother, who lives and reigns with you for ever
and ever. Amen.'

Commentated reading also proves extremely useful as part of a
catechetical instruction. In this case, the best approach is probably a
reading of the text with running commentary whenever it is required.
By the manner in which we vary our tone of voice, by the way we
look at the children whenever we begin a section of commentary, and
by other such small indications, the children will know the difference
between the text actually found in Scripture and the words of explanation we add ourselves. It is an art to do running commentary well.
The running commentary should be interesting and lively, and, above
all, not too drawn out. Ideally speaking, it should be done in such a
natural and unobtrusive manner that the children do not even notice
the commentary. For them it will look as if we are simply reading
from Scripture. Obviously, when we read out a story our commentary
will be much lighter than when we read from the Prophets or the
Book of Wisdom.

It may be that in a lecture we have been discussing liturgical symbols.
Among other things, we may have pointed out that religious rites have no
value unless they correspond to the true feelings of our heart. It is no good
attending Mass if in our daily lives we do not live up to the principles of the

Gospel. In this connection we may want to read from Isaiah 1,11-20. In the next sample of commentated reading, the phrases in italics are the additions made to the text.

'In the next lines we read how God told the people of Israel what he thought of those who covered their sins of injustice and oppression by bringing sacrifices in the Temple.

'What are your endless sacrifices to me?
says Yahweh.
I am sick of your holocausts — *holocausts were one kind of sacrifice in which the victim was completely burnt —*
and the fat of calves — *this refers to another kind of sacrifice in which only the fat of the victim was burnt on the fire —*
I am sick of holocausts of rams and the fat of calves.
The blood of bulls and of goats revolts me.
When you come to present yourselves before me,
who asked you to trample over my courts?
Bring me your worthless offerings no more,
the smoke of them fills me with disgust.
New moons, sabbaths, assemblies —
I cannot endure *your* festivals and solemnities.
— *of course, God did not reject such religious feasts in themselves. He rejected them because people had the wrong disposition of heart —*
Your new moons and your pilgrimages
I hate with all my soul.
They lie heavy on me.
I am tired of bearing them.
When you stretch out your hands *in supplication,*
I turn my eyes away.
You may multiply your prayers,
I shall not listen.
— *Then God explains the reason for his disgust —*
Your hands are covered with blood,
Wash, make yourselves clean.
Take your wrong-doing out of my sight.
Cease to do evil.
Learn to do good,
search for justice,
help the oppressed,
be just to the orphan,
plead for the widow.

— Widows and orphans needed to be protected especially because they had no one to defend their rights —
Then God said how the situation could be rectified. It required a true conversion of heart. God was ready to give people a new chance.
'Come now, let us talk this over',
says Yahweh.
'Though your sins are like scarlet,
they shall be as white as snow;
— that means, they shall be wiped out and forgiven —
though they are red as crimson,
they shall be *clean as* wool.
If you are willing to obey,
you shall eat the good things of the earth.
But if you persist in rebellion,
the sword shall eat you instead.'
— death shall be your punishment.
'The mouth of Yahweh has spoken.'

During the eucharistic celebration we can do justice to most readings with the approach of simple guided reading. But at times only commentated reading can bring out the full meaning. We should then not be afraid to follow this approach. If the text is short and we are not too hard pressed for time, we could read the text a second time, immediately after the commentated reading but now without commentary. If one is not used to the practice, it may seem strange at first. However, I know from experience that it works out quite well. By the double reading of the text, one with a short explanation and another one concentrating on the actual words of Scripture, an appropriate text of which the meaning would otherwise be lost, can now make a deep impression on the audience.

SOME FURTHER SUGGESTIONS

We are all familiar with the 'dramatised reading' of the Passion account in Holy Week. According to liturgical tradition the text is read by three parties: the story-teller, Christ, and a spokesman (who takes all the other spoken parts of the story). Sometimes the parts of the "crowd" are said by the whole community. Such dramatised reading can be extremely effective, as long as we take care that all the persons involved can be clearly heard and understood. The same technique lends itself also to other parts of the Bible where there is a sufficient amount of dialogue.

An approach that has proved its value on many occasions is 'reading illustrated by acting'. Normally, one person will read the text while some others perform the actions described.

At a Confirmation Mass the first reading may be from Ez 37,1-14, the prophet's vision of the dry bones that come to life. A number of children may lie down on the altar steps (the dry bones) with one of them standing up in their midst (the prophet). As the reading proceeds, they gradually raise themselves (the bones are covered with flesh). When the prophet is called to prophesy to the four winds, we see him stretch out his hands in all four directions. When the people receive the full breath of life, we see the children stand up and dance with vitality. The effect can be impressive but it must be carefully practised beforehand and the acting should not be overdone.

At a Eucharistic celebration to mark the beginning of the school year, the Gospel reading could be Jn 4,1-42, which recounts the meeting of Jesus and the Samaritan woman. The text can easily be illustrated with a mime. The actors will be: Jesus, the Samaritan woman, a few apostles and inhabitants of Sichar.

Usually, it is better to concentrate the instructive part of a Holy Mass on one theme. The readings from the lectionary for Sundays have been arranged in such a way that the first and the third readings more or less cover the same theme. If the celebrant plans his homily to be in harmony with this overall theme, there will be some unity of purpose in the whole celebration which will strengthen its overall effect. On the other hand, I do not think it correct to sacrifice the message of a particular reading to the general theme. The second reading on Sundays, for that matter, usually falls outside the scope of the theme that combines the other two. The right way is neither to simply drop the second reading nor to twist its key message to make it fit the general theme. Rather, we should consider each reading on its own merit. Each single reading deserves to be treated as a unit of communication that stands on its own. As long as we go about it slowly and deliberately, the overall theme will not suffer from a second reading that has its own specific message.

For some feasts the selection of the readings goes back to an ancient liturgical practice. Epiphany was a baptismal feast in the Eastern Church. The newly baptised received further initiation in the Christian mysteries.

Fig. 35. Illustration at Epiphany in the lectionary of Limoges (11th cent.).

The age-old theme of the readings was Christ's self revelation ("epiphany" means "manifestation"), His presence in mystery. Three readings traditionally belonged to the feast: the story of the Magi, Christ's baptism in the Jordan and the changing of water and wine in Cana. From the East these readings entered Western lectionaries (see Fig. 35). An ancient antiphon at Vespers records:

"We celebrate a sacred day adorned by three miracles:
today the star led the magi to the manger;
today water was made wine at the wedding;
today Christ wanted to be baptized by John in the Jordan.
Alleluiah!"

The new lectionary has not attempted to retain all the ancient readings. It held on to Mt 2,1-12 (the Magi) as the Gospel text and suggested as complements, readings on Christ's self-revelation: Is 60,1-6 (announces that all nations will come to Jerusalem) and Eph 3, 2-3, 5-6 (the revelation is passed on through the apostles).

A question that arises at times with regard to the lectionary is whether we are bound to stick to the readings suggested or whether we could make our own choice. The answer is that the lectionary itself presupposes a certain amount of freedom and adaptation, even though it is good practice to follow the recommended readings whenever possible. The selection of texts proposed in the lectionary is, after all, the outcome of much study by people who both knew the Bible and were aware of the pastoral needs of the faithful. The whole lectionary presents a programme that highlights different aspects of Scripture. It should be valued also in its entirety. However, because the overriding purpose of the lectionary is its use to people and because, whenever we read Scripture, its relevance for our particular audience should remain our first priority, the recommendations of the lectionary should not be seen as commandments to be followed for their own sakes. When a certain reading is much too difficult for our audience (for instance, if we have a Eucharist for children), it is much better to select a reading that they can understand. If a particular occasion requires a special kind of reading, we are at perfect liberty to select a reading appropriate to the situation. And, of course, in group Masses for specific communities we may select our readings to fit topics of special importance to such communities.

A final word of warning. In many years of pastoral experience I have found that the small introduction, such as we use in simple guided reading, has often proved a big success from the word go. For anyone who puts it into practice its usefulness is immediately apparent. But carried away by enthusiasm at this new discovery, some pastors then fall into the error of making small homilies out of the introductions before the readings. This in turn causes people to grow restless: instead of just one sermon at Mass, they are now presented with a whole series of them! It is good to realise that the words of the priest at various stages of the first part of Mass have a variety of functions. At the beginning of Mass the priest (briefly) welcomes and calls to repentance; before each reading he merely announces the key statement not of his own view but of the gist of the scriptural message; only after the Gospel does the priest add his own reflections, in fidelity to his task of interpreting the Word of God for his people.

If the first reading at Mass is taken by a lay Reader, he (or she) can be asked to prepare the reading according to the approach of simple guided reading explained above. In case the Reader is not able to formulate the key message by himself, the celebrant could write it out for him on a slip of paper or announce it from the celebrant's chair before the Reader takes up his stand.

CHAPTER ELEVEN

STATEMENTS, LAWS AND PROVERBS

In other chapters of this book I have repeatedly drawn attention to the fact that the meaning of passages from Scripture has usually to be judged from the context. If is often quite wrong to lift a sentence from the Bible and maintain that we can understand it by itself. We find in the Bible the sentence, 'There is no God', but its meaning is only clear to us when we read the whole psalm in which this phrase occurs and in which the psalmist exclaims '*The fool* says there is no God' (Ps 35,1). For this reason to understand a biblical story we should search for its main statement first (pp. 97-102). I have suggested that, when preparing a reading from Scripture, we should try to determine its fundamental assertion (pp. 185-189). Generally speaking, it is dangerous practice to focus attention on one particular sentence or phrase, thereby forgetting that the meaning of communication does not reside in isolated phrases but in the unit taken as a whole.

On the other hand, there are exceptions to the rule. It does happen that individual phrases have a special meaning of their own or that they can validly be lifted out of their context and made into a statement on their own. Other units of communication in the Bible are short by their very nature, such as proverbs and laws. In these cases focussing attention on a specific statement is justified and rewarding.

Mahatma Gandhi, the father of Indian Independence, has left an enormous number of works. Most of his speeches, articles and letters have to be understood as total units of communication. But, on account of his constant involvement with the same kind of topic, Gandhi developed certain principles, certain maxims, that can easily be culled from his work. Some examples of these are:

'To me, truth is God and there is no way to find truth except by the way of non-violence.'
'The welfare of India depends on the welfare of her villages.'

'Untouchability is a sin and a blot on Hinduism. Untouchability
has to die if Hinduism is to live.'

From the context of the passages in which such phrases occur it is
clear that they express, by themsleves, an important part of Gandhi's
philosphy of life. We would not do him an injustice if we were to take any
such phrase as the subject matter of a special study.

In this chapter I should like to discuss techniques that are based
upon such a 'one sentence' approach. After considering the merits
and limitations of the classical homily, I will introduce spotlight
exegesis, the study of parallel texts, and the presentation of laws and
proverbs.

THE CLASSICAL HOMILY

The homily was a form of preaching that arose in the Church from
the second century A.D. It was a form of address peculiar to
christians. It differed from the elaborate, technical commentary given
by Rabbis on Sacred Scripture during the Sabbath service. It was also
easily distinguished from the oratory so popular with the Greeks and
the Romans. The homily can best be characterised as a 'familiar
discourse with a group of people'. In a homily the preacher spoke
with great leisure, allowing his thoughts to wander into all kinds of
directions and switching continually from dogmatic instruction to
moral exhortation and back.

To get the feel of what we are discussing in this section I would like you
to creep into St. Augustine's skin. Imagine yourself on a Sunday of the year
420 A.D. in the Church of Hippo in North Africa. There he sits on a throne,
St. Augustine, with his bishop's mitre on, addressing the people. On his
knees rests a codex of sacred Scripture. He gesticulates freely with both
hands.

What would strike us apart from everything else as most different from
our own times is the length of the sermon and people's response. Augustine
continues to preach for half an hour, one hour, yes, even for two hours, if he
is in the mood. The faithful obviously enjoy his performance. They react to
his oratory not unlike crowds today react to a film show or a theatrical play.
Sometimes they are spellbound, and silent; at other times they laugh, or
sigh, or beat their breast. Now and then they interrupt Augustine with the
clapping of hands or cries of support. When Augustine refers to his
favourite psalm text, "Who made peace your aim", people interrupt him

with loud acclamations. We hear him continue: "What? Are you all shout-
ing for joy? Yes, brethren, love this passage! I am so pleased when love for
peace sounds so loudly from the bottom of your hearts! Oh, how pleased
you are yourselves! I have hardly spoken a syllable, I had not explained a
word, I had merely pronounced the verse, and see a storm of applause broke
loose among you!"

And as we watch Augustine and hear him speak, we discover an
interesting fact. We realize that we have found much more than a man
whose words are full of Scripture. Here is a man who lives on Scripture,
whose life and personality are moulded by it. Ever since his conversion,
when he heard the words, "Take and read", the Bible has been his prayer
book, his meditation book, his theological textbook and source book of
preaching. Augustine is a learned man for his own times; he studied the
secular sciences of his days; yet, whatever topic he speaks or writes about, it
is ultimately evaluated in the light of Scripture. Augustine is a man obsessed
by the Word of God, yet his position is not that of a fanatic. The only
purpose of Scripture, he says, is that we learn to love God and our
neighbour. The more a man knows Scripture, the better he can teach. But it
isn't memorizing texts or knowing interesting details that matters. The
important thing is to understand the Word of God, to search for its deeper
meaning, to penetrate its core with the eyes of the heart.

Augustine's attitude is reflected in his preaching. Underneath his long-
winded explanations we discover an enormous desire to understand and
expound the word of God. His homilies are witty and refer to contemporary
life, but they always return to Scripture for their explanation. Here is a man
for whom preaching means "unlocking" the sense of Scripture, whether this
be done by eloquence or straightforward talk, with a golden key or a
wooden one, to use his own words. The preacher is God's servant who
invites people to partake in "the banquet of the sacred books". "In
expounding to you the holy Scriptures, I as it were break bread for you.
What I deal out to you is not my own. What you eat, I eat myself. What you
live on, I live on myself. We have a common storehouse in heaven: it is from
there that the Word of God derives."

In a scriptural homily the biblical text is scrutinised sentence by
sentence, often word for word. One gets the impression that the
preacher moves on to another phrase only when he has exhausted
everything he could possibly say about the previous one. The homily
may well be compared to a film in slow motion, or, rather, a film in
which the frames which are normally projected at a speed of 20 per
second, are projected on the screen one by one and examined in all
their details. Or we could compare it to a theatre in which the whole
stage is in darkness except for a strong beam of light that slowly

travels from left to right and illumines individual persons and objects. Eventually the light will cover everything that is to be seen, but as long as the spotlight rests on a particular place it is as if this place is the only one that exists.

By way of example I will give here some excerpts from a sermon St. Augustine preached on the Lord's prayer, known as Sermon LVI. The audience in this case was a group of so-called 'combatants', i.e. catechumens in their final stage of instruction before being admitted to the reception of Baptism.

'... *"and forgive us our debts, as we also forgive our debtors".*
This petition needs no expounding in order to show that it is for ourselves that we make it, for by it we beg that our debts be forgiven us. And we are debtors, not in money, but in sins. Perhaps you now say to me: "Even you?" The answer, "Yes, even we". "What! Even you holy bishops are debtors?" "Yes, even we are debtors". "Even you? Far be it from you, my Lord; do not so unjustly accuse yourself". "I do not unjustly accuse myself; I am speaking the truth, for we are debtors." 'If we say that we have no sin we deceive ourselves and the truth is not in us' (1 Jn 1,8).

Though we have been baptised, yet we are debtors. Not that anything remains which was not remitted to us in baptism, but because in our lives we are contracting something which needs daily remission. As to those who are baptised and then depart from this life – they come forth from the font without any debt and they go forth from this life without any debt. But, as to those who are baptised and then continue to live – these contract some imperfections through the frailty of mortals. Even though the ship is not lost through these imperfections, the pumps must be used, for if the pumps are not used, there is a gradual leakage that may sink the whole ship. By making this petition, we make use of the pumps. Further, we ought not only to pray, but to give alms as well. For, when we are using the pumps to prevent the ship from sinking, we are using both our voice and our hands. We use our voice when we say: *"Forgive us our debts, as we also forgive our debtors"*, we use our hands when we fulfil this command: "Deal thy bread to the hungry, and bring the homeless needy into thy house" (Is 58,7), and "Shut up alms in the heart of the poor, and it shall intercede for thee before the Lord" (Sir 29,15) ...

Every day, therefore, let us say: *"Forgive us our debts, as we also forgive our debtors".* Let us say it with sincerity of heart, and let us fulfil our promise, for we make a promise, a covenant and pleasing agreement with God. What the Lord your God says to you is this: 'Forgive, and I will forgive. If you have not forgiven, then you yourself – not I – are retaining your sins against yourself'.

Now, my most dearly beloved, give me your attention. I know what is especially applicable to you in the Lord's Prayer, and, above all, in this sentence of it, *"Forgive us our debts, as we also forgive our debtors"*. You are about to be baptised; forgive everything. Whatever anyone of you has in his heart against anyone let him dismiss it from his heart. Come to the font with this disposition, then rest assured that you are forgiven all the sins that you have contracted – both the sin that is yours by reason of your birth from parents with original sin according to Adam (for it is because of this sin that you join with babes hastening to the grace of the Saviour), and also whatever sins you may have committed during your lives, by word, or thought, or deed. All sins are forgiven you, and you shall come forth from the font, as from the presence of your Lord, with the assurance that all your debts are forgiven.

And now, what are you to *do* with regard to those sins of which I have spoken? For, it is on account of those sins that – as though by a kind of daily cleansing – you have to say: *"Forgive us our debts, as we also forgive our debtors"*. Well, you have enemies. Indeed, who could live on this earth without having them? See to it that you love them. In no way can a raging enemy injure you as much as you injure yourself unless you love your enemy. He can damage your farm or your flock; he can injure your household – your man-servant or maid-servant, your son or your wife, or at most, he can injure your body if he has been given the power. But – unlike you – can he injure the soul? Dearly beloved, strive towards this perfection, I exhort you. . . .

You are still saying: "Who can do it, and who has ever done it?" May God do it in your hearts. Very few do it, I know. Those who do it are noble and spiritual. Is it true that all the faithful in the Church, all who approach the altar and receive the Body and Blood of Christ – is it true that all these are such as forgive their enemies? Yet, they all say: *"Forgive us our debts, as we also forgive our debtors"*. Suppose God were to say to them: 'Why do you ask me to do what I have promised, when you are not doing what I have commanded? What have I promised? I have promised to forgive your debts. What have I commanded? I have commanded you to forgive your debtors. How can you do that, unless you love your enemies?'

Brethren, what, therefore, must we do? Is the flock of Christ reduced to such a few? If only those who love their enemies ought to say: *"Forgive us our debts, as we also forgive our debtors"*, then I know not what to say, what to do. Must I tell you that unless you love your enemies, you are not to pray? I would not dare to do that. Rather, pray that you may love them. But must I say to you: unless you love your enemies, then in the Lord's Prayer do not say: *"Forgive us our debts, as we also forgive our debtors?"* Suppose I tell you not to say it? Unless you say it, your debts are not forgiven; if you say it without doing it, your debts are not forgiven. Therefore, in order that our debts be forgiven, we must both *say* and *do* . . . '

The above paragraphs are only a short extract from Augustine's sermon. We can see that such a homily was very much what we would call a lecture or a conference today. Giving such elaborate treatment to each phrase in a longer passage is hardly possible in the time-conscious age in which we live. Rather than trying to imitate the classical homily for ordinary sermons, it may be better to adopt techniques that combine the virtue of thorough exposition with conciseness and brevity.

Yet I would not dismiss Augustine's way of preaching as entirely impractical. For some of the biblical retreats I have been asked to give, I have tried it out with a good measure of success. I have found that the group should not be too big and that the setting should be arranged in such a way that all can feel comfortable (armchairs put in a circle usually creates the right atmosphere). I ask the group beforehand to bring their Bibles with them. The retreat conferences then consist of a slow reading of select books from the Bible, with plenty of explanations and reflections thrown in, not unlike the way St. Augustine did it. After each half hour of such a homily, there are shared reflection, discussions and prayer. The response from quite a few people has been that they have never felt so close to God's Word. The danger is that it may deteriorate into a Scripture class.

SPOTLIGHT EXEGESIS

Spotlight exegesis is an approach in which we work out to the fullest extent possible all the implications of a particular phrase found in

Scripture. It is an offshoot from the classical homily in the sense that it is based on free elaboration. But it differs from the homily by intentionally restricting itself to one particular phrase.

Fig. 36. 'Return of the Prodigal Son' by Rembrandt (1606-1669).
Notice how the artist emphasizes some parts of his painting by making light fall on them.

In its literal sense 'exegesis' means 'drawing out'. Exegesis is the science of drawing the full meaning out of a text, of digging deep to make sure that a particular biblical statement yields up all the teaching it can give. Obviously we will have to select the particular phrase very carefully. It should be a phrase or sentence that contains a statement that can stand on its own. The phrase or sentence in question should almost cover the 'fundamental assertion' the author wants to make.

Spotlight exegesis achieves its purpose by elaborating the meaning in a variety of ways. Apart from adducing philological information, we can study the statement in question from many points of view.

To show how this approach can be worked out in practice, I will give here a rather long excerpt from a sermon preached by S. A Kierkegaard (1813-55) on the lilies of the field.

' . . . In this sermon let us reflect how a person who is beset by anxieties can learn from the lilies in the field and the birds in the sky that he should be content with being human.

"Consider the lilies of the field". Consider, that means: give them close attention, make them the object of careful study, not just of a glance while passing by. That is why Christ here uses the expression which a teacher may use in the most solemn and sacred moment when he says: "Let us in this hour of prayer consider this or that". Christ's invitation now is just as solemn. Perhaps there are many who live in a big city and who never see a lily. Perhaps many live in the country-side and pass the lilies by without giving them a second thought. How many will there be who, in accordance with the word of the Gospel, consider them properly?

"The lilies of the field". There is no question here of rare plants that have been grown by a professional gardener and which are admired by experts. No, go to the field, where no one looks after those abandoned lilies and where one can all the same see so clearly that they have not been abandoned. If this exhortation were not to contain an invitation for a worried man, well then, this man would just be like the abandoned lilies, deserted, forgotten, slighted by others, passed by, lacking the care of other human beings, until by a proper consideration of those lilies he were to understand that in reality he has not been abandoned.

Worried man therefore enters the field and remains standing watching the lilies. He doesn't stand near them as a happy child or a childish adult sometimes does who walks around to find the most beautiful flower to satisfy his curiosity by finding something rare. No, in a silent and elevated mood he considers them as they stand there next to one another, in a numerous, fresh-coloured multitude, one exactly like the other . . .

"How they grow". Well, he doesn't actually see how they grow, for the popular saying is true that one cannot see the grass grow. But all the same he sees *how* they grow, or precisely because he does not understand how they grow, he sees that there must be someone who knows them as well as the gardener who knows his rare plants; someone who watches them day by day, morning and evening, as a gardener keeps watch over his rare plants; someone who gives them the power to grow. Presumably that 'someone' is exactly the same person as the one who gives the power to grow to the rare plants of the gardener, except that in that case the activities of the gardener can so easily lead to misunderstanding. In those places where one sees a gardener at work, where neither cost nor effort is spared to grow the rare plants of a rich landlord, in those places one could perhaps get the impression that it is easy to understand how they grow; but, in contrast, in the fields, where no one, literally no one, bothers about those lilies, how can they grow? And yet they grow.

But then those poor lilies will have to work all the more! No, *"they do not toil"*. It is only the rare flowers that require so much toil to make them blossom. In the place where the tapestry is more precious than in the royal reception rooms, no work needs to be done. When the eye enjoys its beautiful sight, the soul need not be troubled by the enormous amount of work and toil which those poor lilies had to do in order to make the tapestry so beautiful. Only with the product of human artistry one often finds that the eye, while blinded by the splendour of the piece of art, is at the same time filled with tears at the thought of the suffering of those destitute artists who worked at it. . .

So then worried man, who carried his worries to the lilies, now stands in their midst in the field, surprised at the glory with which they are arrayed. He takes one of them into his hands. He did not choose. It did not occur to him to make a choice because he realises that there wouldn't be anyone among them of which it could not be said that even Solomon in all his glory was not clothed like one of these.

Suppose that the lily could speak. Would it not say to this worried man: "Why are you so surprised at me? Is your being human not just as glorious? Could one not say with equal right that Solomon in all his glory is absolutely nothing in comparison with what each human person is, namely being human? Could it not be true that even Solomon, to be the most glorious thing he could be and to be aware of this, would need to detach himself from his external glory and try to be just human? Why would what is true of me, poor creature, not be true of a human being, considering that man is God's masterpiece of creation?"

But the lily cannot speak. But exactly because it cannot speak, just because in the open air there is silence and no one else with it, therefore worried man, if he speaks and if he tries to speak to the lily, is speaking to himself. Yes, gradually he discovers that he is speaking about himself, that whatever he says about the lily, he is actually stating about himself. It is not the lily that tells him this, because it cannot speak; neither is it another human person who says it to him because when we meet another person, disquieting thoughts of comparison intrude so easily. Standing among the lilies, worried man is only man, and it is sufficient for him to be only man. For in exactly the same sense that the lily is lily, he, in spite of all his worries, is man; and in exactly the same sense as the lily — without work and without toil — is more beautiful than Solomon's glory, in that sense man — without toil, without work, without all his own merits — is more glorious than Solomon's glory, simply by being man. By the way, the Gospel doesn't say that the lily is more glorious than Solomon; no, it says that it is better clothed than Solomon in all his glory. But in our daily involvement with other people, because of the many differences and the various relationships, distracted by our anxious sensitivity for comparisons, we forget what it is to be human; we forget it because of all those differences between one man and another. But when one stands in the field among the lilies, where the sky unfolds like a high canopy covering the head of a king, where one is free as the air which one breathes in the open space, where the great thoughts of the clouds chase away all narrow-mindedness, there worried man is the *only* man, and he learns from the lilies what he would perhaps not have been able to learn from another human being . . .

Let us examine the question a little further. Worried man who goes out to the lilies in the field is anxious to avoid any comparison with other people. He doesn't want another human being to speak to him about his worries. That is why I will respect his anxieties. I shall not speak about one or other human person, neither shall I speak about one or other worried person. No, let me speak about *the lily who had worries.*

Fig. 37. 'There was a lily on the bank of a small river . . .'
C. Poggenbeek (1853-1903).

Once upon a time there was a lily that stood in an isolated spot on the bank of a small river near the babbling and rippling water. The lily was a good acquaintance of some nettles and other plants in the neighbourhood. As the Gospel describes so well, the lily was clothed more beautifully than Solomon in all his glory. All day she was happy and without worries. Unnoticed and joyfully time passed on like the water of the river that travelled by, humming its tune.

Now it happened one day that a swallow discovered the spot. He paid a visit to the lily, returned the next day, then stayed away for a few days to come back again at a certain moment. The lily found this surprising and unintelligible; she couldn't understand why the swallow did not stay in the same spot as the flowers in her neighbourhood; she was surprised at the unpredictable way in which the swallow could act. But as things happen so often in life, so it happened to the lily: she started to love the swallow more and more, just because he was so unpredictable.

The swallow was a naughty swallow; instead of showing an understanding for the situation of the lily, instead of rejoicing with her at her beauty and congratulating her on her innocent happiness, the swallow wanted to show off, he wanted to make her feel his freedom, and he wished to make the lily feel how restricted she was. And this is not everything; the swallow was talkative at the same time and he told stories, now about this, now about that; truth and falsehood mixed together, how in other places he had seen great multitudes of other, gorgeous lilies, how in those places he had found a joy and happiness, a smell, a wealth of colours, a music of birds, that defied all description. The swallow kept telling this kind of story; and he loved to finish his descriptions with the remark, so humiliating for the lily, that in comparison with such beauty found elsewhere she had no standing at all; that she was so insignificant that one could rightly ask the question by what right she could be called a lily at all.

In this way the lily got worried. The more she heard from the swallow the more her worries increased. She could no longer sleep peacefully at night. No longer did she awake with joy in the morning. She felt herself hampered and tied down. She started to take a dislike to the rippling sound of the river and the day became long and dreary. She now started to concern herself about her own position and her fate. "It wouldn't be so bad", she told herself, "to hear the sound of the rippling water from time to time, for a change, but actually to have the same thing, day after day, is terribly boring". "No doubt it would be pleasant", she thought "to be alone and by oneself in a quiet and solitary place, but to be forgotten like this for one's whole life time, to spend one's life without company or in the company of nettles, which after all can hardly be called good company for a lily, is hard to endure". "To have such an ugly appearance as I have", the lily remarked to herself, "to be as insignificant as the swallow is telling me I am; Oh, why was I not born somewhere else, under another constellation; why was I not born an orchid!" For the swallow had told the lily that the orchid was considered the most beautiful of all flowers so that all other flowers are jealous of her. To crown her misery, the lily noticed that she was beset with worries; that is why she had a rational argument with herself; not rational in the sense that she dismissed the worries as of no concern, but in the sense that she persuaded herself that her worries were reasonable. "For my wishes are not unreasonable", she said. "I do not desire what is impossible, to become what I am not, for instance a swallow; I only wish to be a beautiful flower, the most beautiful there is".

Meanwhile the swallow kept coming from time to time; with each visit and each departure the lily's disquiet grew. In the end she entrusted herself totally to the swallow. One evening they agreed that they were to take action next morning; they were to make an end of those worries. In the morning the swallow returned; with his beak he dug in the earth round the lily's root so that she could come free. When that had succeeded the swallow put the lily on his wings and flew away. For they had made the plan to fly together to that place where the beautiful lilies were growing. The swallow had promised to re-plant the lily there, and then they thought there would be a chance, because of the change of place and the new surroundings, that the lily would become a really beautiful flower in the company of the other beautiful lilies, or perhaps that she might succeed in becoming an orchid, envied by other lilies.

While they were on the way the lily withered. If only that worried lily had been content to be a lily, she would not have known any worries. Not having any worries, she would have stayed in the place where she was born — where she stood in all her glory. If she had stayed there, she would have been that lily about which the preacher speaks on Sunday morning when he reads the Gospel text: "Consider the lily; I tell you that even Solomon in all his glory was not clothed like one of these" . . . If, being human, we cannot think without a smile of the worries of the lily which wanted to become an orchid but withered while she was on the way, should we not realise at the same time that it is just as ridiculous for a human being to have the same type of irrational worries? No, how would I dare to speak like this? How would I dare in all seriousness to neglect those teachers God has pointed out to me: the lilies of the field. No, the lilies do not have this type of worry; that is why we have to learn from them. If, just like the lilies, a human being is content to be a human being, then he will not be weighed down with temporal worries; and if he has no temporal worries, then he will remain standing in the place that has been allotted to him; and if he remains there, then it will be true that he is more glorious than Solomon in all his glory just by being human . . .

COMPARATIVE GOSPEL STUDY

The Gospel will always remain the most prominent source for our preaching and instruction. Containing the life and teaching of Jesus

Christ it is the part of Scripture we most naturally turn to for reflection and inspiration. But the Gospel's prominence also poses a problem. Because its texts are used so often, because the incidents and examples given in it are so well known, there is a danger that an instruction taken from the Gospel will be experienced by the audience as dull and boring.

If we find ourselves in this predicament and especially if our audience is well educated, it could be an idea to approach the Gospel with a more sophisticated technique. One such technique is the 'comparative Gospel study'. It starts from the recognition that the Gospel has been presented to us in four editions, in four gospels, for a special reason. If the words and deeds of Jesus had been presented to us by only one evangelist, we would have had a rather one-sided interpretation of them. Comparing what is common and what is different between them offers a wealth of material for study and reflection. It is one way of entering more deeply into the essential preaching of the Gospel.

Fig. 38. 'The four evangelists' by J. Jordaens (1593-1678).

The gospels are made up of smaller units, of 'passages'. St. Matthew's gospel, for instance, has a total of 196 passages (18,518 words in the Greek text). Of those passages, about 100 are 'parallel' with Luke and Mark. Matthew has 49 passages 'parallel' with Luke and 47 of his pasages are 'proper' (they have no parallel in another gospel).

As is well known, parallel passages derive from the same tradition in oral catechesis of the early Church (which explains their similarity) while retaining some of the special motifs and interests of the evangelist or the particular school of thought they stand for (and this explains the differences). The variations of expression, the different emphasis, the distinct interpretations of particular words or deeds of Jesus, may seem small and insignificant to a superficial reader of the gospels. But when one makes a close comparative study, it yields a very rich harvest of profound reflections and insights.

Some comparative studies are of considerable theological importance. All the gospels agree in relating that Christ commanded his apostles to preach the Good News to the whole world. But the words used to characterise this mission are different in all of them. In Matthew's Gospel we read that Christ instructed them "to make disciples of all nations" (Mt 28,19). We find here a basic concept according to which Jesus is the Master (Rabbi) and all christians are his disciples (talmudim). It is a Jewish way of thinking and stresses the personal relationship between Christ and each of his followers. In line with his own hellenistic background and missionary experience, Luke reformulates Christ's command as the commission to go as 'witnesses to the ends of the world' (Acts 1,8). In the notion of the 'witness' (martur) a christian is looked upon from the point of view of his personal commitment to the faith he professes. In John's Gospel the dimension stressed is the one of God's self-revelation. Jesus reveals the Father. Every christian too reveals God from the depth of his own experience. These are the implications of Christ's words: "As the Father sent me, so I send you" (Jn 20,21). It is not difficult to see that such a reflection, if properly worked out, can provide the substance for a good sermon. It can also form the basis for a demanding catechetical instruction or conference.

To do justice to this kind of comparative study, each of the following elements is essential:
1. We should first accurately determine the difference between the various parallel passages. Our exposition should be based on the original Greek or at least on a literal translation.
2. We should be aware of what modern commentaries say about

the comparison. A good grasp of present-day research on gospel formation is no luxury.

3. We should work out the implications of the differences for our practical understanding of the Gospel message.

Sometimes a comparative study can be linked with a motif. Suppose I am attending a five day seminar and I have been asked to prepare for each day a small "Bible study" at the opening of the morning sessions. As many of the participants will be persons with responsibility and leadership, I could choose the motif of 'the man in charge' as I find it in Luke's gospel. My approach could be that I show how Luke interprets five short parables of Christ as having a special message for those in charge.

Christ said "If one blind man leads another, both will fall into a pit". In Matthew Christ applied this to the Pharisees who are leading innocent people astray (Mt 15,14). From the context in which it occurs in St. Luke's gospel, we know he applied this text especially to those who had been appointed as elders or leaders over a particular community (Lk 6,39). If we are in charge, we should first take the trouble of acquiring correct knowledge.

Christ has said that the disciple is not superior to his teacher. From Matthew's gospel we learn the original circumstances in which Jesus spoke these words. He meant that, just like himself, his disciple too should expect opposition and suffering (Mt 10,24-25). In Luke's gospel the phrase has been elevated into a universal principle. Whoever is in charge of a christian community should strive to be perfect as Christ was (Lk 6,40).

Christ chided those who see the splinter in their brother's eye, but don't know the plank in their own. In Matthew's gospel it belongs to a precept of charity. No man should judge his brother (Mt 7,1-5). In Luke the text is given special relevance in the context of a christian leader correcting those entrusted to his care. The man in charge should be careful first to correct himself, before correcting his brother (Lk 7,41-42).

Jesus stated that a bad tree could not produce good fruit. His purpose was to teach his disciples how they could distinguish true prophets from false prophets (Mt 7,15-20). The context of Luke's gospel, again, presents it as a warning to christian leaders. If one's own life is not sound, one cannot produce good fruit in others (Lk 6,43-45).

The parable of the servant waiting for his master's return serves as a general exhortation to readiness for the Last Day in Matthew's gospel (Mt 24,45-51). In Luke's gospel the parable is worked out at more length and given a special application to those who are put in charge of others. The christian leader will be judged more severely because a great deal has been given him on trust (Lk 12,41-48).

"No sandals, nor staff . . .": A Conference for Priests (worked out by way of example)

When sending out his twelve apostles, Jesus gave them the following instructions:

> "Do not carry any gold, silver, or copper money in your pockets. Do not carry a travelling bag for the journey or an extra shirt, or sandals, or a walking stick".　　(Mt 10,9-10)

> "Do not take anything with you for the journey: no walking stick, no travelling bag, no food, no money, not even an extra shirt".　　(Lk 9,3)

> The seventy two disciples received the same injunction: "Do not take a purse with you, or a travelling bag, or sandals". (Lk 10,4)

The general purpose of these admonitions seems to be clear enough. Jesus wanted his disciples to be detached, and to practise a high degree of real poverty. He did not want them to worry about their own provisions. He wanted them to be free from the spiritual load of having many possessions. However, are we sure that such general considerations will really do justice to Jesus' words? Do we not too easily pass over the *specific* examples he mentions? Is our tendency to resolve his demands into principles acceptable to all, perhaps not an escape from the *particular* vocation to which he may call us?

If we examine the words of Jesus quoted above, we will notice that he also forbids the use of sandals or of a walking stick. I would like to restrict my reflection to the prohibition of these two articles because the force of the Lord's words speaks most clearly through this prohibition. Wearing sandals and the use of a stick were generally considered necessary for those travelling through the Holy Land in Jesus' time. The Palestinian roads were, as they still are today, covered with small sharp stones. The roads were narrow, dusty and rough on one's feet. One frequently had to walk through thornbushes or jump over holes and ditches. Having sandals on one's feet and a stick in one's hand was no luxury in those circumstances.

It is well known how demanding the Jewish scribes could be in interpreting the strictness of their sacred traditions. One such tradition was that while fasting one was not allowed to wear sandals or use a walking stick. Yet, an exception was made for those persons who went on a journey during a fast: they were allowed to make use of sandals and a staff outside the town: "He who may not wear sandals because of a fast, may put them on when he leaves the town. On the approach of another town he should pull them off again. This also applies to a person who has been put under a ban or who is in mourning" (Taanith, II,6). "Whenever it is stated that it is forbidden to wear sandals, it must be understood as being meant only for walking inside the town. But on a journey one may always wear sandals. What then should one do in practice? When going on a journey, the sandals may be put on; when entering a town, they should be pulled off" (Taanith, 13a). Narrow-minded legalists though they were, the scribes thought it too much hardship for anyone to have to make a journey without sandals or a walking stick!

Only the poorest of the poor could not afford these simple pieces of equipment. The Jews knew the saying: "Who rides on horseback is a king. Who rides a donkey is his own boss. But the person with sandals on his feet is an ordinary man" (Shabbat 152a). Non-Jews who converted to the Jewish faith had no claims to any privilege, because – as the saying went – "they had just passed into Judaism with no more than a travelling bag and a walking stick" (i.e. with nothing to boast of; Shabbat 31a). Rabbi Jehuda (AD 299) repeated what another scribe had handed on to him: "If necessary, one should even sell the crossbeams of one's house to buy sandals for one's feet. Only if a person has just lost blood and has absolutely nothing to eat may he sell the sandals on his feet to buy the food he needs" (Shabbat 129a). The Jewish commentator Rabbi Shelomoh Yitshaki (AD 1105) adds: "For there is nothing so humiliating as having to walk barefoot through the streets".

Sandals and a walking stick then were no signs of luxury at the time of Jesus and they were universally thought indispensable for travel. If we keep this in mind, Jesus' prohibition cannot but strike us as uncommonly strict. What is more, Jesus would not have imposed such a demanding prohibition on his disciples if he were not practising it himself. Jesus and his close followers walked barefoot through Palestine. They did not permit themselves this everyday equipment, which lay within reach of the common man. I believe that there is no need for me to dwell long on the *prophetic value* which this gesture must have had for those who met Jesus. The fact that so many flocked to Jesus may not only be explained by the miracles he performed. His true detachment, clear from the joyful way he could live a life of the utmost simplicity, drew many more. At the Last Supper, Jesus was to ask his disciples: "When I sent you out that time without purse, travelling bag or sandals, did you lack anything?" They were joyfully to respond: "Nothing, Lord" (Lk 22,35). A marvellous disposition to which we may fruitfully compare our own. Does *our* apostolic poverty measure up to this? Is *our* joyful detachment a prophetic sign to others?

To the Jews it was obvious that Jesus and his apostles practised such utter detachment for religious motivations. To them it was a clear sign of self-humiliation, taken upon oneself when fasting, or in mourning, or when entering the courts of the Temple. Thus by their practice Jesus and the apostles were known as people totally dedicated to a sacred task. When

Jesus added that they "should salute anyone on the road" (Lk 10,4), that they "should let the dead bury their own dead" (Lk 9,60), that they should be ready to live "without a stone to lay their heads on" (Lk 9,58), he indicated the same requirement of undivided dedication to their task of proclaiming the Kingdom. While examining the motives for and the expressions of *our* apostolic poverty, let us not forget this element of sacred dedication. Does our detachment identify us, in an unmistakable manner, as persons committed.to Christ and his work and to nothing else?

It may be that we have been somewhat taken aback by the strictness and apparent rigidity of Jesus' practice of apostolic poverty. Perhaps we have asked ourselves: "Will everyone be able to go to such limits of detachment as Jesus demanded?" If so, we will find consolation in the way in which Christ's instructions have been recorded in St. Mark's Gospel. For, in St. Mark's version, Christ *does* allow the use of sandals and a walking stick:

> "Don't take anything with you on the trip, *except a walking stick*; no bread, no travelling bag, no money in your pockets. *You may wear sandals* but do not wear an extra shirt".
> (Mk 6,8-9)

There have been many attempts to explain away the contradiction between this text and Mt 10,9-10 or Lk 9,3; 10,4 which have been quoted above. It has been suggested that Our Lord forbade the use of *boots* or *shoes* (Matthew; Luke), but allowed simple *sandals* (Mark) and that he did not want his apostles to use a stick for self-defence (Matthew; Luke), but permitted a staff for travelling (Mark). However, such explanations fail to do justice to the texts. They do not face up to the fact that Mark does give a different interpretation to Christ's words.

How are we to solve the puzzle? As we have seen above, there is no doubt about the utter strictness of the apostolic poverty practised by Jesus and the apostles. We may also take it for certain that Jesus' original instructions did *not* allow the use of sandals or a walking stick. Matthew or Luke could never have introduced such a strict prohibition if it did not originate from Jesus himself. On the other hand, the words in Mark bear the characteristics of being a pastoral interpretation. They reflect a later stage in the life of the Early Church, a period when it had become obvious that Our Lord's instructions could not be followed by all his followers with the same degree of strictness. The prohibition of sandals and a walking stick, a prohibition which was − remember − extraordinarily hard indeed, had become an obstacle when practical situations had to be judged. In these circumstances St.Peter, whose teaching underlies Mark's Gospel, must have given an authentic interpretation of Our Lord's words, making it clear that it was the mind of Christ to allow sandals and a walking stick for such occasions.

St. Peter may have found the justification for this interpetation in Jesus' own practice. It is quite likely that there have been occasions when – for practical reasons – Jesus allowed some of his disciples to deviate from the common rule by wearing sandals. Had he not made a similar exception to the norm of "not having a purse", by appointing Judas as treasurer for some gifts he and his apostles had received (Jn 13,29)? Moreover, it always was far from Our Lord's mind to replace the formalistic practice of rabbinic rules and regulations by another set of rules. Jesus did not teach rules, but a new spirit, a new ideal of life, new norms and principles of sanctity. Even on his own authority St. Peter could have given an authentic interpretation of what Christ meant. For, like the other apostles, he too had been commissioned to teach Jesus' followers about the things Jesus had taught (Mt 28,20) and this with authority: "Who hears you, hears me" (Lk 10,16). Like the other apostles, he too could teach with the special guidance of the Holy Spirit who would lead them into all truth (Jn 16,13) and who would teach them everything and make them remember all Jesus had told them (Jn 14,26). Through this Spirit Peter could give a new authentic rendering of Jesus' words regarding the sandals and the walking stick too.

The Gospels mutually complement one another. As in other instances, so also in this matter of apostolic poverty we should give a hearing to the fulness of Christ's teaching. We should try to live the various realities that make up the fulness of Christ's life. While maintaining an attitude of common sense and while having consideration for our human limitations (see Mk 6,8-9), we should at the same time leave scope for genuinely prophetic poverty as part of our apostolate (Mt 10,9-10; Lk 9,3,19,4). Jesus' undivided dedication to the preaching of the Kingdom should be made manifest also in the Church of the present day. To do this effectively and with true prophetic vigour may be the special charism of certain individuals and groups who should be helped and encouraged to do so. But even if we have to acknowledge that we ourselves have not received this gift, let us be animated by the same spirit that is expressed by it. If we cannot do without a walking stick, it need not have an ivory knob.

LAWS AND PROVERBS

The Old Testament has six collections of laws, which in order of age and historical composition could be listed as follows:

1. the decalogue (Ex 20,1-17; Dt 5,11-21; cf. Dt 27,11-26);
2. the sanctuary code (Ex 23,20-33; 34,1-28);
3. the book of the covenant (Ex 20,22-23, 33);
4. the deuteronomic code (Dt 5,1-28, 89);
5. the code of sanctity (Lev 17,1-26;46);

6. the priestly code (Ex 25-31; 35-40; Lev 1-16; Num 5-9; 27-36).

The distinct laws contained in these codes, even if we do not subdivide them, amount to over 300.

The Bible has also preserved many proverbs. Most of them can be found in Proverbs, Kohelet (also called Ecclesiastes), Sirach (which has the alternative name Ecclesiasticus) and Wisdom. They contain a total of more than 1500 proverbs.

Some of the laws and proverbs are out-of-date. They have been abolished by the coming of Christ. To this category belong especially the ceremonial laws (such as how to bring a peace offering, Lev 3) and the ritual sanctions ("No Ammonite shall enter the assembly of God"; Dt 23,3). Some proverbs reflect the social prejudices of those times: "One (good) man in a thousand I may find, but never a woman better than the rest" (Koh 7,29); "Fodder, the stick and burdens for a donkey; bread, discipline and work for a slave" (Sir 33,25). Old Testament morality was crude in many ways and such laws and proverbs must be evaluated in the light of the New. They served their purpose long ago. Now they are obsolete.

But the limited value of those abrogated rules of conduct should not make us lose sight of the valuable instruction contained in many others. Many of the prescriptions and suggestions, the commandments and counsels of wisdom contained in the Old Testament have a real message for us today. They touch on many practical and everyday aspects of life which are not mentioned in the New Testament. They give numerous tips on our relationships with other people and how to improve them.

Often a particular law or proverb may prove to be an interesting and profound topic for a biblical instruction. When we make the selection, we make sure that the proverb or law in question is not one of those abrogated through the New Testament. We then gather our material in the following way:

(a) We ask ourselves what the law or proverb meant in the Old Testament situation. Why was it considered important? What did it want to achieve?

(b) We investigate whether the New Testament confirmed it or extended it in any way. How would Christ look upon it?

(c) We apply it to our own situation. What would it mean if we were to put it into effect in our own lives?

To show the usefulness and viability of this approach I will give four examples that have been worked out as short homilies: two are based on laws, two on proverbs. In my experience I have found proverbs easier to explain as they require less technical introduction.

Having leisure for one's family. Reflection on a Law

In ancient times the king had the right to requisition services from his subjects. When a war broke out, he could make them join his army as soldiers. In peace time he could impose work on them both on his agricultural estates and in his palaces. The book of Samuel mentions: "Ploughing the king's land, harvesting his harvest, making his weapons of war, cooking in his palaces and looking after flocks" (1 Sam 8,11-18). King Solomon raised an annual levy of forced labour throughout Israel of 30,000 men, apart from the casual labour that could include as many as 70,000 porters (1 Kings 5,27-32). Rehoboam built 15 fortresses in Judah with requisitioned labour (II Chron 11,5-12). An Old Testament law I should like to reflect on today gives exemption to newly married men from such public services.

"If a man is newly married, he may not be forced to join the army or to perform public service. He shall be left at home free of all obligations for one year to bring joy to the wife he has taken".   (Dt 24,5)

The exemption goes back to a very ancient custom dating from the time of Israel's holy war. It is also known from Ugaritic literature. According to this custom a person who had just built a new house, planted a vineyard and married a wife should not take part in a battle (Dt 20,5-7). If such a person were to die he would be prevented from enjoying the fruits of the new family he was building up. It would amount to the so-called frustration curse (Dt 28,30) for which the Jews nurtured a deep-seated fear.

To put it in simple words: the man who is just building up a new family should not be disturbed. Otherwise the whole of society could be affected. He should have time to give joy to his wife and to get to know her. He should be free to construct his house and to lay out the vineyard on which his wife and children would have to live. The undisturbed peace of a new family was for the Jews an external manifestation of God's blessing. This peace should not be disturbed even for such necessary things as warfare and public services.

"If a man is newly married, he may not be forced to join the army or to perform public service. He shall be left at home free of all obligations for one year to bring joy to the wife he has taken".   (Dt 24,5)

Modern society makes a heavy demand on persons engaged in public services. A feeling of responsibility for his work may leave many a teacher, doctor, social worker or nurse to spend much of his or her time in work outside the home. In fact, it frequently happens that people with many responsibilities and a high record of service find hardly any time to spend at home with their wives and children. The law of Deuteronomy may help such persons to reflect on their basic position in life. However much society may benefit from their services, the building up of their own family should not be neglected. No family can prosper if father or mother has no time for its members. The undisturbed peace of a christian family is in itself a blessing for society and should not be sacrificed to external pressures.

The law tells us that the newly married man should be exempted from all obligations, so as "to give joy to his wife". What a beautiful definition of family life! The secret of a happy family or community does not lie in a self-centred seeking of comfort and security. Rather it lies in the determination of the members to give joy to one another: the husband to his wife, the wife to her husband, the parents to their children and the children to their parents. In human life, family means growth. The giving of joy is the environment in which growth is possible.

It is persons that count, not things. A life without joy is a wasted life. Serving society at the cost of your family is like planting a tree but cutting its roots. Scripture reminds us: "If a man is mean to himself, to whom will he be good?" (Sir 14,5).

Religious tolerance. Reflection on a Law

The Jews were not allowed to eat animals that had died by themselves. The reason was that such animals had died with the blood remaining in their flesh. The Jews were instructed to remove all the blood from the animal after slaughtering it (Gen 9,4: Lev 17,10-14). The blood of the animal to be eaten had to be poured out because the blood was life itself (Lev 17,11; II Sam 23,17). Life was considered to be sacred. It played a special function in sacrifice (Ex 29,16; Lev 1,5.11). Blood could reconcile God and men (Lev 17,11). It could consecrate people to God (Ex 12,22-23; 29,21). It could ratify a covenant (Ex 24,3-8). For all these reasons, Jews were forbidden to eat blood. Their respect for blood gave expression to their respect for life itself and for God, the giver of life.

So we are not suprised to find this law in the Old Testament code:
"You may not eat any animal that dies of itself".
What is remarkable, however, is the addition to the law:
"You may give it as food to the stranger who lives in your community or you may sell it to a foreigner" (Dt 14,21).
The Jews considered themselves an especially "holy" people, a people dedicated to God. At the same time, they realized that some of the obligations put on them by God's covenant did not necessarily apply to others. The interesting element in this particular law is that the lawgiver gives

explicit permission to the Jews to give meat from animals that died by themselves to their non-Jewish brethren. Meat, of course, was rare in Palestine especially for poor people, as it is for many today. It would be a pity if the poor non-Jews were not allowed to benefit from the availability of meat, on account of some special prohibition for the Jews alone.

This illustrates in a concrete instance that Almighty God, the Supreme Lawgiver, acknowledges different applications of morality for different people. God could not tolerate a Jew to eat flesh with blood in it, since the Jew saw the connection between blood, life and God as life-giver. But non-Jews, with their different concepts and their different religious approach, could not be judged by the same moral principle. The non-Jew should be judged by the principle which he had formulated in his conscience and in his religious traditions. As St. Paul was to say much later: Jews will be judged by the Law of Moses, but non-Jews will be judged by their conscience (Rom 2,12-29).

"You may not eat any animal that dies of itself".

"You may give it as food to the stranger who lives in your community or you may sell it to a foreigner".

It is obvious that this law has much application today. When judging Sikhs, Hindus or Muslims, for instance, we should allow them to serve God in the way dictated by their own consciences and by their own religious traditions. Things that may not be allowed to us because of our religious principles, may be perfectly allowable to them on account of the different understanding of morality found with them. We have to tolerate in them things which are not wrong in themselves, but which we ourselves would never do.

The law says that this particular kind of meat should be *given freely* to the stranger or may be sold to the foreigner. Here the lawgiver distinguishes two kinds of persons. In those times there were quite a few poor people, many of them of non-Jewish origin, who lived in Palestinian cities. To such "poor" strangers the meat should be given free of cost. The lawgiver often reminded the people of their duty of charity towards the non-Jewish poor living among them. They should not be oppressed (Dt 24,14). They had to be protected in court (Dt 24,17). They ought to be given a share of the tithe (Dt 14,28-29). They had to be given a share in the sacrifices at Pentecost (Dt 16,11). The command to give this meat freely to such strangers was therefore a reminder that the Jew should not draw financial profit from the fact that his animal died. Rather, he should be happy that his poor non-Jewish neighbour could enjoy the meat which he himself was not allowed to eat.

The "foreigner" to whom he could *sell* the meat was a different person. From a comparative study of the laws we know that he was some kind of businessman, often a money-lender, perhaps representing houses of import and export with the countries of trade. The lawgiver allowed his people to be strict with such "foreigners" when demanding the repayment of debts (Dt 15,3) or the taking of interest (Dt 23,21). Also in this case, he allowed his people to gain financial profit when handing over a dead animal to such a merchant.

"You may not eat any animal that dies of itself"

"You may give it as food to the stranger who lives in your community or you may sell it to a foreigner"

The literal details of this law are no longer applicable to us. Most of us do not possess cattle and even if an animal dies of itself we would be allowed to eat the meat. What remains a lesson for us is the attitude taught with regard to those belonging to other religious traditions. We should be tolerant towards them and not treat them according to our own norms, but according to the norms which they understand and according to which they worship God.

On honesty in business. The lesson of a proverb

The Old Testament has a lovely proverb for shoppers:

" 'Bad, bad' says the buyer,

But when he has gone, then he boasts" (Prov. 20,14).

I remember it as if were yesterday. I was shopping with a friend. He wanted to buy a second-hand army jacket offered in a cheap ready-made garment store. "It is useless", he said to the shop attendant. "It is old, it has stains, it is worn at the elbows". He got it at a forty percent discount. When we had left the shop, he turned to me and said: "This was a very good bargain! The jacket is worth at least twice as much".

I am sure that, like many other people, my friend considers buying and selling a game. They think we can virtually say anything we like, as long as it is to our own advantage. They argue that when closing a deal, we should not rely on the word of the other, but should depend on our own commercial knowledge. If someone else allows himself to be fooled by our talk, it is his own fault!

" 'Bad, bad' says the buyer,

But when he has gone, then he boasts".

There is some truth in the contention that we should not expect straightforward speech between people representing different sides in a business deal. It is *natural* for man to stress what is to his own profit. We cannot realistically expect that a salesman would give an absolutely objective picture of the article he is trying to sell. "Do not ask a merchant for advice about prices, or a buyer about selling" (Sir 37,11).

On the other hand, there is a big difference between stressing our own good points and telling outright lies. However great the temptation may be, neither the buyer nor the seller may say something that they know to be false. It is in this context that the Bible remarks that it is difficult for a merchant to avoid doing wrong in his business (Sir 26,29). But, thanks be to God, honest business men *do exist* and in the long run they will profit from their honesty, even in the commercial sense of the word.

At the same time, we should be aware that there are people who deceive us. If we are constantly being taken in by others, it may be that we lack essential realism. Being a simpleton who is easily deceived by others, is nothing to be proud of, but a defect. If we stand with our two feet on the solid earth, we will know that there are people who pretend to be our friends, while they are only friends in name (Sir 37,1). It is sad, but true, that there are people who flatter us to our face, but who say the opposite when we have turned our back (Sir 27,23). The Bible says: "I have found many things to hate but nothing to equal such a man. And the Lord hates him too" (Sir 27,24). We may dislike such people, but they exist.

" 'Bad, bad' says the buyer,
But when he has gone, then he boasts"

However, we should not make the opposite error of not trusting any person. Rather, we should gladly extend our trust and confidence to others, while remaining realists. Readiness to believe others does not mean that we should take every statement at its face value. Joshua was tricked by the Gibeonites on account of such credulity (Jos 9,4-7). The truly experienced person will learn how to detect the words that cannot be trusted, "just as the palate distinguishes the taste of meat" (Sir 37,19). Not being a simpleton, he will raise his eyebrows when a customer says "bad, bad!"

Love requires speech. The lesson of a proverb

We live in a century that has become aware of man's psychological needs. Freud helped us realize that man's actions are often motivated by what goes on in his subconscious. Through transactional analysis, Berne has demonstrated that people play deep and complicated games under the surface of their everyday relationships. Man's mental make-up is not as simple as it looks. The true reasons for a man's actions are often quite the opposite of what they pretend to be. In psychology one and one don't make two.

The proverb we study today, although it is 2500 years old, offers a remarkably clear insight into the psychological complexity of man. It states the fact that we may hurt other people more by not speaking to them than by telling them off. Or, to put it in different words: human love can only exist where there is communication. The proverb reads:

"Better open scolding
than love without speaking" (Prov 27,5).

In other Wisdom texts, stress is laid on the usefulness of correction. A father may have to show his love by using the stick (Prov 13,24). Punishment can be a true sign of parental affection (Sir 30,1). A teacher who always reproves his pupils will be more appreciated in the end than the person who always flatters (Prov 28,3). Scolding another person can therefore be an expression of one's love. But that isn't precisely the point here.

Every human person needs encouragement and affection. Psychologists tell us that many children are emotionally starved because their parents or teachers do not show them enough attention and interest. All of us have experienced the strain of living with a person who is not "on speaking terms" with us. The lack of spoken affection and love creates a similar tension in those with whom we live. It is this so truly human need which the sacred author is speaking about.

Parents and those who hold similar positions in life often forget this need of speaking to their children or others entrusted to them. A father may be proud of his daughter who is doing well at college. If he *never* expresses his satisfaction, the daughter may feel disillusioned and unhappy without ever realizing the reason for it. A religious sister may do some wonderful work in a difficult mission. If her superior rarely speaks a word of appreciation, the sister may be put under a psychological strain which she herself may find it difficult to understand.

"Better open scolding
than love without speaking"

People who have studied human relations tell us that the lack of sufficient personal communication is a more frequent occurrence than we might think. In his terrifying novel *The Vipers' Nest*, François Mauriac describes a family in which husband and wife have given up direct heart-to-heart conversation with one another. Both of them suffer deeply from the lack of affection which they would like to give and receive. But having begun their routine of petty squabbles and mutual silence, they never come to a personal communication. What a real tragedy! What could have been a happy home has thus been turned into a vipers' nest.

It may be good for each one of us to look around and see if we neglect others by such love-destroying silence. As the inspired author teaches us in the proverb, it is not enough to esteem and love people in secret. By not communicating with others, by not speaking to them in a really human and personal fashion, we may hurt them much more than if we were to scold them with harsh abuse. He who scolds at least treats the other as a person. The silence of non-interest hurts deeper and destroys more. We can be sure that at the last judgement Christ will not only speak of feeding the hungry and clothing the naked. He may well say to us: "I was in need of a human word, but you did not speak to me".

CHAPTER TWELVE

WITNESS AND PROPHECY

Every profession has its "front" which Erving Goffman has defined as "that part of the individual's performance which regularly functions in a general and fixed fashion to define the situation for those who observe the performance". The "front" is that part of our behaviour by which we try to give people a particular kind of impression about our work. The front is maintained by an elaborate social game, sub-consciously or half-consciously adopted by all the members of a profession.

Fig. 39. Façades at the old Market square in Brussels.

Undertakers, for example, carefully distinguish between on-stage and off-stage areas. On-stage areas are accessible to outsiders. They include the showroom where coffins can be sold and the "chapel of rest" where corpses are laid out in state. Outsiders do not see the off-stage places, such as workshops and the room where bodies are dressed and prepared for burial. In the on-stage area a certain dignity and solemnity is fostered. Service personnel will be formally dressed. Curtains and other ornamentation will reflect sobriety and mourning. The manner of conducting business will be dignified and subdued. All evidence of the "dirty work" that necessarily needs to be done will be suppressed as far as possible. By charging a higher fee for the coffin, the undertaker does not need to dramatize the other costs of conducting a funeral that somehow would seem to upset the front. In short, an undertaker is an ordinary human person, an individual who laughs and jokes like everyone else, but who in the exercise of his profession is forced to maintain a certain front that covers and obscures his own person.

This is true of all professions to a greater or lesser extent. It is certainly the case for all those engaged in teaching or preaching the Gospel message. Whether they want it or not, a certain "front" has been constructed by society which they are expected to maintain. A clergyman who ascends the pulpit on a Sunday morning assumes the front of a preacher. He may confirm this by his terminology, "dear brethren . . .", by his vestments, by the topic selected for his sermon and a hundred and one other small things that mark him off as a "preacher". There is nothing surprising in this, you will say, and it can hardly be avoided. That may be true, but we should be aware of some of the undesirable consequences.

As soon as people realize that we are maintaining a front we lose credibility. People know that it is our professed aim to convince them of some truths and to persuade them to adopt certain modes of action. Almost instinctively this knowledge calls into operation a kind of defence mechanism by which people will be somewhat sceptical about everything we say.

Psychological research confirms this to be a fact. To make people adopt a message, the honesty and credibility of the speaker are more important than his competence or the intrinsic value of his words (Kelman and Hovland, 1953). A speaker loses credibility whenever the hearer knows he wants to persuade him (Hovland 1953). People are much more inclined to accept a message if they hear it accidentally, because they are then convinced that the speaker did not intend to influence their thinking (Walster and Festinger 1962). However one tries to explain it, the fact seems clear that the professional masters of the word, the politician, the barrister, the salesman and the preacher, are listened to with a certain amount of scepticism and distrust.

A shy and ill-at-ease farmer was called as a witness in a Kansas court. The counsel for the defence was anxious to get a good account out of him. "Now, sir, stand up and tell your story like a preacher!" The judge is said to have intervened by exclaiming, "Like a preacher?! No sir! None of that; I want you to tell the truth".

Religious studies about teenagers around the world confirm that credibility should be of especial concern to preachers and teachers of religion in our own times. Modern youth seem to have an inborn aversion to everything that smacks of dogmatism. Perhaps this arises from a profound awareness of the limitations of conditions and structures. Our young intellectuals know that doctrines affirmed by one authority are contradicted by another. They realize they are part of a society that is self-contradicting and constantly changing. They are exposed all the time to the business of making bold assertions which later prove false or erroneous. As a result they are distrustful of anything that is self-perpetuating and static, of institutions and traditions, of *a priori* ideologies and structures of power. They will not readily believe anything that is presented as traditional doctrine or the teaching of an official Church. Thus, in a person who speaks about religion they will immediately sense whether he is presenting a front or his real self.

SPEAKING ABOUT OURSELVES

In his booklet *How to prepare a sermon* Francis S. MacNutt rightly stresses that in our preaching today we should by all means introduce a personal element. Rather than represent the official Teaching Church by presenting an intellectual and objective lecture on faith or morals, the preacher or teacher should speak from his own experience and present a personal witness. As long as the preacher is not personally involved, his word lacks credibility. Francis MacNutt, quoting John Wesley, defines a preacher as a man who can say: "I set myself on fire; and people come to watch me burn". This is indeed a powerful image of a preacher. It reminds me of the 73 year-old Buddhist monk who immolated himself at Saigon in protest against the Diem regime. (Fig. 40). Nobody could doubt that this preacher believed in what he was saying.

To break down the front that we present, we have to lead people to the off-stage areas where we let our hair down and where we are ourselves. We share with people what we have experienced, our searching, our failings and our discoveries. We give our personal views and evaluations. We talk about our likes and dislikes, the things that encourage or discourage us. We communicate faith as we believe it and love as we feel it. We reveal ourselves as much as the topic about which we speak.

Fig. 40. Self-immolation by a 73 year-old Buddhist monk at Saigon in 1962.

It is my conviction that such a "personal" approach to our religious preaching and teaching is a necessary element in every presentation. There are obviously limits to what can and what should be done in this regard. Ultimately we are not preaching ourselves. There will be times when a very personal involvement is called for and other times when a more detached presentation is required. There are ways of bringing in personal matters that offend good taste or obstruct effective communication. No exact rules can be given about this.

Knowing precisely where the personal element should begin and where it should end is the outcome of informed wisdom and a good amount of experience.

In this chapter I would like to discuss two approaches in which the personal element predominates: witness and prophecy. I have brought together various suggestions which result from my own experience in trying to communicate scriptural messages or from observing the process in others. In giving some thoughts and hints as to how one should be a witness or a prophet, I may seem to contradict my own purpose. By teaching people how to be a prophet or witness, it may look as if I am making these things into new professions with their tricks and skills. We are indeed on thin ice when making a study of what is by nature unstudied and spontaneous. Perhaps, we should formulate our attempt in this way: by looking at what witness and prophecy mean, we could liberate ourselves from our professional mask, from the preacher's front, to be ourselves when the occasion demands this from us.

WHAT IS WITNESS?

In every day English, giving witness to an event means that we testify that we have seen this event with our own eyes. We have experienced it. We can vouch for its being true for we were present and have seen what happened or heard what was said. In court practice, the eye-witness account ranks as the highest form of evidence. We speak of someone who vouches for qualities in a person as a character witness.

In the book of Acts, the apostles testified both as eyewitnesses and as character witnesses. They are eye-witnesses of the Resurrection. "The Apostles continued to testify to the Resurrection of the Lord Jesus with great power" (4,33). They also gave witness to Jesus himself as a person, thus executing Jesus' command "You shall be my witnesses to the ends of the earth" (1,8). Their witness about Jesus is a complex statement. It asserts the truth of the historical events they relate. It vouches for Jesus' credibility. It attests, on the strength of experience, that Jesus can truly save. All these elements are part of the testimony.

> "We are witnesses of everything that Jesus did in the land of Israel and in Jerusalem. Then they put him to death by nailing him to a cross. But God raised him from death three days later and caused him to appear, not to everyone, but only to the wit-

nesses that God had already chosen, that is, to us who ate and drank with him after he rose from death. And he commanded us to preach the gospel to the people and to testify that he is the one whom God has appointed judge of the living and the dead. All the prophets spoke about him, saying that everyone who believes in him will have his sins forgiven through the power of his name." (10,39-43)

Christ is central to the idea of witness in the New Testament sense of the word. To give witness in this sense simply means to share with others our experience of Christ.

In his very first sermon on the day of Pentecost (2,14-39), Peter presents the pattern that must have been well-known in the Early Church. At first he explains the outpouring of the Spirit which was so manifest in the behaviour of the Apostles, then he reminds his audience of what Jesus has done and finally he testifies to the Resurrection. Peter, therefore, relates a threefold experience; his experience of the Holy Spirit, his experience of living with Christ, and his experience of Jesus as the Risen One. His words make such a great impression precisely because he is giving a testimony of something he himself has seen.

And John writes in his Letter:
"We write to you about the Word of life, which has existed from the very beginning. We have heard it, and we have seen it with our eyes; yes we have seen it, and our hands have touched it. When this life became visible, we saw it; so we speak of it and tell you about the eternal life which was with the Father and was made known to us. What we have seen and heard we announce to you also, so that you will join with us in the fellowship that we have with the Father and with his Son Jesus Christ" (1 John 1,1-3).

We will appreciate the force of such testimony. There is a big difference between what we simply pass on as a traditionally held doctrine and the message which we convey as witnesses of what we have personally experienced. An objection here would seem unavoidable. It may be said: "but how can *we* witness to what we have not experienced? Have *we* actually seen the Risen Christ?" The answer is that although we have not actually seen the Risen Christ in flesh and blood, we too can witness to what Christ, through his Spirit, is doing in us. The New Testament is emphatic on this point. In his Eucharistic farewell address, Jesus said that we will know him because of the Spirit of Truth that will be in us. "I will ask the Father and he will give you another helper, the Spirit of Truth to stay with you for ever. The world cannot receive him because it cannot see him or know him, but you know him, for he remains with you and lives in you" (Jn 14,16-17). Jesus says he will reveal himself to us: "My Father will love him who loves me. I too will love him and reveal myself to him" (Jn 14,21). The Holy Spirit will teach us everything: "The helper, the Holy Spirit, whom the Father will send in my name, will teach you everything and make you remember all that I have told you" (Jn 14,26). The early christians were aware that in this way every christian could know God directly and therefore could give witness of him. "This is how we are sure that we live in God and that he lives in us: he has given us his Spirit. And we have seen and will tell others that the Father sent his Son to be the Saviour of the world" (1 Jn 4, 13-14).

Whenever we give witness, our testimony is related to this experience of Christ and his Spirit. I am not thinking of something deeply mystical or dramatic. I believe that all of us, if we become sufficiently sensitive to the work of the Spirit, will discover that we have a real experience of Christ in this way. It is here that the roots of our christian witness lie even if the immediate topic discussed may not cover the whole christian message. There is no dichotomy here between the words we preach and the life we live. In early christian parlance, the preacher was a witness (in Greek "martur") who was ready to die for his testimony. Our word "martyr" derives from this.

WITNESS IN COMMUNICATION

In practice, when speaking about the Bible, how can we witness to what we say? What will a testimony look like in an ordinary Sunday sermon or in a catechism class?

Having observed and analysed what seemed to be genuine cases of witness, I always found these four ingredients: personal involvement, the touch of true life, a favourite Scripture text and experience of the Spirit.

Personal involvement:

The person speaks about himself. He talks in terms of "I" and "me". The subject in hand obviously means a lot to him.

The touch of true life:
> What he says fits in with ordinary human life as we know it. He acknowledges his own limitations and defects. He admits doubts and mistakes. His account includes true elements of life which are not easily captured by definition but which are yet very important, such as emotion, a sense of mystery, poetry and the voice of conscience.

A favourite Scripture text:
> Some word of Christ or some other passage from the Bible has made a deep impression on the person. The truth or attitude implied has become part and parcel of his view of life.

Experience of the Spirit:
> The person has been affected by the profound stirrings of the soul that are caused by the Holy Spirit: love, joy, peace, patience, kindness, goodness, faithfulness, humility or self control (Gal 5,22).

> Six weeks before she died, St. Theresa of Lisieux said: "You know, those words of Isaiah, 'There is no beauty or majesty in him. We saw him, but he has no looks to attract our eyes. He is despised, the least among men, a man of sorrows, familiar with suffering, who hides his face from shame. That is why we despise him. . .' (Is 53,2-3); these words have been the foundation of all my devotion to the Sacred Face, or I may even say the foundation of all my religious life . . . I too wanted to be without beauty, without looks, lonely, treading the winepress while being unknown to all creatures".

This was a personal testimony. Devotion to the Sacred Face of Christ was something dear to Theresa. When she became a novice as a girl of sixteen years old she had already asked to receive as her religious name "Theresa of the Sacred Face". Theresa kept a picture of the Sacred Face of Christ in her prayerbook and during her final sickness she asked that such a picture be pinned to the curtain at the side of her bed so that she could look at it from time to time. Frequently we find prayers and poems of hers that make reference to this special devotion. She understood her whole life in the convent as a hidden life chosen on purpose to live up to the example of self negation given by Christ. "To console you, oh Jesus, I want to live unknown and lonely. Your beauty, which you cover with a veil, reveals to me the depth of your mystery and makes me want to approach nearer to you! Your face is my only riches. I want to possess nothing else. Hiding myself in your face I will be like you, oh Jesus!"

Such reflections of Theresa had great consequences for her practical

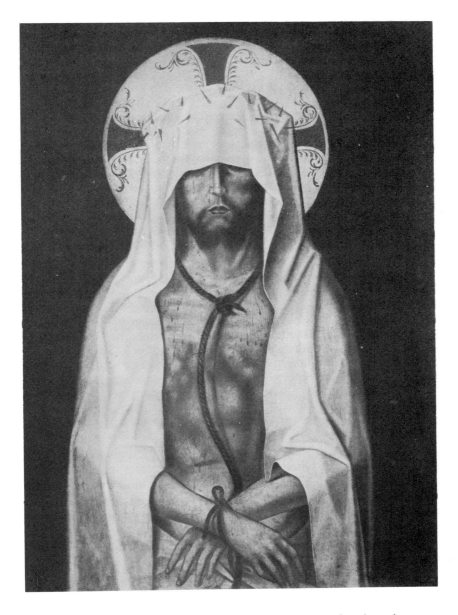

Fig. 41. Painting of the Veiled Christ (15th cent., Portugal, artist unknown).

and spiritual life. Theresa's biographers agree that one of her most remarkable virtues was her talent of hiding all her internal struggles, tensions and anxieties, but also her visions and exalted spiritual experiences, under the veil of a kind and childlike smile. This corresponded to her philosophy of life.

> "Our face is a mirror of the soul. That is why you must always show a happy, relaxed face as a small and contented child. All the more so when you are alone, for there are always angels who watch you."

> "Our dear Lord is sorry enough to have to test us here on earth, even though he loves us so much. Why should we cause him more sorrow by telling him how difficult we find life? That is why we should not let him notice what we feel. We should not be so tactless as to complain of heat or cold, to wipe the sweat from our face, or to rub our hands together when we are cold. Or, if we do these things, we should do them as it were without drawing his attention to them so that he knows we don't blame him for it."

In our age of gut-level communication and of finding Christ in intimate communion with others, Theresa's ideal of life may be beyond our understanding. We may not be able to say, as she did, "may my face like that of Christ remain hidden from all creatures on earth so that no one may recognise me!" Be that as it may. The point here is that when Theresa spoke about these things she presented something that had become part and parcel of her life. The sacred face of Jesus meant something to her. The words of Isaiah, "There was no beauty nor majesty in him", etc. had become a reality in her life. That is why Theresa could be a true witness about it. And however much our inclinations may be different from hers, she presents us with a genuine experience of Christ which no one will treat with disrespect.

Witness is such a personal thing that each individual can only do it in his own way. Often we may not feel strong enough about a certain point to be able to give witness to it. But, unless we are utterly spineless creatures who have no christian principles of our own, there will be issues on which we can give a genuine witness and about which, in fact, we may *have* to give witness. To help us recognise the opportunities that may come our way, I will briefly describe four more examples I have come across myself.

Confession is quite a problem nowadays, even with practising Catholics. A chaplain addressed a group of college students about the sacrament of penance. He did not dogmatize or moralize. Instead he told them in simple words what confession meant in his own life. He was quite honest about it. He admitted his own difficulties and reluctance at various stages of his life, and told them how he had come to appreciate the real value of confession. In this context he said that the story of the woman who wept at Jesus' feet (Lk 7,36-50) had made a deep impression on him. He had really felt the power of Jesus' sacramental words, "Your sins are forgiven". He was consoled by Jesus' assurance that sin might lead to greater love if the experience had brought us nearer to him. He added to all this an explanation of the various practical, pastoral rulings laid down by the Church. The students were wrapt in attention throughout his talk. Everyone felt that the chaplain was not putting up a front, but communicating a part of himself.

In religious instruction classes at school the matter of the relationship with parents repeatedly came up for discussion. After some of the usual teenager problems had been aired and looked at, the discussion moved towards grandparents and looking after people when they get old. Some students imitated and ridiculed old people. At this stage the teacher intervened. She narrated how she had felt about her own parents at various periods in her life. She told them that both her parents were now dead, and how she was happy about any small pleasure she had given them in their old age. She gave some examples of this and referred also to Sir 3,12-16 which discusses the blessings for children who respect their parents when they are old. She said she was especially struck by the promise that kindness to a father or mother shall not be forgotten but will serve as a reparation for our own sins.

I remember attending a congress in Madras at which a government official was to speak about education. In the course of his address he mentioned the fact that he himself was of Pariah descent and had been born in a small village. Through the christian mission his family had been baptized and he himself had been given the chance of attending various schools. He then continued to give a straightforward witness about Christ. "Without Christ I would not be a human person. Christ gave me everything I have and made me a child of God because he loved me." He then quoted 1 Cor 1,26-30 in which Scripture says that God chooses what is common and contemptible in the eyes of the world and that Jesus Christ has become our wisdom and our virtue and our holiness and our freedom. It was a moving testimony, which I will never forget.

A certain youth leader spoke about drugs. He himself had gone through a period when he occasionally used drugs and was on the way to getting hooked for good. He gave an interesting account of the agonizing struggle he went through. One of the things that helped him break the habit altogether was hearing a short sermon on the blind man of Jericho (Mk 10,46-52). The blind man called after Jesus, "Have pity on me!" When

Jesus invited him to come, he was so full of confidence that he threw off his cloak, jumped up and went to Jesus. It is difficult for a blind man to find his cloak when he has let it drop. Throwing off the cloak symbolized his abandoning himself to Jesus. The youth leader said that he had felt that breaking with his habit would require a similar act of trust.

PROPHECY AS FOUND IN SCRIPTURE

We are all familiar with prophecy as a phenomenom described in Scripture. We know that it means "pronouncing in the name of God a judgment on a specific situation, uttered on the strength of the prophet's inspired conviction". The prophets condemned or praised, threatened or consoled, according to the needs of their times. Prophecy was ranked as an important charism in the Early Church: after the ministry of the apostles and before that of the teachers (1 Cor 12,28).

The distinctive feature of prophecy was that a man of God told certain people what God thought of them in a particular situation. The prophet's vision always had a bearing on people's life.

The prototype of all prophets in the Old Testament was Moses. Moses' charismatic leadership inspired the Hebrews to such an extent that they left Egypt under his guidance and concluded a covenant with God at Sinai. According to the Old Testament books that describe Moses' activities, Moses always spoke on behalf of God. "This is what Yahweh has commanded me to say to the children of Israel . . ." Moses was so close to God that after speaking to Yahweh on the holy mountain, "the skin on his face was radiant with light" (Ex 34,29). And at his death we find recorded: "Since then, never has there been such a prophet in Israel as Moses, the man Yahweh knew face to face. What signs and wonders Yahweh caused him to perform in the land of Egypt against Pharaoh and all his servants and his whole land! How mighty the hand and great the fear that Moses wielded in the sight of all Israel!" (Dt 34,10-12).

Jesus too was a prophet

On one occasion many simple and poor people had gathered to listen to Jesus. Looking at them Jesus proclaimed: "Happy are you who are poor, the kingdom of God is yours! Happy are you who are hungry now, you will be filled!" (Lk 6,20-21). These simple god-fearing people did not realize how happy they really were. Jesus, acting as a prophet, told them what God thought about their situation. When confronted with the pharisees however, Jesus had a different judgment to give. He said: "Woe to you teachers of the

Fig. 42. "Moses" by Michelangelo (1515).

law and pharisees! Imposters!" (repeated seven times in Mt 23,13-28). Jesus proclaimed God's disapproval of the hypocrisy and formalism of Jewish religious leaders.

Prophets have sometimes been called "the voice of God and the conscience of society". Prophecy had two aspects: the social dimension, by which one person expressed what was present in the consciousness of the whole community; and the inspiration of an individual who felt called upon to make a statement on behalf of God. Both elements had to be there to make it a real prophecy. Condemning society or some abuses in it on purely humanitarian grounds did not make it prophecy. It was the reference to the judgement of God that changed a democratic protest into real prophecy.

As Christ's followers, we have been sent to teach people to obey everything Jesus has commanded us (Mt 28,20). We have been commissioned to continue his own prophetic task (Jn 20,21). So we too may occasionally be called upon to exercise the function of prophecy ourselves. In what kind of conditions would we be required to do so? What would such a prophecy look like? No doubt Christ promised his apostles, "When they bring you to trial, don't worry about what you are going to say or how you will say it; when the time comes, you will be given what you will say. For the words you speak will not be yours; they will come from the Spirit of your Father speaking in you" (Mt 10,19-20). But Christ spoke to men for whom prophecy was familiar. Will *we* be able to recognize its moment and allow the Spirit of the Father to speak in us?

PROPHECY TODAY

Before analyzing the elements that always seem to be present in a prophetic statement, I would like to present two examples of prophecy in our own times. For some mysterious reason or other we always associate prophecy with biblical times: more readily with the Old Testament and hesitatingly with the New. Prophecy, having become a scriptural category, has been made to look unreal, out of place, in our present-day running of the Church. Paul's injunction not to disregard prophecy (1 Thess 5,20) is perhaps taken too lightly by us. Seeing some examples of prophecy outside a scriptural context may make us aware again of its function in our own lives.

Girolamo Savonarola was a Dominican monk preaching in Florence. Being a saintly man he was utterly appalled by the conditions of his time. christian life had been ruined by prosperity and materialism. People freely indulged in pleasure-seeking and extravagances that would have shamed pagan Rome. With prophetic zeal Savonarola set about remedying the situation. He pronounced doom and divine wrath on all forms of degeneration and called for a universal renewal. The effect of his repeated messages was unparalleled. It brought about a revolution of life within the city, replacing pagan indulgence with pious austerity. It is unfortunate that Savonarola in his fanaticism overstepped the mark and was to die at odds with the Church. However, he certainly had the stature of a prophet and spoke as one, as can be seen from these extracts from a sermon he preached in the Duomo at Florence on 12th May 1496.

"In everything I am oppressed: even the spiritual power is against me with Peter's mighty key. Narrow is my path and full of trouble: like Balaam's ass, I must throw myself on the ground and cry: 'See here I am: I am ready to die for the truth'. But when Balaam beat his fallen beast, it said to him: 'What have I done to you?' So I say to you: "Come here and tell me: 'What have I done to you? Why do you beat me? I have spoken the truth to you: I have warned you to choose a virtuous life: I have led many souls to Christ". . . "The ass alone saw the angel, the others did not; so open your eyes. Thank God, many have them open. You have seen many learned men whom you thought wise and they have withstood our cause: now they believe; many noted masters who were hard and proud against us: now humility casts them down. You have also seen many women turn from their vanity to simplicity; vicious youths who are now improved and conduct themselves in a new way. Many indeed, have received this doctrine with humility. This doctrine has stood firm, no matter how attacked with the intention of showing that it was a doctrine opposed to Christ. God does that to manifest his Wisdom, to show how it finally overcomes all other wisdom. And he is willing that his servants be spoken against that they may show their patience and humility, and for the sake of his love not be afraid of martyrdom.

Oh you men and women, I bid you to this truth: let those who are in captivity contradict you as much as they will, God will come and oppose their pride. You who are proud, however, if you do not turn about and become better, then will the sword and the pestilence fall upon you; with famine and war will Italy be turned upside down. I foretell you this because I am sure of it: if I were not, I would not mention it. Open your eyes as Balaam opened his eyes when the angel said to him: "Had it not been for your ass, I would have killed you". So I say to you, you captives: 'Had it not been for the good and their preaching it would have been woe unto you'. . . . 'What will you have of us, brother?' you ask. I desire that you serve Christ with zeal and not with sloth and indifference. . . ."

William Wilberforce addressed the House of Commons in London on the African slave trade on 12th May in 1789. Wilberforce was a statesman and humanitarian leader who had pursued the abolitionist cause with great enthusiasm. Being a profoundly religious person he saw his task as not only dictated by principles of human dignity, but also imposed by the teaching of the Gospel. It has been said that in his lifetime struggle against slavery Wilberforce personified the conscience of contemporary England. The prophetic nature of his message will be clear from this extract of his address.

"I trust, therefore, I have shown that upon every ground total abolition ought to take place. I have urged many things which are not my leading objects for proposing it, since I have wished to show every description of gentlemen, and particularly the West Indian planters, who deserve every attention, that the abolition is politic upon their own principles also. Policy, however, sir, is not my principle, and I am not ashamed to say it. There is a principle above everything that is political, and when I reflect on the command which says: 'Thou shalt do no murder', believing the authority to be Divine, how can I dare to set up any reasonings of my own against it? And, sir, when we think of eternity, and of the future consequences of all human conduct, what is there in this life that should make any man contradict the dictates of his conscience, the principles of justice, the laws of religion and of God?
Sir, the nature and all the circumstances of this trade are now laid open to us; we can no longer plead ignorance, we cannot evade it, it is now an object case before us, we cannot pass it; we may spurn it, we may kick it out of our way, but we cannot turn aside so as to avoid seeing it; for it is brought now so directly before our eyes that this House must decide, and must justify to all the world, and to their own consciences, the rectitude of the grounds and principles of their decision. A Society has been established for the abolition of this trade, in which dissenters, Quakers, Churchmen – in which the most conscientious of all persuasions – have all united and made a common cause in this

greater question. Let not parliament be the only body that is insensible to the principles of natural justice."

Prophecies of this nature usually seem to contain five elements which I have called: endangered value, particular situation, direct address, judgment of God and support from scripture.

Endangered value:
> The immediate occasion for a "prophet" to intervene is the fact that a human value or a Gospel value is in need of being defended.

Particular situation:
> What is at stake is never a purely theoretical or abstract question. The problem arises from very specific conditions, peculiar to a particular country and time.

Direct address:
> In his statement the "prophet" directly addresses a particular person or group of persons who are involved in the particular situation.

Judgment of God:
> The authority with which the "prophet" is speaking is a kind of charismatic leadership arising from the fact that at this moment he knows himself to be inspired by God. He knows that he is the one most capable of expressing God's judgment on the situation. He is deeply convinced that he is empowered by God to speak on God's behalf.

Support from Scripture:
> If at all possible, the christian prophet will base his judgment not only on his own personal inner conviction, but on the manifest meaning of God's Word.

I remember a prophetic statement made by a religious sister at a staff meeting of an urban high school in India. The school catered for two thousand pupils; there were around sixty teachers on the staff. In a low voice, but with great determination, the sister pointed out to her colleagues that she had noticed discrimination in the treatment given to children of rich and poor families. She produced some examples: children whose parents were influential got better marks, received less punishment, were granted special privileges on the sports field and given top positions in the school organisation. Sister said she understood quite well the advantages individual teachers might reap from giving such preferential treatment to children from well-to-do families, but she asked them whether this was a truly christian attitude. Quoting Jesus' words "When you give a feast, invite the poor, the crippled, the lame, and the blind, and you will be blessed: for they are not able to pay you back" (Lk 14,13), she said that she felt Jesus would thoroughly disapprove of what was being done in the school. If any children were to be given preferential treatment, these should be children belonging to the poor and backward families. Some teachers who attended the meeting told me that it had opened their eyes to the unjust habits of favouritism they had gradually acquired.

At a meeting of professors teaching theology at major seminaries the discussion had been on rather humanistic lines. A lot of the discussion was dominated by the God-is-dead theology and secular thinking. At the con-celebrated mass in the evening, the main celebrant confessed in his homily that he had felt uneasy the whole day. "At the back of my mind", he said "I kept hearing the words of Christ: if a man is ashamed of me and of my teaching, then I will be ashamed of him" (Lk 9,26). While we should try to formulate theology in terms understandable to modern society, we should never allow ourselves to disown Christ or to deny him the central place in salvation which is his. We are not doing justice to the Gospel if we describe Christ only as the most perfect man. Christian faith cannot be resolved into charity towards the neighbour without more. It contains as an essential element submission to God and to Jesus Christ, the Saviour and mediator between God and us! He ended up by saying: "I feel that in today's discussion we have not sufficiently owned up to Christ".

In a tribal area of India the Bible Society had launched a plan for bringing out an ecumenical translation of the New Testament in a local language. Baptists, Methodists, Lutherans, Roman Catholics and Evangelicals had been called together to discuss cooperation. Especially among the representatives from the Evangelical groups there were strong reservations about Roman Catholic participation. It looked as if the meeting would end in an atmosphere of distrust and without coming to practical resolutions. At that moment an old Baptist minister asked to be allowed to speak. He said that all day he had felt the presence of the Holy Spirit in the coming together of these members of different Christian Churches. He stated it to be his deep conviction that Christ himself would welcome this kind of cooperation. "When the Disciples on one occasion wanted to stop a man driving out demons in Jesus' Name, because he didn't belong to their group, Jesus said: 'Whoever is not against you is for you' (Lk 9,49-50). Jesus prayed for unity. He wanted unity. Translating the Bible together and so bringing out one christian version would clearly be the mind of the Lord". This prophetic intervention helped to arouse the christian con-science of all present and the ecumenical translation was accepted as a common project.

SAMPLE SYLLABUS

The purpose of this section is not to give a 'model' or 'ideal' syllabus, but to show how an individual teacher could build up his or her own syllabus for a particular class.

Suppose I have a class of juniors and it is my task to give them religious instruction for about 20 minutes every day. With ten weeks in the term and five schooldays per week I will need to prepare fifty short instructions. Instead of blindly relying on a ready-made syllabus (which may not meet the particular needs of this group) or of fixing the topic from day to day (which is altogether too haphazard and costly in time) I could sit down at the beginning of the term and draw up a plan of what I intend to do.

For my children the obvious unit is the week. Each Monday means a new beginning; each Friday a close, so I could fix one overall theme for each week and thus ensure simplicity and continuity. With an eye on some existing syllabuses or on what I have done in previous years, and keeping in mind the special needs of the group I am dealing with now, I start jotting down some of the themes I would like to do. When I have found ten, I put them in order. It becomes the backbone of my new syllabus:

'Beginnings'	'Sharing'
'Living together'	'Prayer'
'God loves us'	'Holy Mass'
'Jesus'	'Forgiving one another'
'Baptism'	'Gratitude'

To complete the plan I will need to work out roughly for each day, which passage from Scripture I will draw on and what technique I will use. I will also want to make sure that the plan offers sufficient variation: both Old and New Testament; stories as well as portraits; from time to time commentated reading and discussion. While concentrating on input during the first four days, I could reserve each Friday for discussion and feedback. After reading a short and relevant Scripture passage I could ask the children to summarise what they learned during the previous days. I might ask them what they remember of the stories, what they liked most, and so on. It could also consist in a re-play of a story narrated during the week. I will call this 'wrapping-up' operation on Friday a 'sharing session'.

A syllabus based on such principles could look like this:

"BEGINNINGS"

topic	text	technique
1. God gave Joshua a new task. He assumed leadership.	Jos 1,1-18	Simple free narration
2. Ruth was a courageous woman. Out of love for her mother-in-law she began a new life.	Ruth 1,1-22	Simple portrait
3. Paul travelled to Greece because he saw in a vision how people needed his help.	Acts 16,6-12	Simple free narration
4. Jesus performed his first miracle at Cana because he had come to make people happy.	Jn 2,1-11	Simple free narration
5. ' If you have a high ideal, you will achieve it. You will put it on as a feastday dress '	Prov 27,8	Sharing session

'LIVING TOGETHER'

6. David and Nabal clashed because both were proud.	1 Sam 25,2-35	Simple free narration
7. We must help our neighbour when he is in trouble.	Dt 22,1-4	Commentated reading
8. The Early Christians lived together as one big family.	Acts 4,32-35	Simple portrait

9. When the apostles quarreled, Jesus taught that we need to be humble.	Mt 20,20-28	Simple free narration
10. ' Where two or three of you meet in my name, I shall be there with them. '	Mt 18,20	Sharing session

'GOD LOVES US'

11. God loves us as tenderly as a father.	Ps 103,1-22	Commentated reading
12. As God told Jeremiah, he loves each person even before he is born.	Jer 1,4-8	Simple portrait
13. God often shows his love by testing us, as he did when he wrestled with Jacob.	Gen 32,23-33	Simple free narration
14. God showed his love through Jesus who died for us.	Rom 5,5-11	Commentated reading
15. ' Think of the love that the Father has lavished on us, by letting us be called God's children '.	1 Jn 3,1	Sharing session

'JESUS'

16. ' I am the light of the world!' Jesus saves.	Jn 8,1-12	Simple free narration
17. ' I am the good shepherd ' Jesus protects us.	Jn 10,1-14	Commentated reading
18. ' I am the vine!' We should stay close to Jesus.	Mt 14,22-33 Jn 15,1-7	Simple free narration
19. ' The Father and I are one!' Jesus proves he is God.	Mt 9,1-8 Jn 10,22-39	Simple free narration
20. ' Who do you say I am '?	Mt 16,15	Sharing session

'BAPTISM'

21. God adopts us, as Moses was adopted when he was 'lifted from the water'.	Ex 2,1-10	Simple free narration

22. Jesus gives us new life, as he gave life to Jairus' daughter.	Mk 5,21-24; 35-43	Simple free narration
23. Jesus makes us see new things, as he gave sight to the blind man.	Jn 9,1-34	Simple free narration
24. Jesus' baptism and ours: the Holy Spirit comes on us.	Mk 1,9-11; 7-8.	Commentated reading
25. ' He who believes and is baptised will be saved '.	Mk 16,16	Sharing session

'SHARING'

26. Tobit gave us an example of sharing.	Tob 1,10- 2,8	Simple free narration
27. Abraham gave Lot the best part of the land.	Gen 13,1-17	Simple free narration
28. When God gave manna to the Hebrews, they had to take just enough for the day.	Ex 16,1-21	Simple free narration (One-point example)
29. Every Christian should share his property with the poor.	Lk 3,1-6; 10-14	Commentated reading
30. ' A brother helped by a brother is a fortress '.	Prov 18,19	Sharing session

'PRAYER'

31. Prayer means meeting God, as Moses used to do.	Ex 33,7-17	Simple Portrait
32. We should pray with confidence and using our own words, as Esther did.	Est 4-5	Simple free narration
33. We should make time for prayer. Prayer means sitting at Jesus' feet.	Lk 10,38-42	Simple free narration
34. Our prayer should be humble.	Lk 18,9-14	Simple free portrait

35. ' Lord, teach us to pray '.	Lk 11,1	Sharing session

'HOLY MASS'

36. Like Abraham we show our love for God through sacrifice.	Gen 22,1-19	Simple free narration
37. Jesus offered himself for us on Calvary	Mt 26,36-46	Simple free narration
38. The Eucharist makes Jesus' sacrifice present.	1 Cor 11,23-27	Commentated reading
39. If we offer ourselves to God at Mass, he will bless us, as he blessed Solomon.	1 Kgs 3,4-15	Simple free narration
40. ' Do this to remember me '.	Lk 22,19	Sharing session

'FORGIVING ONE ANOTHER'

41. David forgave Shimei, even though Shimei had treated him badly.	2 Sam 16,5-14; 19,16-24	Simple free narration
42. We should learn how to restore a broken friendship.	Sir 22,19-26	Commentated reading
43. We should forgive others, because God forgives us.	Mt 18,23-35	Simple free narration
44. It is no good praying to God, if we don't forgive others.	Mt 5,23-24; 6,12-15	Thematic exposition
45. ' Forgive us our sins as we forgive others '.	Lk 11,3-4	Sharing session

'GRATITUDE'

46. Elijah performs a miracle out of gratitude.	1 Kgs 17,8-24	Simple free narration
47. Hannah was grateful to God.	1 Sam 1,9-2,3	Simple portrait
48. Jesus expects gratitude.	Lk 17,11-19	Simple free narration

49. We should thank God for   Ps 107   Commentated
    all the good things he   reading
    gives us.

50. ' I thank God through Jesus   Rom 1,8   Sharing
    for all of you '.   session

ACKNOWLEDGEMENTS

We gratefully acknowledge permission to use the following copyright material:

Text
Sermon by Girolamo Savonarola and speech by William Wilberforce from *A Treasury of the World's Great Speeches,* Houston Peterson (ed.), Simon and Schuster (New York) 1965, pp. 80-2 & 219. Reprinted by permission of Simon and Schuster.

Dar Senflkorn von Lisieux, I. F. Goerees, Herder (Freibourg) 1958. Reprinted, in translation by J. M. N. Wijngaards, by permission of Herder.

God is for Real, Man, Carl Burke, Fontana 1974, pp. 32-3. Reprinted by permission of Williams Collins Sons & Co. Ltd.

The City of God and *Sermon 56* by Saint Augustine, in *Fathers of the Church Volumes XIV* and *XII* respectively, Catholic University of America Press 1953 and 1951. Reprinted by permission of the Catholic University of America Press.

The New Being, Paul Tillich, SCM Press 1964, pp. 85-6. Reprinted by permission of SCM Press Ltd., and Charles Scribner's Sons.

The Presentation of Self in Everyday Life, Erving Goffman, Penguin Books 1959, pp. 32ff. Reprinted by permission of Penguin Books Ltd., and Doubleday & Company, Inc.

'An answer of Jesus' from Attar of Nishapur from *The Way of the Sufi,* Idris Shah, Penguin 1974, p. 69. Reprinted by permission of the author.

Women of the Bible, H. V. Morton, Methuen Educational Ltd. 1940, p. 4. Reprinted by permission of the author, and the publishers.

Illustrations
Figs. 1, 2, 4, 7, 8, 9, 11, 25, 26, 27, 34, 36, 37, 38, 39 & 42 are reproduced from *Archief Kunst in Beeld.*

Figs. 3 & 19, *Bhakti* and *Khrist Prasad* by A. de Fonseca are reproduced by permission of Art India.

REFERENCE NOTES

Page
30   *De Imitatione Christi,* Thomas à Kempis, (Book III, Chapter 2), [author's translation].
36–8   *The New Book,* P. Tillich, (pp. 85-6).
40   *Kierkegaard, Een Keuze uit zijn Dagboeken,* H. A. van Munster, (pp. 174ff), [author's translation].
40–1   *Het Einde van het Conventionele Christendom,* W. H. van de Pol, (p. 74), [author's translation].
41   *Kerk in Opstand,* S. Jelsma, (p. 88), [author's translation].
53   *De Lof der Zotheid,* Erasmus ed. A. H. Kan, (pp. 116-21), [author's translation].
65–7   Freely adapted from H. Arens, F. Richardt, J. Shulte, 'Die Predigt als Kommunikationsmedium' in *Communicatio Sozialis* 6 (1973) (pp. 123-33).
82   *Le Palais Royal d'Ugarit,* J. Nougayrol, (Vol. IV, pp. 48ff), [author's translation].
108–10   *The City of God,* St. Augustine ed. G. G. Walsh and G. Monahan *Fathers of the Church* (Vol. XIV, p. 334).
134   *Women of the Bible,* H. V. Morton, (p. 4).
142   *De Archaische Glimlach,* C. W. M. Verhoeven, (pp. 129-54).
169   *The Way of the Sufi,* I. Shah, (p. 69).
182–3   *God is for Real, Man,* C. Burke, (pp. 32-3).
201–2   *Epigrams from Gandhiji,* S. R. Tikekar, (*passim*).
204–6   *Selected Sermons,* St. Augustine in *The Fathers of the Church* ed. D. J. Kavanagh, (Vol. XII, Sermon 56).
208–13   *Kierkegaard's Redevoeringen,* H. A. van Munster, (pp. 96-105), [author's translation].
230   *Presentation of Self in Everyday Life,* E. Goffman, (pp. 32-40).
230–1   *Over Overtuigen,* W. Drop et al, (pp. 38-40).
231   *How to Prepare a Sermon,* F. S. MacNutt, (*passim*).
236   *Dar Senflkorn von Lisieux,* I. F. Goerres.
243–5   *The World's Great Speeches,* ed. H. Peterson, (pp. 80-2 & 219).